THE BOOK OF MARRIAGE

FROM THE EXPLANATION OF BULUGH AL-MARAAM

PART 1

SHAYKH MUHAMMAD IBN SAALIH AL-UTHAYMEEN

Softcover ISBN: 978-1-6358-7510-2
Hardcover ISBN: 978-1-6382-1685-8

First Edition: Jumaada Awwal 1438 A.H. /February 2017 C.E.

Cover Design: Pario Studios UK

Translation by: Mustafa Lamei ʿAbdul Hakim al-Misri

Revision & Editing by ʿAbdullāh Omran

Typesetting & formatting by Abū Sulaymān Muhammad ''Abdul-Azim Ibn Joshua Baker

Subject: Marriage/ Family

Website : www.maktabatul-irshad.com

00316 41 58 59 64

مكتبة الإرشاد
Maktabatul-Irshad
PUBLICATIONS

فهرس

Table of Contents

TRANSLITERATION TABLE ... 7

BIOGRAPHY OF THE EXPLAINER OF BULUGH AL-MARAAM ... 10

CHAPTER OF MARRIAGE ... 15

THE RULING OF MARRIAGE ... 16

Explanation ... 16

ḤADĪTH 971 ... 33

Explanation ... 33

ḤADĪTH 972 ... 49

Explanation ... 49

THE WOMAN IS MARRIED FOR FOUR REASONS ... 60

Explanation ... 60

CONGRATULATIONS FOR THE ONE WHO GOT MARRIED ... 66

Explanation ... 66

ḤADĪTH 975 ... 73

Explanation ... 74

THE ETIQUETTES OF PROPOSAL: THE RULE OF LOOKING AT THE FIANCÉE ... 103

Explanation 103

ḤADĪTH 977 AND 978 112

Explanation 112

ḤADĪTH 979: A MUSLIM SHOULD NOT PROPOSE TO AN ENGAGED WOMAN 115

Explanation 115

THE ḤADĪTH OF THE WOMAN WHO OFFERED HERSELF FOR MARRIAGE 124

Explanation 126

ḤADĪTH 981 160

Explanation 160

PUBLICIZING THE NIKĀH 161

Explanation 161

THE CONDITION OF A WALI (GUARDIAN) 164

Explanation 164

HADITH 983 169

MARRIAGE WITHOUT THE GUARDIAN'S PERMISSION 170

Explanation 171

THE CONDITION OF THE WIFE'S APPROVAL 182

Explanation 184

THE RULING OF *ASH-SHIGHAR* 193

Explanation 193

FREEDOM OF CHOICE FOR THE ONE WHO WAS MARRIED AGAINST HER WILL 206

Explanation 206

WHAT IF A WOMAN WAS MARRIED BY TWO GUARDIANS TO TWO DIFERENT MEN? 211

Explanation 211

WHAT IS THE RULING OF A SLAVE'S MARRIAGE WITHOUT THE MASTER'S PERMISSION? 216

Explanation 216

THE RULING OF MARRYING THE WOMAN AND HER PATERNAL AUNT, HER MATERNAL AUNT AND HER SISTER OR THE SAME TIME 220

Explanation 220

THE RULING ON ENGAGMENT AND MARRIAGE OF AL-MUHRIM 226

Explanation 227

NIKĀH CONDITIONS 235

Explanation 235

THE RULING OF NIKAH AL-MUT'AH (TEMPORARY MARRIAGE) 244

Explanation 244

ḤADĪTH 998 247

Explanation 247

ḤADĪTH 999 256

Explanation 256

ḤADĪTH 1000 263

Explanation 263

THE RULING OF NIKAH *AT-TAHLIL* MARRIAGE 267

Explanation 268

MARRIAGE OF THE ADULTERER AND ADULTERESS 275

Explanation 275
ḤADĪTH 1004 284
Explantion 284

TRANSLITERATION TABLE

Consonants

ء	ʾ	د	d	ض	ḍ	ك	k
ب	b	ذ	dh	ط	ṭ	ل	l
ت	t	ر	r	ظ	ẓ	م	m
ث	th	ز	z	ع	ʿ	ن	n
ج	j	س	s	غ	gh	هـ	h
ح	ḥ	ش	sh	ف	f	و	w
خ	kh	ص	ṣ	ق	q	ي	y

Vowels

Short	ـَ	a	ـِ	i	ـُ	u
Long	ـَا	ā	ـِي	ī	ـُو	ū
Diphthongs	ـَوْ	aw	ـَيْ	ay		

Arabic Symbols & their meanings

عَزَّوَجَلَّ (Allāh) the Mighty & Sublime	سُبْحَانَهُ وَتَعَالَىٰ Glorified & Exalted is Allāh	رَحِمَهُ ٱللَّهُ May Allāh have mercy on him	حَفِظَهُ الله May Allāh preserve him
صَلَّىٰ ٱللَّهُ عَلَيْهِ وَعَلَىٰ آلِهِ وَسَلَّمَ May Allāh elevate his rank & grant him peace	جَلَّ جَلَالُهُ (Allāh) His Majesty is Exalted	جَلَّ وَعَلَا (Allāh) the Sublime & Exalted	تَبَارَكَ وَتَعَالَىٰ (Allāh) the Blessed & Exalted
رَضِيَ ٱللَّهُ عَنْهُمْ May Allāh be pleased with them	رَضِيَ ٱللَّهُ عَنْهَا May Allāh be pleased with her	رَضِيَ ٱللَّهُ عَنْهُ May Allāh be pleased with him	عَلَيْهِ ٱلصَّلَاةُ وَٱلسَّلَامُ May Allāh elevate his rank & grant him peace
			رَحِمَهُمُ ٱللَّهُ May Allāh have mercy upon them

BIOGRAPHY OF THE EXPLAINER OF BULUGH AL-MARAAM

Al-Allaamah Muhammad Bin Saleh Al-'Uthaymeen (1347-1421AH)

His lineage and birth: He is the noble scholar, verifier, Faqeeh, a scholar of Tafsir, Allah-fearing, ascetic, Muhammad Bin Saleh Bin Muhammad bin Sulaymaan bin 'Abd-Rahman Ali 'Uthaymeen from *Al-Wahbah* of Bani Tameem. He was born on the 27th night of the blessed month Ramadan in the year 1347AH in 'Unayzah - one of the cities of Al-Qaseem - in the kingdom of Saudia Arabia.

His scholastic upbringing: His father, may Allāh have mercy upon him, enrolled him to study the Noble Qur'ān with his maternal grandfather, the teacher ʿAbdur-Raḥmān Bin Sulaymān Ad-Dāmigh', may Allāh have mercy upon him. Then he studied writing, some arithmetic, and Arabic literature at *"Al-Ustaadh 'Abdul-Azeez Bin Saleh Ad-Daāmigh's school"*; and that was before he enrolled in *"Al-Mu'allim 'Ali Bin 'Abdillah Ash-Shahaytan's School"* where he memorized the Noble Qur'ān with him, and he had not reached fourteen years of age yet.

Under the direction of his father, may Allāh have mercy upon him, he embarked upon seeking religious knowledge; and the noble Shaykh Al-'Allamah 'Abdur Rahman Bin Nasir As-

Sa'dee, may Allāh have mercy upon him, used to teach religious sciences and Arabic at *"Jaame' Kabeer"* (i.e. Grand masjid where Jumu'ah is held) in 'Unayzah. He arranged two of his senior students to teach the beginning students. Therefore, the Shaykh (i.e. Al-'Uthaymeen) would join Shaykh Muhammad Bin 'Abdul-'Azeez Al-Mutawwa's circle of knowledge, may Allāh have mercy upon him, until he attained what he attained from the knowledge of *Tawheed, Fiqh* and *Nahw* (i.e. Arabic grammar related to the ending of words).

Then he sat in the circles of knowledge of his Shaykh 'Abdur Rahman Bin Nasir As-Sa'dee, may Allāh have mercy upon him. He studied with him Tafsir, Ḥadīth, Seerah of the Prophet, At-Tawheed, Al-Fiqh, Al-'Usool, Al-Faraa'id, An-Nahw and memorized concise texts on these sciences.

The noble Shaykh Al-'Allamah 'Abdur Rahman Bin Nasir As-Sa'dee, May Allāh have mercy upon him, was considered to be his first Shaykh. Since he acquired knowledge, experience and methods (of learning) from him more so than anyone else; and he was impressed by his methodology, his principles, his way of teaching and his adherence to proofs and evidence.

When Shaykh 'Abdur-Rahman Bin 'Ali Bin 'Awdaan, may Allāh have mercy upon him, was a judge in 'Unayzah he (i.e. Shaykh Al-'Uthaymeen) would study the science of Al-Faraa'id with him, just like he would study An-Nahw and Al-Balaghah with Shaykh 'Abdur-Razzaaq 'Afeefee, may Allāh have mercy upon him, during his presence as a teacher in that city.

When the academic institute opened in Riyadh, some of his brothers urged him to enroll. So, he sought his Shaykh's, 'Abdur Rahman Bin Nasir As-Sa'dee, may Allāh have mercy upon him, permission. He gave him permission and he enrolled in the institute from 1372AH to 1373AH.

Indeed, he took advantage of the scholars who used to teach there at that time throughout the two years that he was enrolled in the academic institute in Riyadh. Among them was Al-'Allamah, the scholar in Tafsir, Shaykh Muhammad Al-Ameen As-Shanqitee, Shaykh Al-Faqeeh 'Abdul-'Azeez Bin Nasir Bin Rasheed and Shaykh, the scholar in Ḥadīth, 'Abdur-Rahman Al-Ifreekee, may Allāh have mercy on them.

During that time, he would stick with His eminence Shaykh Al-'Allamah 'Abdul-'Azeez Bin 'Abdillah Bin Baaz, may Allāh have mercy upon him, and he studied with him Saheeh Bukhārī and some treatises of Shaykhul-Islam Ibn Taymiyyah in the masjid. He benefited from him in the science of Ḥadīth, analyzing the views of the scholars of Fiqh and the relationship between them. He considered Shaykh 'Abdul-'Azeez Bin Baaz, may Allāh have mercy upon him, to be his second Shaykh in obtaining knowledge and being influenced by him.

Then he returned to 'Unayzah in 1374AH and he commenced studying under his Shaykh Al-'Allamah ʿAbdur-Raḥmān Bin Nasir As-Sa'dee and he followed up his studies in the faculty of Sharee'ah, which had become a subsidiary of Imam Muhammad Bin Saud Islamic University until he obtained a high-ranking degree.

His teaching: His Shaykh saw in him nobleness and quickness in the acquisition of knowledge, so he encouraged him to teach while he was still a student in his circles of knowledge. So, he began teaching in 1370AH at the "*Jaamee Kabeer*" in 'Unayzah.

When he graduated from the institute in Riyadh in 1374AH, he was appointed as a teacher at the institute in 'Unayzah.

In 1376AH, his Shaykh Al-'Allamah 'Abdur-Rahman Bin Nasir as-Sa'dee, may Allāh have mercy upon him, died. Therefore, he (i.e. Al-'Uthaymeen) was appointed the imamate of "Jaamee Kabeer" in 'Unayzah and he was also appointed the imamate of two 'Eid there and he was appointed to teach in the library of 'Unayzah Al-Wataniyah next to Jaamee Kabeer, which his Shaykh founded in 1359AH.

When the number of students increased and the library could not suffice them, the noble Shaykh began teaching in Masjid Al-Jaamee. The students gathered there and they would flock together from the Kingdom of Saudia Arabia and outside of the Kingdom until they reached in the hundreds for some of the classes. These people studied seriously and they did not just simply listen to the classes. He (i.e., 'Uthaymeen) remained upon that as an Imam, a Khateeb and a teacher until his passing, may Allāh have mercy upon him.

The Shaykh remained a teacher in the institute from 1374AH to 1398AH until he transferred to teaching in the faculty of *Sharee'ah* and *Usūl-Dīn* in the Al-Qaseem branch of Muhammad Bin Saud Islamic University and remained there as a teacher until his passing, May Allāh, the Most High, have mercy upon him.

He would lecture in *Masjid Al-Haram* and *Masjid An-Nabawi* during the seasons of Hajj, Ramadan and the summer vacations from 1402AH until his passing, may Allāh have mercy upon him.

The Shaykh had a particular teaching practice in his open-handedness and integrity. He would raise questions to his students, receive their questions and hold classes and lectures with a lofty concern, a composed mind and delight at his propagation of religious knowledge and his closeness to the people.

His passing away: He passed away, may Allaah have mercy upon him, in the city of Jeddah, shortly before Maghrib on a Wednesday, the 15th of the month of Shawwal, 1421AH. He was prayed over in *Masjid Al-Haram* after 'Asr on Thursday. Then he was followed by the thousands who had prayed over him and he was buried in *Mecca Al-Mukaramah.* [1]

---

[1] The source of this is biography was from the Shaykh's website (www.ibnothaimeen.com)

CHAPTER OF MARRIAGE

A **"chapter"** contains many sections. The scholars categorize a book structure into chapter, section and article. There are some differences between them. "Chapter" is a generic term that includes many subcategories. For example, the chapter of purification (Taharah) includes water, pots, cleaning after defecation, performing Wudu', washing (Ghusl), performing tayammum, removal of dirt and hayd (menstruation). Then a "section" is a part of a chapter. For example, the water section and the Wuḍu' section are both included within the chapter of purification. As for an "article", it includes a collection of points in a singular topic. It is used because either the section is very large or to highlight crucial points inside the section. Interestingly, this framework is meant to avoid boredom.' The author mentions here the chapter of marriage as it is a category that contains many things.

First, let's discuss the ruling of marriage (nikāh) which will be mentioned in Ibn Mas'ūd's *Ḥadīth* (رَضِيَ اللَّهُ عَنْهُ). What is the definition of marriage? According to the definition in Sharia law, it is a meeting between a male and a female in a designated manner. This manner is designated by Sharia in the form of the marriage contract with certain conditions.

THE RULING OF MARRIAGE

970- On the authority of ʿAbdullāh ibn Masʿūd (رَضِيَ اللَّهُ عَنْهُ), the Messenger of Allāh (صَلَّى اللَّهُ عَلَيْهِ وَسَلَّمَ) told us,

يَا مَعْشَرَ الشَّبَابِ مَنِ اسْتَطَاعَ مِنْكُمُ الْبَاءَةَ فَلْيَتَزَوَّجْ فَإِنَّهُ أَغَضُّ لِلْبَصَرِ وَأَحْصَنُ لِلْفَرْجِ وَمَنْ لَمْ يَسْتَطِعْ فَعَلَيْهِ بِالصِّيَامِ فَإِنَّهُ لَهُ وِجَاءٌ

"O young men! Those among you who can afford to marry a wife should marry for it restrains eyes from casting (evil glances) and fortifies oneself against immorality, but those who cannot should devote themselves to fasting for it is a means of controlling sexual desire." Related by Bukhārī and Muslim.[2]

Explanation

"Told us" refers to the young people, the young Companions. The word **'young'** refers to a man who has reached puberty but has not yet reached thirty years of age. Others maintained

[2] Related by al-Bukhārī: Book of Saum, the unit of fasting for those who are afraid to stay unmarried, No. (1905), Muslim: Book of Marriage, the unit of marriage being allowed for the one who is in a dire need of, No. (1400)

it extends to forty years of age, when he becomes middle-aged and eventually becomes old.

مَنِ اسْتَطَاعَ مِنْكُمُ الْبَاءَةَ فَلْيَتَزَوَّجْ

"Who can afford to marry a wife should marry,"

The young people are specifically addressed because they are in dire need of that and because they have a stronger sexual desire than the elderly. So, in a prophetic *Ḥadīth* (This *Ḥadīth* may be weak),

إِنَّ رَبَّكَ لَيَعْجَبُ لِلشَّابِ لَيْسَ لَهُ صَبْوَةٌ

"Allāh has been wondering about the young man who has no sexual desire,"[3]

Meaning the desire of the young people. This ruling is also applied to young women. However, because it is traditional that the young woman is the one who is proposed to, she is not particularly addressed.

مَنِ اسْتَطَاعَ مِنْكُمُ الْبَاءَةَ

"Those among you who can afford to marry a wife."

This affordance includes the physical and financial capacity. If the young man has no physical capacity, he will have no

---

[3] Related by Ahmad No. (16920).

need of marriage. And if he has physical capacity, but he has no money, he is not able to marry.

One can argue that *capacity* here is meant to be the financial capacity only because the Prophet (ﷺ) said,

وَ مَنْ لَمْ يَسْتَطِعْ فَعَلَيْهِ بِالصَّوْمِ

> **"But those who have no ability should devote themselves to fasting."**

This indicates that the speech is intended for the one who has physical capacity with no financial capacity.

أَغَضُّ لِلْبَصَرِ، وَ أَحْصَنُ لِلْفَرْجِ

> **"For it restrains eyes from casting (evil glances) and fortifies oneself against immorality."**

"It" refers to marriage.

The Prophet did not say marriage is the entered into for more children, though it is important. Rather, most young people are more interested in restraining their eyes from evil glances and fortifying themselves against immorality. For this reason, when people congratulate the husband, they do not congratulate him on finding a wife that can give birth to children. They can advise him to wait for two, three or four years concerning giving birth to children. Instead, they congratulate him on restraining his eyes from casting evil glances and fortifying himself against immorality. The Prophet (ﷺ) did not mention this great benefit because he is addressing the young who are highly interested in those two matters (mentioned in the *Ḥadīth*).

أَغَضُّ لِلْبَصَرِ

"For it restrains eyes from casting (evil glances)": It helps restrain eyes from casting evil glances. It is clear that if the man gets married, he would not gaze at women. Before marriage he may gaze at them out of instinct, but his faith may protect him. Allāh (سُبْحَانَهُۥوَتَعَالَىٰ) said,

﴿ قُل لِّلْمُؤْمِنِينَ يَغُضُّوا۟ مِنْ أَبْصَٰرِهِمْ ﴾

> **"Tell the believing men to lower their gaze (from looking at forbidden things)."** [*Sūrah An-Nūr* 24:30]

وَ أَحْصَنُ لِلْفَرْجِ

"**Fortifies oneself against immorality**": Meaning more protective. It is derived from the fort that protects the people in it. It prevents from sinful acts and adultery. The Prophet (صَلَّى ٱللَّهُ عَلَيْهِ وَسَلَّمَ) ordered the man who sees something seducing in a woman (to gratify his desires) by means of consummation. Where he (صَلَّى ٱللَّهُ عَلَيْهِ وَسَلَّمَ) said,

إِنْ مَـا مَعَهَا مِثْلُ الَّذِي مَعَهَا

"**Both of them are the same**"[4], meaning this wife is similar to that woman one was seduced by.

وَ مَنْ لَمْ يَسْتَطِعْ

"**But those who cannot":** Meaning those who cannot marry. Marriage cover both meanings of consummation and the expenses of consummation, as he (صَلَّى ٱللَّهُ عَلَيْهِ وَسَلَّمَ) said,

وَ مَنْ لَمْ يَسْتَطِعْ

"But those who cannot." It is incorrect to say that, **"But those who cannot"** does not mean consummation because the one who is not able to consummate is not in need of marriage. So, it refers to the expenses that helps one consummate.

بِالصَّوْمِ

"Devote themselves to fasting": Meaning he should keep fasting, which means not to eat or drink as an act of worship from the sunrise to the sunset. Here, Saum is used in its legal sense, as opposed to its linguistic sense, which, if it is used here, would be meaningless. This follows the established rule, which states "Speaker's words are to be understood contextually in the light of his local tradition"

If the Prophet (صَلَّى ٱللَّهُ عَلَيْهِ وَسَلَّمَ) delivers a speech, it shall be interpreted according to Sharia as he (صَلَّى ٱللَّهُ عَلَيْهِ وَسَلَّمَ) is a legislator.

[4] Related by at-Tirmidhi in book of suckling, under the chapter: what is mentioned concerning the man who see a that pleases him No. (1158)

But if the speech is delivered by a linguist, it shall be explained according to the linguistic meaning.

فَإِنَّهُ لَهُ وِجَاءٌ

"**For it is a means of controlling sexual desire.** "It" refers to Saum. "for" refers to one who cannot.

وِجَاءٌ

"**A means of controlling.**" It controls the sexual desire and its arousal. Saum controls the sexual desire which makes one no longer feel aroused.

In this *Ḥadīth*, the Prophet (صَلَّى ٱللَّٰهُ عَلَيْهِ وَسَلَّمَ) addresses the youth specifically because they are more in need of this speech than elderly people and because the youth are more sexually aroused than the elderly people.

The benefits of the Ḥadīth:

1. **The speech of the Prophet (صَلَّى ٱللَّٰهُ عَلَيْهِ وَسَلَّمَ)** is so convenient that it is addressed to the targeted group.

2. **The young man who is able to marry must marry.** The Prophet (صَلَّى ٱللَّٰهُ عَلَيْهِ وَسَلَّمَ) said,

   فَلْيَتَزَوَّجْ

   "**should marry**", This form is used to confirm inevitability since many scholars believe that the one who is able to marry must do that to obtain the great benefits.

Other scholars believe that this is desirable because marriage is beneficial because, after all, there is a physical need related to sexual desire. So, this command is meant for guiding and desirability.

This command may also indicate inevitability because marriage is an act of worship and the Prophet (ﷺ) urged doing it. It is also a tradition of the Messengers, as Allāh (سُبْحَانَهُ وَتَعَالَى) said,

﴿ وَلَقَدْ أَرْسَلْنَا رُسُلًا مِّن قَبْلِكَ وَجَعَلْنَا لَهُمْ أَزْوَاجًا وَذُرِّيَّةً ﴾

"And indeed, We sent Messengers before you (O Muhammad (ﷺ) and made for them wives and offspring." [*Sūrah* ar-*Ra'd* 13:38]

The Prophet (ﷺ) said when speaking about himself,

وَأَتَزَوَّجُ النِّسَاءَ فَمَنْ رَغِبَ عَنْ سُنَّتِي فَلَيْسَ مِنِّي

"and take wives. So, whoever turns away from Sunnah does not belong to me."[5]

However, Muslim Jurists (رحمهم الله), divided marriage (nikāh) into many categories. They said it is obligatory

---

5 Related by al-Bukhārī: Book of marriage, the section of calling for marriage No. (5063), and Muslim: Book of marriage, the section of the desirability of marriage for one who is eager to, No. (1401).

(wājib), forbidden (haram), undesirable, allowed and supererogatory, as the case may be. Thus, the Muslim Jurists (ﷺ) hold the opinion that the ruling of marriage is originally supererogatory' and cannot be obligatory without a reason.

So, what is meant by obligatory (wājib)?

First: It is said that the **obligatory** marriage is meant for those who fear committing adultery if they do not marry, because, in marriage, one abstains from committing the prohibtions that must be avoided. **"The rule states whatever is integral to an obligatory act is as obligatory as the action itself**." So, if one fears committing adultery, he must marry. This is related to what is mentioned before. The obligation of marriage upon those who are able to marry is due to the fact that those who maintained that marriage is obligatory hold it as such. even if they do not fear to commit adultery. Whenever one has sexual desire, they shall marry.

Second: It is said that marriage is **prohibited** in enemy territory. For example, if we are in war against the disbelievers in their country, marriage is prohibited in such cases for fear of enslaving the Muslim children. The disbelievers may gain control over the Muslims and capture their children so that they can enslave their children. "**The rule states measures that help fend off forbidden acts are obligatory to take**." Thus, staying unmarried in such cases is obligatory. But it is said that it is permissible if he fears to commit adultery.

Third: It is **undesirable** for the needy who have no sexual desire, why? This marriage will result in nothing but burden (to support a wife). There is no doubt that it is an unnecessary burden. Marriage is unnecessary if a person has no sexual desire.

Fourth: it is **allowed** in the case of a man with a sexual desire, but has no money and is unable to support a wife. In this case, it is allowed, but undesirable, to marry if he can borrow money to marry. Also, for a man who has a lot of money, but has no sexual desire, marriage is allowed because he has no sexual desire. But if he gets married, he would get benefit because the wife will be at his service and the wife's sexual desire will be satisfied. This is beneficial.

Fifth: To be **supererogatory** is the **original basic ruling**. So, we can find that the above-mentioned four rulings are vulnerable to be changed into desirable, obligatory, prohibited, undesirable and allowed.

3. **The Prophet's teaching of the Muslim Ummah is superb** because when he (صَلَّى ٱللَّهُ عَلَيْهِ وَسَلَّمَ) mentioned the ruling, he mentioned its rationale and mentioning the rationale has three benefits:

   First: Islamic Sharia is so highly prestigious that its rulings are based on caring for interests.

   Second: Knowing the rationale behind the ruling gives more assurance to the listener and motivates him as well. So, when the Prophet (صَلَّى ٱللَّهُ عَلَيْهِ وَسَلَّمَ) said,

فَإِنَّهُ أَغَضُّ لِلْبَصَرِ، وَأَحْصَنُ لِلْفَرْجِ

"For it restrains eyes from casting (evil glances) and fortifies oneself against immorality."

It motivates the man to marry.

<u>**Third:**</u> **Cases that share the same rationale follow the same ruling**. When we find the very rationale in another situation, we shall say that the ruling for this situation should be identical to the other situation that has the identical rationale. The Islamic Sharia, owing to being perfect and methodical, does not differentiate between two identical things nor combine between two opposites. If the rationale of the mentioned ruling is found in another situation, this mentioned ruling will extend to this other situation because we know that Islamic Sharia does not differentiate between the identical things.

4. <u>**It is necessary to lower the gaze**</u>, because one is ordered to marry for the sake of lowering the gaze. So, the rationale of the ruling is more important than the ruling. So, marriage is required for lowering the gaze. In addition, gaze lowering is necessary because Allāh says,

﴿ قُل لِّلْمُؤْمِنِينَ يَغُضُّوا۟ مِنْ أَبْصَٰرِهِمْ ﴾

"Tell the believing men to lower their gaze (from looking at forbidden things)." [*Sūrah an-Nūr* 24:30]

And,

﴿ وَقُل لِّلْمُؤْمِنَٰتِ يَغْضُضْنَ مِنْ أَبْصَٰرِهِنَّ ﴾

"And tell the believing women to lower their gaze (from looking at forbidden things)." [*Sūrah an-Nūr* 24:31]

So, we need to take the rulings from this *Ḥadīth*.

5. **The lawfulness of fortifying oneself against immorality** as the Prophet (صَلَّى ٱللَّٰهُ عَلَيْهِ وَسَلَّمَ) said,

وَ أَحْصَنُ لِلْفَرْجِ

"And fortifies oneself against immorality."

6. **To avoid all that leads to looking at forbidden things or doing immoral acts**. Since marriage is obligated for purposes of lowering the gaze and preserving one's honor, anything that leads to otherwise is automatically unlawful.

From this ruling, we can say that if the man has found himself tempted because of newspapers including bad photos, then he must avoid them because they may lead to looking at forbidden things or committing adultery, may Allāh preserve us.

7. **It is permissible if one does not mention all the benefits related to a particular issue if the situation does not require it.** This benefit is taken from the rationale that the benefits the Prophet (ﷺ) provided for marriage, namely, lowering the gaze and fortifying oneself against immorality are the only ones mentioned despite the fact that marriage has another rationale highly considered by the legislator, which is having children. But because Allāh addresses the youth who are interested in nothing but sexual desire, marriage and lowering the gaze, the suitable rationale is appropriately addressed to the appropriate addressee, namely, young people.

8. **The Prophet (ﷺ) is so wise that when anything is difficult**, the Prophet (ﷺ) provides the alternative, as the Prophet (ﷺ) said,

وَ مَنْ لَمْ يَسْتَطِعْ فَعَلَيْهِ بِالصَّوْمِ

"But those who have no ability should devote themselves to fasting,"

If one is not able to marry because of poverty, they shall devote themselves to fasting.

9. **The man shall not borrow in order to marry** because the Prophet (ﷺ) said,

وَ مَنْ لَمْ يَسْتَطِعْ فَعَلَيْهِ بِالصَّوْمِ

"But those who have no ability should devote themselves to fasting",

He does not say that he shall borrow money, and Allāh (سُبْحَانَهُ وَتَعَالَى) says,

﴿ وَلْيَسْتَعْفِفِ ٱلَّذِينَ لَا يَجِدُونَ نِكَاحًا حَتَّىٰ يُغْنِيَهُمُ ٱللَّهُ مِن فَضْلِهِۦ ﴾

"And let those who find not the financial means for marriage keep themselves chaste until Allāh enriches them of His Bounty." [*Sūrah an-Nūr* 24: 33]

Meaning without human interference. He does not say: until Allāh enriches them anyway, but Allāh says,

﴿ حَتَّىٰ يُغْنِيَهُمُ ٱللَّهُ مِن فَضْلِهِۦ ﴾

"Until Allāh enriches them of His Bounty."

Another piece of evidence is mentioned in the *Ḥadīth* of Sahl ibn Sa'd (رَضِيَ ٱللَّهُ عَنْهُ) concerning the woman who herself proposed to the Prophet (صَلَّى ٱللَّهُ عَلَيْهِ وَسَلَّمَ), but the Prophet (صَلَّى ٱللَّهُ عَلَيْهِ وَسَلَّمَ) had no desire of her. Some people said, "If you are not in need of this woman, let me marry her". The Prophet (صَلَّى ٱللَّهُ عَلَيْهِ وَسَلَّمَ) asked him,

هَلْ عِنْدَكَ مِنْ شَىْءٍ ". فَقَالَ لاَ وَاللَّهِ يَا رَسُولَ اللَّهِ. قَالَ " اذْهَبْ إِلَى أَهْلِكَ فَانْظُرْ هَلْ تَجِدُ شَيْئًا ". فَذَهَبَ ثُمَّ رَجَعَ فَقَالَ لاَ وَاللَّهِ يَا رَسُولَ اللَّهِ مَا وَجَدْتُ شَيْئًا. قَالَ " انْظُرْ وَلَوْ خَاتَمًا مِنْ حَدِيدٍ ".

فَذَهَبَ ثُمَّ رَجَعَ فَقَالَ لاَ وَاللَّهِ يَا رَسُولَ اللَّهِ وَلاَ خَاتَمًا مِنْ حَدِيدٍ وَلَكِنْ هَذَا إِزَارِي ـ قَالَ سَهْلٌ مَا لَهُ رِدَاءٌ ـ فَلَهَا نِصْفُهُ. فَقَالَ رَسُولُ اللَّهِ صلى الله عليه وسلم " مَا تَصْنَعُ بِإِزَارِكَ إِنْ لَبِسْتَهُ لَمْ يَكُنْ عَلَيْهَا مِنْهُ شَىْءٌ وَإِنْ لَبِسَتْهُ لَمْ يَكُنْ عَلَيْكَ شَىْءٌ ". فَجَلَسَ الرَّجُلُ حَتَّى طَالَ مَجْلِسُهُ ثُمَّ قَامَ فَرَآهُ رَسُولُ اللَّهِ صلى الله عليه وسلم مُوَلِّيًا فَأَمَرَ بِهِ فَدُعِيَ فَلَمَّا جَاءَ قَالَ " مَاذَا مَعَكَ مِنَ الْقُرْآنِ ". قَالَ مَعِي سُورَةُ كَذَا وَسُورَةُ كَذَا وَسُورَةُ كَذَا عَدَّهَا قَالَ " أَتَقْرَؤُهُنَّ عَنْ ظَهْرِ قَلْبِكَ ". قَالَ نَعَمْ. قَالَ " اذْهَبْ فَقَدْ مَلَّكْتُكَهَا بِمَا مَعَكَ مِنَ الْقُرْآنِ

"Do you have anything to offer her?" He replied. "No, by Allāh, O' Allāh's Messenger!" The Prophet (ﷺ) said to him, "Go to your family and see if you can find something." The man went and returned, saying, "No, by Allāh, O' Allāh's Messenger! I have not found anything." The Prophet (ﷺ) said, "Try to find something, even if it is an iron ring." He went again and returned, saying, "No, by Allāh, O' Allāh's Messenger, not even an iron ring, but I have this waist sheet of mine." The man had no upper garment, so he intended to give her, half his waist sheet. So Allāh's Messenger (ﷺ) said, "What would she do with your waist sheet? If you wear it, she will have nothing of it over her body and, if she wears it, you will have nothing over your body." So, that

man sat for a long period and then got up and Allāh's Messenger (صَلَّىٰ ٱللَّٰهُ عَلَيْهِ وَسَلَّمَ) saw him going away, so he ordered somebody to call him. When he came, the Prophet (صَلَّىٰ ٱللَّٰهُ عَلَيْهِ وَسَلَّمَ) asked him, "How much of the Qur'ān do you know?" He replied, "I know such Surat and such Surat and such Surat," and went on counting them, The Prophet (صَلَّىٰ ٱللَّٰهُ عَلَيْهِ وَسَلَّمَ) asked him, "Can you recite it by heart?" he replied, "Yes." The Prophet (صَلَّىٰ ٱللَّٰهُ عَلَيْهِ وَسَلَّمَ) said, "Go. I have married this woman to you for the amount of the Qur'ān you know by heart."

The Prophet (صَلَّىٰ ٱللَّٰهُ عَلَيْهِ وَسَلَّمَ) did not instruct him to borrow. This proves that the one who is not able to marry should not borrow.

If it is asked, "What is the reason for not borrowing, doesn't this serve the person's best interests?"

The answer: Yes, but borrowing makes one humiliated, especially when he is seen by the lender who looks down on him as a slave. So, the Prophet (صَلَّىٰ ٱللَّٰهُ عَلَيْهِ وَسَلَّمَ) instructed the poor against borrowing.

10. **The prohibition of the masturbation**. Notice that the Prophet (صَلَّىٰ ٱللَّٰهُ عَلَيْهِ وَسَلَّمَ) has not instructed it even in the case of inability to marry. Had it been permissible, he would have advised it. Certainly, it is easier than fasting and an action in which one can find pleasure. Whereas in Saum, one only suffers from the pain of thirst and hunger. It is known that the Prophet

(صَلَّى ٱللَّهُ عَلَيْهِ وَسَلَّمَ) always selects the easier as long as it is not prohibited[6]. So, this indicates that masturbation is prohibited because marriage is easier than both fasting and masturbation. This (proves that) masturbation is prohibited because the Prophet had not chosen it.

If one asks, "What should the man do if he has a sexual desire in spite of fasting?"

<u>The answer:</u> He can do masturbation because it is less harmful than adultery. Imām Ahmad (رَحِمَهُ ٱللَّهُ) made it allowed if one fears committing adultery and is unable to fast because it is less harmful. Some scholars believe that masturbation is allowed when necessary, saying that the Companions (رَضِيَ ٱللَّهُ عَنْهُمْ) did such acts in battles when necessary and out of fear of adultery.

If it asked, "Is it allowed to have medications to lessen sexual desire to an extent that is not harmful?"

<u>The answer:</u> If the doctors have said it is not harmful, then there is no problem when Saum is difficult for him. But if they have said it is harmful, those medications are therefore not allowed to be used because they may be needed when one ages. The young man believes that the sexual desire cannot be weakened whereas it will be weak in the future. So, such medications may have a bad effect.

---

[6] Related by al-Bukhārī: Book of outstanding traits, the unit of the biography of the Prophet (صَلَّى ٱللَّهُ عَلَيْهِ وَسَلَّمَ) م No (3560), and Muslim: Book of virtues, the unit that the Prophet (صَلَّى ٱللَّهُ عَلَيْهِ وَسَلَّمَ) avoids sins, No (2327).

ḤADĪTH 971

971- On the authority of Anas Ibn Mālik (رَضِيَ ٱللَّهُ عَنْهُ),

أَنَّ النَّبِيَّ صَلَّى اللهُ عَلَيْهِ وَسَلَّمَ حَمِدَ اللَّهَ وَأَثْنَى عَلَيْهِ . فَقَالَ : لَكِنِّي أُصَلِّي وَأَنَامُ وَأَصُومُ وَأُفْطِرُ وَأَتَزَوَّجُ النِّسَاءَ فَمَنْ رَغِبَ عَنْ سُنَّتِي فَلَيْسَ مِنِّي

The Prophet (صَلَّى ٱللَّهُ عَلَيْهِ وَسَلَّمَ) gives thanks and praises to Allāh **and** said, **"But still I observe fast and break it, perform Salat and sleep at night and take wives. So, whoever turns away from my Sunnah does not belong to me."** Bukhārī and Muslim[7].

Explanation

The reason behind this *Ḥadīth* is that three companions, because of loving righteousness, asked the Prophets' wives about his worship at home. When they knew about it, they consider it to be little. They said that the previous and future sins of the Prophet (صَلَّى ٱللَّهُ عَلَيْهِ وَسَلَّمَ) were forgiven and we are not as such. One said, "I will fast and won't break." The other said, "I shall perform Salāt all the night and won't sleep." The third said, "I will not take wives," meaning that he will never

[7] Related by Bukhari: Book of Nikaah (marriage), the unit of calling for marriage, No (5063), and Muslim: Book of Nikaah (marriage), the unit of the desirability of marriage for who has sexual desire, No (1401).

marry so that he can do acts of worship. They thought they were doing their best. When the Prophet (صَلَّى ٱللَّهُ عَلَيْهِ وَسَلَّمَ) heard of it, he delivered a speech, praised Allāh and then said what is above mentioned. What is said by those young men is a highly dangerous matter. It is similar to the monasticism which was innovated by the Christians. It is not prescribed for them, but they thought it would please Allāh. They carried themselves to extremes and Allah made it difficult for them. So, when one stresses himself, he will fail at the end.

These young people came to the Prophet (صَلَّى ٱللَّهُ عَلَيْهِ وَسَلَّمَ) who usually gave thanks and praises to Allāh in his speeches. "Alhamdulillah" is to give thanks to Allah. "Praise" is to declare the perfect qualities over and over again. If describing the praised one is repeated, it will be a praise of Allah. The Prophet (صَلَّى ٱللَّهُ عَلَيْهِ وَسَلَّمَ) said about Allāh (سُبْحَانَهُ وَتَعَالَىٰ),

قَسَمْتُ الصَّلاَةَ بَيْنِي وَبَيْنَ عَبْدِي نِصْفَيْنِ فَنِصْفُهَا لِي وَنِصْفُهَا لِعَبْدِي وَلِعَبْدِي مَا سَأَلَ " . فَإِذا قَالَ الْعَبْدُ : الْحَمْدُ لِلَّهِ رَبِّ الْعَالَمِينَ : يَقُولُ اللَّهُ عَزَّ وَجَلَّ حَمِدَنِي عَبْدِي . يَقُولُ الْعَبْدُ :الرَّحْمَنِ الرَّحِيمِ يَقُولُ اللَّهُ عَزَّ وَجَلَّ أَثْنَى عَلَيَّ عَبْدِي

"I have divided the prayer between Myself and My servant into two halves and My servant shall have what he has asked for. When the servant says, 'Al-hamdu lillahi rabbi l-alamin.' Allāh, Mighty and Sublime be He, says, 'My servant has praised Me.' And when he says, 'Ar-rahmani r-rahim,' Allāh, Mighty

and Sublime be He, says, 'My servant has extolled Me.'"[8]

And then he said that,

لَكِنِّي أَنَا أُصَلِّي وَ أَنَامُ

"He performs Salāt and sleeps at night." This is his way of life. Allāh (سُبْحَانَهُ وَتَعَالَى) said in Sūrah al-Muzzammil,

﴿ ۞ إِنَّ رَبَّكَ يَعْلَمُ أَنَّكَ تَقُومُ أَدْنَىٰ مِن ثُلُثَيِ ٱلَّيْلِ وَنِصْفَهُۥ وَثُلُثَهُۥ ﴾

"Verily, your Lord knows that you do stand (to pray at night) a little less than two-thirds of the night, or half the night, or a third of the night." [*Sūrah al-Muzzammil* 73:20]

"Less two-thirds of the night" means more than half of the night. Then **"Half the night."** And **"Third of the night"** means less than half of the night. So, the Prophet (صَلَّى ٱللَّهُ عَلَيْهِ وَسَلَّمَ) had never prayed the two-thirds of the night except in Ramadan. The Prophet (صَلَّى ٱللَّهُ عَلَيْهِ وَسَلَّمَ) used to pray all the night when the last ten days of Ramadan came.[9]. The Prophet

[8] Related by Muslim: Book of Salat (prayer), the unit of the necessity of reciting Surat Al-Fatiha in every Raka' No (395).

[9] On the authority of Ā'ishah (رَضِيَ ٱللَّهُ عَنْهَا) said, "When the last ten days of Ramadan came, he (صَلَّى ٱللَّهُ عَلَيْهِ وَسَلَّمَ) used to prepare himself rigorously for devotion, remain awake at night and (also) keep his family awake." Related by al-Bukhārī: Book of Tarawih (the extra night prayer performed in Ramadan), the unit of praying in the last ten days in Ramadan, No (2024), and Muslim: Book of I'tikaf, the unit of worshipping in the last ten days of Ramadan, No (1174).

(صَلَّى ٱللَّهُ عَلَيْهِ وَسَلَّمَ) used to get back to sleep (after praying) by the end of the night as Ā'ishah (رَضِيَ ٱللَّهُ عَنْهَا) said,

مَا أَلْفَاهُ السَّحَرُ عِنْدِي إِلاَّ نَائِمًا

> **"Never have I ever seen the Prophet awake in the late night before daybreak"[10],**

Meaning that he slept a little late at night. He (صَلَّى ٱللَّهُ عَلَيْهِ وَسَلَّمَ) said that the best prayers are those of Dāwud (عَلَيْهِ ٱلصَّلَاةُ وَٱلسَّلَامُ) who used to sleep half the night, get up to perform Salāt for one-third of it and then sleep through the remaining one-sixth of it"[11]

أُصَلِّي وَ أَنَامُ

"He performs Salāt and sleeps at night." This applies to one night. He sometimes prayed the whole night every night to the degree where one was left to think he doesn't sleep. At other times he would sleep so much as it would seem like he doesn't pray. The reason behind this is that the Prophet (صَلَّى ٱللَّهُ عَلَيْهِ وَسَلَّمَ) was worshipping Allāh (سُبْحَانَهُ وَتَعَالَىٰ) in the most appropriate manner. He had always committed himself to obligatory prayer. But he performs the Supererogatory

---

[10] Related by al-Bukhārī, the unit of who slept at early dawn, No (1133), and Muslim: Book of travelers' prayers and being shortened, the unit of night prayer and the number of Raka's of the Prophet (صَلَّى ٱللَّهُ عَلَيْهِ وَسَلَّمَ), No (742).

[11] Related by al-Bukhārī: Book of al-Jumu'ah, the unit of who sleeps at early dawn, No (1131), and Muslim: Book of Saum, the unit of not to usually observe Saum for who is harmed by which, No (1159).

prayers at the right time. Sometimes it was better to host the guests and to stay with them a bit late.

The Prophet once delayed the supererogatory prayer of Dhuhr until after Asr due to hosting a guest.[12] Sometimes a person may be busied by researching a scholarly matter earlier at night, and then sleeps late at night.

So, other than the obligatory prayers, one should choose which is better. So, every voluntary prayer is performed at the right time.

وَ أَصُومُ وَ أُفْطِرُ

"But still I observe fast and break it." The Prophet (صَلَّى ٱللَّٰهُ عَلَيْهِ وَسَلَّمَ) used to fast three days every month. He used to fast at the beginning of the month, at the middle of the month or the end of the month[13]. He (صَلَّى ٱللَّٰهُ عَلَيْهِ وَسَلَّمَ) used to fast on Mondays and Thursdays.[14] He (صَلَّى ٱللَّٰهُ عَلَيْهِ وَسَلَّمَ) used to observe Saum in the favorite days, such as the Day of Arafah and the Day of Ashura. He said,

لَئِنْ بَقِيتُ إِلَى قَابِلٍ لأَصُومَنَّ التَّاسِعَ

---

[12] Related by al-Bukhārī: Book of al-Jumu'ah', the unit of what he speaks when praying, so he signed with his hand and listened, No (1233), and Muslim: Book of traveler's Salat, the unit of praying two Rak'as which are prayed by the Prophet (صَلَّى ٱللَّٰهُ عَلَيْهِ وَسَلَّمَ), No (834).

[13] Related by Muslim: Book of Saum, the unit of the desirability of fasting three days every month, No (1160).

[14] Related by Muslim: Book of Saum, the unit of the desirability of fasting three days every month, No (1162).

"If I remain alive till the next year, I shall also observe fasting on the ninth of Muharram." [15]

Thus, he (صَلَّى ٱللَّهُ عَلَيْهِ وَسَلَّمَ) used to observe Saum and break it. He also said that the best Saum is that of Dāwud (عَلَيْهِ ٱلصَّلَاةُ وَٱلسَّلَامُ) who used to fast on alternative days. When Abdullah Ibn Amr Ibn al-A's (رَضِيَ ٱللَّهُ عَنْهُمْ) said I will perform night prayers and never sleep, observe Saum and never break it, the Prophet (صَلَّى ٱللَّهُ عَلَيْهِ وَسَلَّمَ) told him this is against the Sunnah. The Prophet (صَلَّى ٱللَّهُ عَلَيْهِ وَسَلَّمَ) kept discussing such matters with him until he gave him permission to observe fasting on alternative days. Abdullah (رَضِيَ ٱللَّهُ عَنْهُمْ) said, "I can do more", the Prophet (صَلَّى ٱللَّهُ عَلَيْهِ وَسَلَّمَ) said,

لَا أَفْضَلَ مِنْ ذَلِكَ

"There is no better than this." Meaning there is nothing better than Saum of Dāwud (عَلَيْهِ ٱلصَّلَاةُ وَٱلسَّلَامُ) who used to fast on alternative days. When Abdullah ibn Amr (عَلَيْهِ ٱلصَّلَاةُ وَٱلسَّلَامُ) grew older, he said,

لَيْتَنِي قَبِلْتُ رُخْصَةَ النَّبِيِّ صلى الله عليه وسلم

"I wish I had accepted the concession granted to me by the Prophet (صَلَّى ٱللَّهُ عَلَيْهِ وَسَلَّمَ)."

---

[15] Related by Muslim: Book of Saum, the unit of the desirability of fasting three days every month, No (1134).

When he became older, fasting on alternative days was difficult for him. Later, he was fasting for fifteen days and breaking for the other fifteen days.

He (صَلَّىٰ ٱللَّٰهُ عَلَيْهِ وَسَلَّمَ) said,

وَ أَتَزَوَّجُ النِّسَاءَ

"I take wives." Meaning I will not commit to worship all the time as those young men. He (صَلَّىٰ ٱللَّٰهُ عَلَيْهِ وَسَلَّمَ) took wives just as the Messengers before him. Allāh (سُبْحَانَهُ وَتَعَالَىٰ) said,

﴿ وَلَقَدْ أَرْسَلْنَا رُسُلًا مِّن قَبْلِكَ وَجَعَلْنَا لَهُمْ أَزْوَاجًا وَذُرِّيَّةً ﴾

> **"And indeed, We sent Messengers before you (O Muhammad (صَلَّىٰ ٱللَّٰهُ عَلَيْهِ وَسَلَّمَ), and made for them wives and offspring."** [*Sūrah ar-Ra'd* 13:38]

He (صَلَّىٰ ٱللَّٰهُ عَلَيْهِ وَسَلَّمَ) did not marry because of sexual desire, so he did not marry a virgin wife except Ā'ishah (رَضِيَ ٱللَّٰهُ عَنْهَا). However, had he wished to marry virgins, he would have done it. But he (صَلَّىٰ ٱللَّٰهُ عَلَيْهِ وَسَلَّمَ) got married for the great legitimate interest rather than sexual desire. Allāh (سُبْحَانَهُ وَتَعَالَىٰ) made women beloved to him. He (صَلَّىٰ ٱللَّٰهُ عَلَيْهِ وَسَلَّمَ) said,

حُبِّبَ إِلَيَّ مِنَ الدُّنْيَا النِّسَاءُ وَالطِّيبُ وَجُعِلَ قُرَّةُ عَيْنِي فِي الصَّلَاةِ

"Women and perfumes in your worldly life are beloved to me and my comfort was in prayer."[16]

Thus, the Prophet (صَلَّىٰ ٱللَّهُ عَلَيْهِ وَسَلَّمَ) had ties with every tribe of the Arabs, ties of kin by blood and by marriage. Allāh (سُبْحَانَهُ وَتَعَالَىٰ) said,

﴿ وَهُوَ ٱلَّذِى خَلَقَ مِنَ ٱلْمَآءِ بَشَرًا فَجَعَلَهُۥ نَسَبًا وَصِهْرًا ﴾

"And it is He Who has created man from water, and has appointed for him kindred by blood, and kindred by marriage." [*Sūrah al-Furqān* 25:54]

Women are beloved to the Prophet (صَلَّىٰ ٱللَّهُ عَلَيْهِ وَسَلَّمَ) and he (صَلَّىٰ ٱللَّهُ عَلَيْهِ وَسَلَّمَ) has been given the (sexual) potency of thirty young men.[17] He (صَلَّىٰ ٱللَّهُ عَلَيْهِ وَسَلَّمَ) took wives for the sake of making ties with the tribes of the Arabs. Those wives got virtues and privileges because of being married to the Prophet (صَلَّىٰ ٱللَّهُ عَلَيْهِ وَسَلَّمَ). The Prophet's knowledge which was delivered at home was conveyed by his wives. Thus, it is the Sunnah of the Prophet (صَلَّىٰ ٱللَّهُ عَلَيْهِ وَسَلَّمَ) to take wives.

He (صَلَّىٰ ٱللَّهُ عَلَيْهِ وَسَلَّمَ) said,

فَمَنْ رَغِبَ عَنْ سُنَّتِي فَلَيْسَ مِنِّي

"Whoever turns away from my Sunnah is not of me."

[16] Related by Ahmad No. (11884); also, related by an-Nisaaee' No. (3939).
[17] Related by al-Bukhārī (268) on the authority of Anas who said, We used to say that the Prophet was given the strength of thirty (men), Tuhfat Al-Ashraf (1365).

Meaning whoever turns away from his way of life regarding Saum and breaking it, praying and sleeping and taking wives is **"Not of me."** Meaning," I am free of such a person." According to the Prophet (صَلَّى ٱللَّهُ عَلَيْهِ وَسَلَّمَ), this is in accordance with the Fitrah. Whoever turns away from one's way of life, such a person is undoubtedly not on the same side and has no ties whatsoever. But he who sticks to one's way is on the same side.

So, in fact, a strong bond is forged when a person is a follower of another person in both sayings and actions. Therefore, if anyone loves a person, he will follow his steps. So is the friendship. So, whoever wants to be one of the Awliya of Allāh and His Messenger, he shall follow the Sharia that is conveyed by the Prophet (صَلَّى ٱللَّهُ عَلَيْهِ وَسَلَّمَ).

فَمَنْ رَغِبَ عَنْ سُنَّتِي فَلَيْسَ مِنِّي

"Whoever turns away from my Sunnah."

Here "**Whoever turns away from my Sunnah,"** meaning abandons it and keeps away from it. "**Is not of me.**" Meaning he does not belong to my nation because the one who really belongs to his nation is the one who follows his Sunnah.

<u>There are many benefits in this *Ḥadīth*:</u>

1. **<u>Islam combats monasticism</u>** because the Prophet (صَلَّى ٱللَّهُ عَلَيْهِ وَسَلَّمَ) condemned abstinence from marriage and excessive worship (prayers and Saum).

2. **Worship may be classified as undesirable, not because of an intrinsic factor, but for contingent reasons**. Prayer, for example, is highly desired by Allāh but it may be prohibited or undesirable if it is performed in an innovative way. Moreover, what innovators argue when one condemns the innovation of celebrating the Prophet's birth, they say, "Are you calling for the turning away from the Prophet (صَلَّى ٱللَّهُ عَلَيْهِ وَسَلَّمَ) and from the saying of prayers upon him?" You will say, "I am calling for the saying of prayers upon the Prophet (صَلَّى ٱللَّهُ عَلَيْهِ وَسَلَّمَ), but I am also calling for the turning away from innovation (bid'a). Are these prayers and praise upon the Prophet (صَلَّى ٱللَّهُ عَلَيْهِ وَسَلَّمَ) on that night in accordance with the Prophet's Sunnah? No. So, it is innovation (bid'a) and all innovations are considered misguidance. Thus, everything against Sunnah of the Prophet (صَلَّى ٱللَّهُ عَلَيْهِ وَسَلَّمَ) is considered bid'a even if it is originally an act of worship."

3. **The Prophet (صَلَّى ٱللَّهُ عَلَيْهِ وَسَلَّمَ) quickly nullified the falsehood** that he delivered a speech in order to denounce the falsehood. We should follow his steps because it is difficult to remove falsehood, to root it out, if it becomes public. It is easier to do so if it's caught at its inception.

4. **It is important and necessary to denounce a falsehood in public** when the falsehood is widespread. The Prophet (صَلَّى ٱللَّهُ عَلَيْهِ وَسَلَّمَ) has delivered a speech even though he was able to speak in private to those

involved. He did so because he was worried about spreading misconceptions.

5. **In addition, it is important to begin with thanks and praises upon Allāh in speeches**. This is in accordance with the Sunnah of the Prophet (صَلَّى ٱللَّهُ عَلَيْهِ وَسَلَّمَ). However, the scholars have different views about the speeches of the two Eids, whether to begin them with praising Allah or with Takbir (i.e. Allah is the Greatest). In this regard, there are two different views. The most probable is to begin with praises and thanks,[18] even though *takbīr* contains praises and thanks because you say,

اللهُ أَكْبَرُ ، اللهُ أَكْبَرُ ، لَا إِلَهَ إِلَّا اللهُ ، اللهُ أَكْبَرُ ، اللهُ أَكْبَرُ ، وَ للهِ الْحَمْدُ

"Allāh is the Greatest. Allāh is the Greatest. No one is worshipped truly but Allāh. Allāh is the Greatest. Allāh is the Greatest. Praise is due to Allāh."

However, this was not the habit of the Prophet (صَلَّى ٱللَّهُ عَلَيْهِ وَسَلَّمَ) whenever he delivered a speech.

6. **Clarifying the easiness of the religion. He (صَلَّى ٱللَّهُ عَلَيْهِ وَسَلَّمَ) said**,

[18] This is what Sheikh Al-Islam Ibn Taymiyyah (رَحِمَهُ ٱللَّهُ) chooses in "almobd'i" (2/187), "Alforou'a " (2/205), and "alinsaaf" (2/430).

أُصَلِّي وَ أَنَامُ ، وَ أَصُومُ وَ أُفْطِرُ

"But still I observe fast and break it, perform Salat and sleep at night."

7. **<u>One should not be worshipping Allāh too laboriously</u>** because the Prophet (ﷺ) clarified in his Sunnah that he always balanced between resting the body and worshipping Allah. If one is praying at night and fell asleep, he should stop praying and go to sleep[19]. This is the command of the Prophet (ﷺ). He clarified the reason for that when he said,

رُبَمَا يَذْهَبُ لِيَدْعَوَ لِنَفْسِهِ فَيَسُبُهَا

"He may abuse himself instead of seeking pardon (as a result of drowsiness)."

This is right. He may want to say, **"O My Lord! Forgive my sins"** and instead he says, **"O My Lord! Get me destroyed (as a result of drowsiness)."** So, the man should not worship too laboriously.

8. **<u>Fasting can be performed at all times</u>** because he (ﷺ) said,

---

[19] Related by al-Bukhārī (213) and Muslim (786) on the authority of Anas (رضي الله عنه), Tuhfat Al-Ashraf (953), but Bukhārī (212) related on the authority of Aisha (رضي الله عنها): "When one of you dozes off while performing Salāt, he should lie down till his drowsiness has gone away from him. When one of you performs Salāt while dozing, he may abuse himself instead of seeking pardon (as a result of drowsiness)."

وَ أَصُومُ وَ أُفْطِرُ

"But still I observe fast and break it."

This includes the indefinite fasting and definite fasting, including the Saum of Mondays and Thursdays, three days every month, the white days, six days in Shawwal, the Day of Arafat and Day of Ashura.

9. **Marriage (nikāh) is legislated** because it is the Sunnah of the Prophet (صَلَّىٰٱللَّهُعَلَيۡهِوَسَلَّمَ) who said,

وَ أَتَزَوَّجُ النِّسَاءَ

"I take wives."

If one argues that this act is naturally and instinctively needed, just like eating and drinking. So, it may not be legislated itself.

The answer is that there is a difference between them. The Prophet (صَلَّىٰٱللَّهُعَلَيۡهِوَسَلَّمَ) presented this ḥadīth as an act of worship. The Prophet (صَلَّىٰٱللَّهُعَلَيۡهِوَسَلَّمَ) did not say, "I eat and drink." Moreover, marriage (nikāh) has many advantages such as being responsible for the wife and children whom he shall bring up. This is not like eating and drinking.

10. **He who turns away from the Prophet's Sunnah has no relationship with him**. He (صَلَّىٰٱللَّهُعَلَيۡهِوَسَلَّمَ) said,

فَمَنْ رَغِبَ عَنْ سُنَّتِي فَلَيْسَ مِنِّي

"And he who turns away from my Sunnah, he has no relation with me."

This indicates that turning away from the Prophet's Sunnah is a major sin. The major sin is identified by Sheikh Al-Islām Ibn Taymiyyah (رَحِمَهُ ٱللَّهُ) as what is denounced by the Legislator. We have to know that abandoning the Sunnah is divided into two types. To abandon the Sunnah, as in turning away from it, is considered a major sin. To abandon the Sunnah, owing to carelessness but believeing that it is legislated and loving it, this is not a major sin unless the act itself is a major sin. To stop practicing a supererogatory act is not a major sin.

So, what can we say if someone stops raising his hands when saying the opening *takbīr* due to a dislike of following the Sunnah? This is a major sin. However, if the Sunnah is abandoned because of laziness, this is not a major sin. So, notice he who abandons it out of reluctance to follow it because, in such case, a person might do that out of dislike for it and that influences him until he no longer practices it. Such reluctance is considered a major sin.

What If one argues, **"And he who turns away from my Sunnah"** means the Sunnah whose practice is a must?

The answer: if the *Ḥadīth* is understood in such way, then abandoning the obligatory act is regarded a major sin depending on its importance and its scale. But turning away from the Sunnah is undoubtedly a major sin if one is asked why he does not practice it and he were to reply that he did not want to perform it as it is nonsense.

11. **Whoever sticks to the Sunnah will be closely related to the Prophet (صَلَّى ٱللَّهُ عَلَيْهِ وَسَلَّمَ)**. Is this a concrete or abstract relation? It is abstract because it indicates entire adherence. So, the more you stick to the Sunnah of the Prophet (صَلَّى ٱللَّهُ عَلَيْهِ وَسَلَّمَ), the more you will be related to Him. Allāh (سُبْحَانَهُ وَتَعَالَىٰ) said,

﴿ إِنَّ أَوْلَى ٱلنَّاسِ بِإِبْرَٰهِيمَ لَلَّذِينَ ٱتَّبَعُوهُ وَهَٰذَا ٱلنَّبِىُّ وَٱلَّذِينَ ءَامَنُوا۟ ۗ وَٱللَّهُ وَلِىُّ ٱلْمُؤْمِنِينَ ٦٨ ﴾

"Verily, among mankind who have the best claim to Ibrahīm (Abraham) are those who followed him, and this Prophet (Muhammad صَلَّى ٱللَّهُ عَلَيْهِ وَسَلَّمَ) and those who have believed (Muslims). And Allāh is the Wali (Protector and Helper) of the believers." [*Sūrah Ali 'Imrān* 3:68]

12. **The way of the Prophet (صَلَّى ٱللَّهُ عَلَيْهِ وَسَلَّمَ) is called the Sunnah**. It includes the obligatory and desirable acts of worship. In a similar regard, what do you say about one who does not marry (nikāh) out of turning away from the Sunnah? He is a sinner and commits a major sin. However, whoever abandons marriage out of fear

is not a sinner. And whoever abandons it out of fear of poverty, we say he mistrusts Allāh because there is no living creature on earth but its provision is due from Allāh. So, if you marry, Allāh will increase your living for the sake of your wife. Marriage (nikāh) cannot be a reason for poverty.[20]

[20] Shaykh was asked if this is a major sin (i.e. to believe that marriage is a reason for poverty). He said, "I believe that it is not a major sin but if this is caused by mistrusting Allah or His Promise, it may be a major sin regarding 'Aqīdah."

ḤADĪTH 972

972- On the authority of Abdullāh ibn Mas'ūd (رَضِيَ ٱللَّهُ عَنْهُ),

كَانَ رَسُولُ اللهِ صَلَّى اللهُ عَلَيْهِ وَ سَلَّمَ يَأْمُرُنَا بِالْبَاءَةِ ، وَ يَنْهَى عَنِ التَّبَتُّلِ نَهْيًا شَدِيداً ، وَ يَقُولُ : زَوَّجُوا الْوَدُودَ الْوَلُودَ فَإِنِّي مُكَاثِرٌ بِكُمُ الْأَنْبِيَاءَ يَوْمَ الْقِيَامَةِ .

"The Prophet (صَلَّى ٱللَّهُ عَلَيْهِ وَسَلَّمَ) used to order us to marry and strongly advised against celibacy and said, "Marry the one who is fertile and loving for I will be proud of your great number before the Prophets on the Day of Resurrection."[21] Related by Ahmad and graded as Ṣaḥīḥ by Ibn Hibbān.

And there is another *Hadīth* related by Abū Dawud, An-Nasai and Ibn Hibbān also on the authority of Maaqel ibn Yassār (رَضِيَ ٱللَّهُ عَنْهُ).[22]

Explanation

[21] al-Musnad (3/158), authenticated by Ibn Hibbān (4028), and said to be Hassan by AlDiaa (5/261), and appendage by AlHaithami in Almajmaa (4/258).

[22] Abu Dawud (2050), Annassai (6/65), Ibn Hibbān (4056) and authenticated by al-Hākim (2/176).

كَانَ يَأْمُرُ

"Used to."

Scholars of Usul al-Fiqh said that **"used to"** expresses what happened often, but not all the time. Thus, the Companions have not always used the phrase: The Prophet (صَلَّىٰٱللَّهُعَلَيۡهِوَسَلَّمَ) used to recite surah of 'Sabbeh' and Al-Ghashia on Friday prayers. Others said that he used to recite surah al-Jumu'ah and al-Munafiqun. If we were to say "used to" expresses a continuous habit, then there would be contradiction between the two ḥadīths. This evidently leads to a single conclusion that "used to", as used here, expresses a habit that was not necessarily exercised all the time.

الْبَاءَةِ

"He used to order us to marry" indicates nikāh because the Prophet (صَلَّىٰٱللَّهُعَلَيۡهِوَسَلَّمَ) said,

مَنِ اسْتَطَاعَ مِنْكُمُ الْبَاءَةَ فَلْيَتَزَوَّجْ

"Whoever can afford to marry a wife..."

وَ يَنْهَى عَنِ التَّبَتُّلِ

"He prohibits celibacy." "Order" is the opposite of "instruct against" because the former expresses taking an action, while the latter expresses refraining from an action.

التَّبَتُّل

"Celibacy" means to abstain from marriage which he (صَلَّى ٱللَّٰهُ عَلَيْهِ وَسَلَّمَ) strongly instructed against it.

In addition to ordering them to marry, he said,

تَزَوَّجُوا الْوَدُودَ الْوَلُودَ

"Marry the one who is fertile ..." Here, the Prophet (صَلَّى ٱللَّٰهُ عَلَيْهِ وَسَلَّمَ) clarified the characteristics of the wife one shall marry.

الْوَدُودَ

"**Loving**" indicates the one who is friendly to her husband. Some women are friendly by way of being gentle and beautiful and so on. These are the women who, when their husbands get in trouble and feel sorrow, they please them and try to make them feel at ease. Other women frown which makes matters worse. So, they are two types. One of them is bad and the other is good. The Prophet (صَلَّى ٱللَّٰهُ عَلَيْهِ وَسَلَّمَ) ordered us to marry the fertile and loving woman. The reason for that is not only enjoying a happy life, but also for having more children. If the man loves his wife, he likes to be more intimate with her and then many children will be born. So, he said later:

الْوَلُود

"Fertile" meaning able to beget many children. It is known that women are married as (virgin or non-virgin who were previously married). The previously married one is known to be fertile because she has begotten children before. But the virgin is not known to be fertile except through her relatives with whom she shares similar genetic features including her physical appearance and personality. Thus, if the woman is from a family whose women are known to be fertile, she will be fertile. So, if she is virgin, one may know by considering how it runs in her family.

إِنِّي مُكَاثِرٌ بِكُمُ الْأَنْبِيَاءَ يَوْمَ الْقِيَامَةِ

"For I will be proud of your great number before the Prophets on the Day of Resurrection" indicates I (i.e., Prophet Muhammad (صَلَّى ٱللَّٰهُ عَلَيْهِ وَسَلَّمَ) will be proud of your great number before the Prophets. It is known that our Prophet's followers are more than that of any other Prophet. The Prophet (صَلَّى ٱللَّٰهُ عَلَيْهِ وَسَلَّمَ) had a dream in which he saw all nations. He saw some Prophets whose followers were only one or two, while others had none. Then he raised his head and saw a big crowd covering the horizon which he thought to be his nation. He is told, This is Musa and his nation." And he (صَلَّى ٱللَّٰهُ عَلَيْهِ وَسَلَّمَ) raised his head seeing a bigger crowd covering the horizon and he was told, "This is your nation."[23]

And he (صَلَّى ٱللَّٰهُ عَلَيْهِ وَسَلَّمَ) said,

---

[23] Related by al-Bukhārī (6541) and Muslim (220) on the authority of Ibn 'Abbās (رَضِيَ ٱللَّٰهُ عَنْهُ), Tuhfat Al-Ashraf (5493).

إِنِّي لَأَرْجُو أَنْ تَكُونُوا شَطْرَ أَهْلِ الْـجَنَّةِ

"I hope that you would constitute half of the inhabitants of Paradise."[24]

All the other nations will constitute the other half. The Prophet (صَلَّى ٱللَّٰهُ عَلَيْهِ وَسَلَّمَ) said that Paradise is made up of one hundred and twenty ranks, and eighty are from this nation.[25] Thus, this Ummah will form two-thirds of the all the nations. So, to make this a reality, you shall beget more children. The more children there are, the greater the number of the Ummah will be.

<u>There are some benefits in this *Ḥadīth*:</u>

1. **<u>It is obligatory to marry</u>** because the Prophet (صَلَّى ٱللَّٰهُ عَلَيْهِ وَسَلَّمَ)

يَأْمُرُ بِالْبَاءَةِ

"used to order us to marry."

---

[24] Related by al-Bukhārī (3348) and Muslim (222) on the authority of Abu Said (رَضِيَ ٱللَّٰهُ عَنْهُ), Tuhfat al-Ashraf (4005).

[25] Related by Ahmad (5/361), atThirmidhi (2645) on the authority of Abu Musa (رَضِيَ ٱللَّٰهُ عَنْهُ)with a supporting hadith on the authority of Ibn Masoud (رَضِيَ ٱللَّٰهُ عَنْهُ) related by Ahmad (1/453), Abu Ya'la (5358), Albazzar (1999), AtTabarani (539) in Al-Aswat, the narrators are mentioned in Sahih except Al-Hārith Ibn Hassira who is trustful, mentioned by Al-Haithami (10/403).

The commands of the Prophet are originally obligatory. He (ﷺ) prohibited celibacy which is the opposite of marriage (nikāh). If the Prophet (ﷺ) prohibited celibacy, then marriage is be obligatory. So, the right opinion is that nikāh is obligatory depending on one's ability. If one is not able, then it is not obligatory because Allāh (سُبْحَانَهُ وَتَعَالَى) said,

﴿ لَا يُكَلِّفُ ٱللَّهُ نَفْسًا إِلَّا وُسْعَهَا ﴾

"Allāh burdens not a person beyond his ability." [*Sūrah al-Baqarah* 2:286]

2. **<u>Celibacy is prohibited</u>**. Everybody must marry even if his wife is dead or he is divorced. Some people may stick to the religion after being married and think there is no need for women which makes them divorce their wives. We say it is prohibited to worship Allāh by way of abstaining from marriage. The Prophet (ﷺ) said,

مَنْ رَغِبَ عَنْ سُنَّتِي فَلَيْسَ مِنِّي

"And he who turns away from my Sunnah, he has no relation with Me"

So, celibacy is prohibited.

3. **Prohibition is divided into strong and weak types.** The weak prohibition entails undesirability but the strong prohibition entails a complete prohibition.

4. **There are different levels concerning commands and prohibitions**. Some prohibitions are stricter than others. He said,

   نَهْيًا شَدِيدًا

   "Strict forbiddance." Similarly, sins are divided into minor and major ones. There are different grades of minor sins and major ones as well.

5. **According to the Sharia, one can select the loving and fertile woman**. If one argues that the qualities of loving and fertile were in contrast with the religion, which is to be preferred? We say that religion is to be preferred. The Prophet (صَلَّى ٱللَّهُ عَلَيْهِ وَسَلَّمَ) said,

   اِظْفَرْ بِذَاتِ الدِّينِ تَرِبَتْ يَمِينُكَ

   "Select the pious, may your hand be rubbed in the dust!" [26]

6. **The more the woman loves her husband, the happier his life is**. Allāh (سُبْحَانَهُ وَتَعَالَى) says,

[26] This is the next Hadīth in this book.

﴿ وَمِنْ ءَايَـٰتِهِۦٓ أَنْ خَلَقَ لَكُم مِّنْ أَنفُسِكُمْ أَزْوَٰجًا لِّتَسْكُنُوٓا۟ إِلَيْهَا وَجَعَلَ بَيْنَكُم مَّوَدَّةً وَرَحْمَةً ﴾

"And among His Signs is that He created for you wives from among yourselves, that you may find repose in them. And He has put between you affection and mercy." [*Sūrah ar-Rūm* 30:21]

So, the cordiality is rooted in the heart, which is the controller of the organs. If the heart loves, the organs will love. If it hates, they will hate. It is the manager. Happiness and cordiality are bound to happen when Allah blesses both spouses with mutual friendliness, which would not happen by any other way.

7. **The Prophet (صَلَّى ٱللَّهُ عَلَيْهِ وَسَلَّمَ) is so proud of His Ummah** that he said,

إِنِّي مُكَاثِرٌ بِكُمُ

"I will be proud of your great number." So, the scholars mentioned among the benefits of marriage is that the Prophet (صَلَّى ٱللَّهُ عَلَيْهِ وَسَلَّمَ) will be proud of His Ummah. And we will be happy if we strive to accomplish what fulfills the Prophet's wish.

8. **<u>The Lawmaker is longing for more children</u>** so he said **"fertile"** because begetting more children establishes a great and dignified Ummah. Allāh (سُبْحَانَهُ وَتَعَالَىٰ) has blessed the Children of Israel with lots of children. He said,

﴿ وَجَعَلْنَاكُمْ أَكْثَرَ نَفِيرًا ﴾

"And made you more numerous in manpower." [*Sūrah* al-Isrā' 17:6]

And Shuaib (عَلَيْهِ ٱلصَّلَاةُ وَٱلسَّلَامُ) reminded his people of this when he said,

﴿ وَٱذْكُرُوٓا۟ إِذْ كُنتُمْ قَلِيلًا فَكَثَّرَكُمْ ﴾

"And remember when you were but few, and He multiplied you." [*Sūrah al-A'rāf* 7: 86]

It is noteworthy that calling for birth control is taken over by a disbeliever who wants to decrease the Muslim Ummah or by an ignorant one who does not know the consequences of birth control or by one who is not interested in anything but gratifying his sexual desire and is not concerned with the growth of the Muslim children. Today, we see many people are interested in having a small number of children. They think this makes the husband gratify his sexual desire. Also, if she is an employee, she will have more time for her job. These are all narrow-minded. Having children is good. And Allāh will enlarge your provision because of your children. Allāh (سُبۡحَانَهُۥوَتَعَالَىٰ) said,

﴿ ۞ وَمَا مِن دَآبَّةٖ فِي ٱلۡأَرۡضِ إِلَّا عَلَى ٱللَّهِ رِزۡقُهَا ﴾

"And no moving (living) creature is there on earth, but its provision is due from Allāh." [*Sūrah Hud* 11:6]

And some women take the contraceptive pills which are medically harmful and negatively affect the birth in addition to being against the Sharia law.

9. **The Prophet (صَلَّىٰٱللَّهُعَلَيۡهِوَسَلَّمَ) is highly interested in multiplying his Ummah** as he gave an order and mentioned the reason for it. He used to order men to marry the fertile and loving so that he (صَلَّىٰٱللَّهُعَلَيۡهِوَسَلَّمَ) would be proud of His Ummah on the Day of Judgment.

10. **The Prophets (عَلَيۡهِمُٱلسَّلَامُ) will be boasting with one another over who has more followers**. Why? Because the more followers the Prophet has, the more he will be rewarded. If they followed him and practiced his teachings, he would have the reward of the followers:

مَنْ سَنَّ فِي الْإِسْلَامِ سُنَّةً حَسَنَةً كَانَ لَهُ أَجْرِهَا وَ أَجْر مَنْ عَمِلَ بِهَا إِلَى يَوْمِ الْقِيَامَةِ

> **"He who introduced some good practice in Islam which was followed after him (by people), he would be assured of a reward like he who followed it."** [27]

[27] Related by Muslim on the authority of Jarīr (رَضِيَٱللَّهُعَنْهُ).

THE WOMAN IS MARRIED FOR FOUR REASONS

973- Abu Hurairah (رَضِيَ ٱللَّهُ عَنْهُ) reported, the Prophet (صَلَّىٰ ٱللَّهُ عَلَيْهِ وَسَلَّمَ) said,

تُنْكَحُ الْمَرْأَةُ لأَرْبَعٍ لِمَالِهَا وَلِحَسَبِهَا وَلِجَمَالِهَا وَلِدِينِهَا فَاظْفَرْ بِذَاتِ الدِّينِ تَرِبَتْ يَدَاكَ

"A woman is married for four reasons: for her wealth, for her class, for her beauty or for her piety. Select the pious, may your hand be rubbed in the dust!"[28] Related by Bukhari and Muslim.

Explanation

The purposes of people regarding marriage are different. Women are often married for these four reasons: for her wealth, class, beauty or piety.

First: "For her wealth." For example, an old woman is married for her big fortune because she will die sooner or later. If she is childless, he will take half of her wealth or all of it according to a weak point of view.

---

[28] Related by al-Bukhārī (5090), Muslim (1466), Abū Dawud (2047), Annassai (6/68), Ibn Majah (1858), Ahmad (2/428), but related by Tirmidhi (1086) on the authority of Jabir (رَضِيَ ٱللَّهُ عَنْهُ), Tuhfat Al-Ashraf (14305).

Second: "For her class." Tribes are different from each other regarding superiority and inferiority. A man who is inferior can marry from a tribe superior to his in order to upgrade himself. So, people will say that he married this one to upgrade himself and his children.

Third: "For her beauty." The beautiful woman is married in spite of her low class and being penniless.

Fourth: "For her religion." This refers to the religious woman, especially a knowledgeable one. The Muslim has to marry a woman who helps him to obey Allāh. The religious woman helps her husband to obey Allāh and she is obedient to her husband. Some religious women can choose another wife for her husband if she notices his desire for her. If she is not religious, she will make troubles if her husband has dreamt of marrying another woman. A religious woman is an honest one. When her husband is absent, she will not betray him. Also, she will care for his wealth, children and family. The Prophet (صَلَّى ٱللَّهُ عَلَيْهِ وَسَلَّمَ) said,

فَاظْفَرْ بِذَاتِ الدِّينِ

"Select the pious," meaning to look upon her as a prize you want to win. **"The pious"** meaning the religious one. One should know that if they follow this advice, this religious woman will turn out to be the most beautiful in one's eyes even if she is only slightly beautiful. Beauty is not the only criterion. Sometimes the woman looks very beautiful, but Allāh makes her look ugly in her husband's view. And he hears people talk about her beauty, but, in fact, she is not beautiful because hearts are controlled by Allāh. So, if one follows this advice, he will be in good state because he followed the Prophet's advice (صَلَّى ٱللَّهُ عَلَيْهِ وَسَلَّمَ) when he told him to select the pious.

تَرِبَتْ يَدَاكَ

"May your hand be rubbed in dust." This indicates that dust will stick to your hand or your hand will be filled with dust or the dust is caught by your hand. All these meanings are relevant. It means you will be poor because the poor man is the only one in whose hand you can find dust. This is a figurative phrase and is not used to express its literal or connotational implication, but to urge one to do something. It is also said that it means may your hands be (literally) rubbed in dust because you didn't marry the religious one.

So, the second meaning indicates that it is an invocatory sentence. The Prophet (صَلَّى ٱللَّهُ عَلَيْهِ وَسَلَّمَ) invocated against the man who does not win the religious wife. But the first sentence is invitatory sentence. Its own purpose is to urge anyone to do so, such as what the Prophet (صَلَّى ٱللَّهُ عَلَيْهِ وَسَلَّمَ) said to Mu'ādh ibn Jabal (رَضِيَ ٱللَّهُ عَنْهُ):

ثَكِلَتْكَ أُمُّكَ يَا مُعَاذُ ، وَ هَلْ يَكُبُّ النَّاسَ عَلَى وُجُوهِهِمْ فِي النَّارِ إِلَّا حَصَائِدُ أَلْسِنَتِهِمْ

"May your mother not find you, O Mu'ādh! Are people thrown onto their faces in Hell for anything other than the harvest of their tongues?'"[29].

ثَكِلَتْكَ أُمُّكَ

"May your mother not find you" means lose you. The Prophet (صَلَّىٰٱللَّهُعَلَيْهِوَسَلَّمَ) did not invoke against anyone being lost, but it is an invitatory sentence. Others argue that it is an invocative sentence which means he is supplicating this would happen were he fail to understand.

تَرِبَتْ يَدَاكَ

"May your hand be rubbed in the dust." The dust will be stuck to your hand, your hand is filled with dust or the dust is caught by your hand. These are all figurative for poverty. **There are some benefits in this *Ḥadīth*:**

1. **This is a reference that men's most desirable marriage purposes revolve around these four**: wealth, class, beauty and piety.

2. **There is no problem if anyone marries a woman for her wealth** because the Prophet (صَلَّىٰٱللَّهُعَلَيْهِوَسَلَّمَ) approved this but he urged to marry the religious woman.

---

[29] Related by Ahmad (5/231), Tirmidhi (2616), Annassai in Assunan al-Kubrā (11394), Ibn Majah (3973), and authenticated by Ibn Hibbān (214), al-Hākim (2/413), and we mentioned their narrations in "Jami' Al-Oloum" (J/29), see our investigation.

3. **There is no problem if the man marries a woman for her class** to upgrade himself and his children.

4. **The woman can be married for her beauty**. So, there is no problem if she is married for her beauty. Maybe the man likes beauty and cannot stand looking at a woman who is not as men are so different in this respect.

5. **A woman may be married for her piety** even if this is the only purpose.

6. **The best one of these purposes is to marry a woman for her piety** as he (صَلَّىٱللَّهُعَلَيْهِوَسَلَّمَ) said,

فَاظْفَرْ بِذَاتِ الدِّينِ تَرِبَتْ يَدَاكَ

"Select the pious, may your hand be rubbed in the dust."

7. **Everyone should follow the Prophet's advice.** However, nowadays, most people marry a woman for her beauty and others for her wealth and class. Are these the only purposes? No, the proof is in the above-mentioned *Ḥadīth,*

تَزَوَّجُوا الْوَدُودَ الْوَلُودَ

"Marry the one who is fertile and loving."

The man can marry a woman because she is known to be loving to her husband and satisfying to his desires. And he can marry a woman because she is known to be fertile. One can marry a woman for being educated. A knowledgeable woman who has earned her Bachelor's degree can be married, even if the man only has a primary certificate.

He also may marry her for the upbringing of his children with his dead wife.

The purposes for men marrying are different. But the Prophet (صَلَّى ٱللَّهُ عَلَيْهِ وَسَلَّمَ) mentioned the most common ones. So, whenever the man marries a woman for a legally recognized purpose, this is allowed. However, it is better to marry her for piety. What if a man marries a woman because she is a singer and he loves songs? This is (prohibited) haram unless he wants to call her to abandoning singing. But we are afraid he may be led astray.

CONGRATULATIONS FOR THE ONE WHO GOT MARRIED

974- Narrated Abu Hurairah (رَضِيَ ٱللَّهُ عَنْهُ) reported,

أَنَّ النَّبِيَّ صلى الله عليه وسلم كَانَ إِذَا رَفَّأَ الإِنْسَانَ إِذَا تَزَوَّجَ قَالَ : بَارَكَ اللَّهُ لَكَ وَبَارَكَ عَلَيْكَ وَجَمَعَ بَيْنَكُمَا فِي خَيْرٍ

When the Prophet (صَلَّى ٱللَّهُ عَلَيْهِ وَسَلَّمَ) congratulated a man on his marriage, he (صَلَّى ٱللَّهُ عَلَيْهِ وَسَلَّمَ) said,

Baarak Allahu laka wa baarak 'alayk wa jama' baynakumaa fi khayrin

"May Allāh bless for you and may He bless on you and bring goodness between you in good (works)."[30] Related by Ahmad and the four Imams and graded as Ṣaḥīḥ by At-Tirmidhi, Ibn Khuzaymah and Ibn Hibbān.

Explanation

كَانَ إِذَا رَفَّأَ إِنْسَانًا

[30] Al-Musnad (2/381), Abū Dāwud (2130), at-Tirmidhi (1091), an-Nasai in as-Sunan al-Kubra (10089), Ibn Majah (1905), Al-Busiri said, authentic Isnād, its men are trustful, authenticated by Ibn Hibbān (4052), and al-Hākim (2/199) said, in accordance with the conditions of Muslim, it is also authenticated by the author.

"When the Prophet (صَلَّى ٱللَّهُ عَلَيْهِ وَسَلَّمَ) congratulated a man" indicates that he can invocate for his marriage and say so-and-so. In the pre-Islamic period of ignorance, when they congratulate each other, they say may you be blessed with harmony and children. I wish you harmony and children. They always hate females:

﴿ وَإِذَا بُشِّرَ أَحَدُهُم بِٱلْأُنثَىٰ ظَلَّ وَجْهُهُۥ مُسْوَدًّا وَهُوَ كَظِيمٌ ﴿٥٨﴾ يَتَوَارَىٰ مِنَ ٱلْقَوْمِ مِن سُوٓءِ مَا بُشِّرَ بِهِۦٓ ۚ أَيُمْسِكُهُۥ عَلَىٰ هُونٍ أَمْ يَدُسُّهُۥ فِى ٱلتُّرَابِ ۗ أَلَا سَآءَ مَا يَحْكُمُونَ ﴿٥٩﴾ ﴾

"And when the news of (the birth of) a female (child) is brought to any of them, his face becomes dark, and he is filled with inward grief! * He hides himself from the People because of the evil of that whereof he has been informed. Shall he keep her with dishonor or bury her in the earth? Certainly, evil is their decision." [*Sūrah an-Nahl* 16: 58-59]

In such period, they also buried the females alive when they were born. However, they assigned them to Allāh and they said they are the daughters of Allāh:

﴿ وَيَجْعَلُونَ لِلَّهِ مَا يَكْرَهُونَ ۚ وَتَصِفُ أَلْسِنَتُهُمُ ٱلْكَذِبَ أَنَّ لَهُمُ ٱلْحُسْنَىٰ ۖ لَا جَرَمَ أَنَّ لَهُمُ ٱلنَّارَ وَأَنَّهُم مُّفْرَطُونَ ﴿٦٢﴾ ﴾

"They assign to Allah that which they dislike (for themselves), and their tongues assert the falsehood

that the better things will be theirs. No doubt for them is the Fire, and they will be the first to be hastened on into it, and left there neglected." [*Sūrah an-Nahl* 16:62]

إِذَا تَزَوَّجَ

"On his marriage" refers to a marriage contract made between him and a woman whether he consummated the marriage or not. If this is the case, one may offer congratulations. But if he proposed to a woman who accepted him, one should not say that because marriage is not concluded then. The Prophet said **"On his marriage."**

إِذَا رَفَّأَ إِنْسَانًا

"When the Prophet (صَلَّى ٱللَّٰهُ عَلَيْهِ وَسَلَّمَ) congratulated a man on his marriage" and the females may be congratulated by their friends and colleagues.

بَارَكَ اللهُ لَكَ

Baarak Allāh laka **"May Allāh bless for you"** includes your wife. Blessing is found in knowledge and morals besides care and children. Concerning **"blessing,"** the scholars have said it indicates much more fertility. It is derived from a pool which is plentiful and full of still water. It is not like water in a glass, and still not running.

وَ بَارَك عَلَيْك

"And may He bless on you." He blessed you for your wife. So, the Prophet (صَلَّى ٱللَّهُ عَلَيْهِ وَسَلَّمَ) prayed for the husband and his wife. Is it probable that the word 'blessing' here indicates a general prayer for the husband and his wife, and everything else? Yes, we can say this is a general prayer. It may also refer to this particular situation given this context of this ḥadīth.

So, those who congratulate the man who married, they do not congratulate him on wealth, but only on marriage. Thus, the generalization here is not intended even if the word is likely to be considered as such because the context requires particularization.

وَ جَمَعَ بَيْنَكُمَا فِي خَيْرٍ

"And bring goodness between you in good (works)." Meaning combine both of you in good works in this life and the life to come. So, it includes all kinds of goodness. These are three sentences:

بَارَكَ اللهُ لَكَ ، وَ بَارَكَ عَلَيْكَ ، وَ جَمَعَ بَيْنَكُمَا فِي خَيْرٍ

"May Allāh bless for you, and may He bless on you, and bring goodness between you in good (works)."

How many sentences are in the congratulation of the Jāhiliyyah? They are two poor sentences (in meaning and utterance). It is strange that some uneducated people say, when they congratulate one another, **"May you be blessed**

with harmony and many children." This is the congratulation of the Jāhiliyyah. This is not allowed because replacing the Islāmic congratulation said by the Prophet (ﷺ) with an abrogated congratulation of Jāhiliyyah indicates that they turn away from the Sunnah. And they are often ignorant of what is said by the Prophet (ﷺ) and they do not know how it is dangerous to go back to Jāhiliyyah. So, all matters of Jāhiliyyah must be eradicated unless it is approved by Islam. The Prophet (ﷺ) said,

لَيْسَ مِنَّا مَنْ ضَرَبَ الْـخُدُودَ ، وَ شَقَّ الْـجُيُوبَ ، وَ دَعَا بِدَعْوَى الْـجَاهِلِيَّةِ

"He who (on befalling a calamity) slaps his cheeks, tears his clothes and follows the ways and traditions of the Days of Ignorance is none of us."[31]

So, in this *Ḥadīth*:

First: "May Allāh bless for you." The hadith maintains that one asks Allah, upon congratulating, to encompass the married person with His blessings.

Second: Is this allowed for men and women? We can say that this is allowed for men, but women can congratulate only the bride.

The benefits of the Ḥadīth:

1. **This duaa is only related with the married** not with those who are still engaged.

---

[31] Related by al-Bukhārī (1294, 1297), Muslim (103) on the authority of Ibn Mas'ūd (رضي الله عنه), and Tuhfat Al-Ashraf (9569).

2. **The one who got married, but has not consummated the marriage**, can be congratulated with such because as soon as the marriage contract is concluded, both couples are married. And they will inherit from each other in case of death.

3. **Shaking hands is not allowed during congratulating** because there is no existing proof. The Prophet (صَلَّىٰ ٱللَّهُ عَلَيْهِ وَسَلَّمَ) had not done it. Had he done it, it would have been narrated. It is highly unlikely to say that the Prophet (صَلَّىٰ ٱللَّهُ عَلَيْهِ وَسَلَّمَ) used to shake hands simultaneously with saying the Duā. The duā is transmitted while the handshake is overlooked, since handshake would be out of context in this case. Instead, a handshake is reasonably made during meeting and greeting. In addition, giving kisses is not allowed. However, it is people's habits today that they shake hands, give kisses and they may give hugs. Anyway, this is inconsistent with the Sunnah.

4. **Furthermore, Islāmic greetings and congratulations are better than non-Islāmic ones**. For example, saying, "Hello" is just a greeting. But saying, "Peace be upon you (as-Salām Alaykum)" is a greeting and a prayer. Likewise, **"May you be blessed with harmony and many children"** implies a duā for a worldly matter only. Moreover,

بَارَكَ اللهُ لَكَ ، وَ بَارَكَ عَلَيْكَ ، وَ جَمَعَ بَيْنَكُمَا فِي خَيْرٍ

"May Allāh bless for you and may He bless on you and bring goodness between you in good (works)"

Includes good in this life and the afterlife. When you think about the traditions of the Prophet (صَلَّى ٱللَّهُ عَلَيْهِ وَسَلَّمَ) in these situations, you find praying, blessing, goodness and setting matters right.

5. **Moreover, you shall resort to Allāh (عَزَّ وَجَلَّ) whenever you are sad or happy**. When one gets married, beseeches Allāh to bless on and for the husband and combine him and his wife in good (works).

ḤADĪTH 975

975- On the authority of Abdullāh Ibn Mas'ūd (رَضِيَ ٱللَّهُ عَنْهُ),

قَالَ عَلَّمَنَا رَسُولُ اللَّهِ صلى الله عليه وسلم التَّشَهُّدَ فِي الْحَاجَةِ قَالَ التَّشَهُّدُ فِي الْحَاجَةِ " إِنَّ الْحَمْدَ لِلَّهِ نَسْتَعِينُهُ وَنَسْتَغْفِرُهُ وَنَعُوذُ بِاللَّهِ مِنْ شُرُورِ أَنْفُسِنَا مَنْ يَهْدِهِ اللَّهُ فَلاَ مُضِلَّ لَهُ وَمَنْ يُضْلِلِ اللَّهُ فَلاَ هَادِيَ لَهُ وَأَشْهَدُ أَنْ لاَ إِلَهَ إِلاَّ اللَّهُ وَأَشْهَدُ أَنَّ مُحَمَّدًا عَبْدُهُ وَرَسُولُهُ " . وَيَقْرَأُ ثَلاَثَ آيَاتٍ .

"The Prophet (صَلَّى ٱللَّهُ عَلَيْهِ وَسَلَّمَ) taught us At-Tashahhud (The Testimonial) in case of some need. The Khutbah of need is indeed. Praise is due to Allāh. We praise Him and we seek His help and His forgiveness. We seek refuge with Allāh from the evil of our own souls. Whomsoever Allāh guides will never be led astray and whomsoever is led astray, no one can guide. I bear witness that none has the right to be worshiped in truth but Allāh and that Muhammad (صَلَّى ٱللَّهُ عَلَيْهِ وَسَلَّمَ) is His servant and His Messenger). Then to recite three verses."[32]

Related by Ahmad, the four Imāms, graded as Hassan by at-Tirmidhi and al-Hākim.

---

[32] Al-Musnad (1/350), Abu Dawud (2130), At-Tirmidhi (1091), An-Nassai in Assunan Al-kobra (750), Ibn Majah (1905), Al-Hakim (2/199) on the authority of Abu Ubaida Ibn Abdullah Ibn Mas'ūd ((رَضِيَ ٱللَّهُ عَنْهُمْ)on the authority of his father but never heard from him, see Al-Elal by Ad-Daraqotni (5/313).

Explanation

عَلَّمَنَا

"Taught us." It is habitual that the Prophet (صَلَّى ٱللَّٰهُ عَلَيْهِ وَسَلَّمَ) taught his Companions either for answering a question or for no reason.

التَّشَهُّدَ

"Testimonial." When you read what he had taught, you find phrases like **"I bear witness that none has the right to be worshiped but Allāh."** He named this remembrance At-Tashahhud because it contains the word of Tawḥīd by which one can embrace Islam. This word is said also in At-Tashahud in prayers because of the superb words contained in it.

أَشْهَدُ أَنْ لَا إِلَهَ إِلَّا اللهُ وَ أَشْهَدُ أَنَّ مُحَمَّداً عَبْدُهُ وَ رَسُولُهُ

> **"I bear witness that none has the right to be worshipped but Allāh and Muhammad is his servant and Messenger"**

فِي الْـحَاجَةِ

"In case of some need." This indicates that it is said at times of dire need, not at every situation. The Prophet (صَلَّى ٱللَّٰهُ عَلَيْهِ وَسَلَّمَ) may be asked about worldly matters and did not say this

Khutbah. However, it is to be observed in times of need, like sermons (Jumu'ah' speeches) and so on.

إِنَّ الْـحَمْدَ لله

"Indeed praise is due to Allāh." The word "indeed" is for emphasis just like when it is used in *Talbiyah,* "Indeed, all praise and blessings are Yours." This is because Allah is the only One praised in all circumstances and He is the One worthy of all praise. The word "due" is for singling out Allah and expressing that He merits this praise.

Praise, in its absolute sense, is exclusive to Allah. Whereas others are praised for a limited reason. Also, Allah is praiseworthy no matter the situation. In contrast, there are people who are praised while they are not praiseworthy.

لله

"is due to Allāh" is meant to describe the praised one with perfection. Indeed, none has the right to be praised but Allāh (عَزَّوَجَلَّ). Anyone else who is praised, it is because of a favor by the help of Allah. But the only one who merits praise is Allāh (عَزَّوَجَلَّ). "**Praise**" in its absolute sense is exclusive for Allah. Those other than Allah merit praise for something they did as well as merit dispraise for other things. No one has the right to be praised whenever and wherever but Allāh (سُبْحَانَهُوَتَعَالَىٰ).

وَ نَسْتَعِينُهُ

"**We seek His help**" in all matters, particularly in this present situation for which such an introduction is used.

﴿ إِيَّاكَ نَعْبُدُ وَإِيَّاكَ نَسْتَعِينُ ۝٥ ﴾

"You (Alone) we worship, and You (Alone) we ask for help (for each and everything)." [*Sūrah* al-Fātihah 1:5]

We worship You alone in each and everything, particularly in acts of worship.

وَ نَسْتَغْفِرُهُ

"**And His forgiveness.**" Forgiveness indicates that Allāh conceals one's sins in this life and in the Hereafter in addition to bestowing His forgiveness. So, forgiveness can only be achieved by these two things: Concealment of sins and forgiveness. We seek His forgiveness for all sins, because sinning leads to failure. If anyone constantly seeks pardon (from Allāh), Allāh will provide him a way out of every distress and a relief out of every anxiety. Moreover, sinning stands in the way of making right decisions. Allāh (سُبْحَانَهُ وَتَعَالَى) said,

﴿ إِنَّآ أَنزَلْنَآ إِلَيْكَ ٱلْكِتَـٰبَ بِٱلْحَقِّ لِتَحْكُمَ بَيْنَ ٱلنَّاسِ بِمَآ أَرَىٰكَ ٱللَّهُ ۚ وَلَا تَكُن لِّلْخَآئِنِينَ خَصِيمًا ۝١٠٥ وَٱسْتَغْفِرِ ٱللَّهَ ۖ إِنَّ ٱللَّهَ كَانَ غَفُورًا رَّحِيمًا ۝١٠٦ ﴾

"Surely, We have sent down to you (O Muḥammad (صَلَّى ٱللَّهُ عَلَيْهِ وَسَلَّمَ) the Book (this Qur'ān) in truth that you

might judge between men by that which Allāh has shown you (i.e. has taught you through Divine Revelation). So be not a pleader for the treacherous. And seek the Forgiveness of Allāh, certainly, Allāh is Ever Oft-Forgiving, Most Merciful." [*Sūrah an-Nisā'* 4: 105-106]

Some scholars stated, "This indicates that sins stand in the way of making right decisions."[31] Everybody should seek forgiveness in order to diminish the effects of sins when giving a fatwa or judgment.

"We seek His Guidance, and we repent." This is not mentioned in this *Ḥadīth,* but some people say it. However, since this sentence is not mentioned in this *Ḥadīth,* people should not say it. When anyone wants to deliver a speech of his own, he may do whatever he wants whenever it is allowed, but constant delivery of a particular speech while incorporating something foreign to it is disputable. So, we need not say, **"We seek His guidance and repent to Him,"** because this is not transmitted in this *Ḥadīth.*

وَ نَعُوذُ بِاللهِ مِنْ شُرُورِ أَنْفُسِنَا

"We seek refuge with Allāh from the evil of our own souls." There is evil and good in human souls. Allāh (سُبْحَانَهُ وَتَعَالَى) has divided souls into restful, devilish and self-reproaching. All of them are mentioned in the Qur'ān:

﴿ لَآ أُقْسِمُ بِيَوْمِ ٱلْقِيَٰمَةِ ۝١ وَلَآ أُقْسِمُ بِٱلنَّفْسِ ٱللَّوَّامَةِ ۝٢ ﴾

"I swear by the Day of Resurrection. And I swear by the self-reproaching person (a believer)." [*Sūrah* al-Qiyāmah 75: 1-2]

And,

﴿ يَٰٓأَيَّتُهَا ٱلنَّفْسُ ٱلْمُطْمَئِنَّةُ ﴿٢٧﴾ ٱرْجِعِىٓ إِلَىٰ رَبِّكِ رَاضِيَةً مَّرْضِيَّةً ﴿٢٨﴾ ﴾

"(It will be said to the pious - believers of Islamic Monotheism): "O (you) the one in (complete) rest and satisfaction! Come back to your Lord - well pleased (yourself) and well-pleasing unto Him)!" [*Sūrah* Al-Fajr 89: 27-28]

And,

﴿ ۞ وَمَآ أُبَرِّئُ نَفْسِىٓ ۚ إِنَّ ٱلنَّفْسَ لَأَمَّارَةٌۢ بِٱلسُّوٓءِ ﴾

"And I free not myself (from the blame). Verily, the (human) self is inclined to evil." [*Sūrah* Yūsuf 12:53]

These three kinds of souls exist in the human being. They are recognizable by their influence.

1. The restful one urges doing good deeds and forbids doing evil deeds.

2. The devilish one urges doing evil and bad deeds.

3. Lastly, the self-reproaching soul can describe the other two souls, which excludes it as a third soul.

To clarify, one side of the self-reproaching soul blames itself for missing an evil deed while the other side blames itself for missing a good deed. The former covers the devilish one while the other covers the restful soul. The soul that conceals evil is regarded as a devilish one. The evils of the soul start with making offenses and abandoning commandments which eventually leads to disastrous consequences. Consider the following verse where Allāh (سُبْحَانَهُۥوَتَعَالَىٰ) said,

﴿ فَإِن تَوَلَّوْا۟ فَٱعْلَمْ أَنَّمَا يُرِيدُ ٱللَّهُ أَن يُصِيبَهُم بِبَعْضِ ذُنُوبِهِمْ ﴾

"And if they turn away, then know that Allāh's Will is to punish them for some sins of theirs." [*Sūrah al-Mā'idah* 5: 49]

So, turning away from righteousness is a result of previous sins but not all sins. Allah says,

﴿ بِبَعْضِ ذُنُوبِهِمْ ۗ وَإِنَّ كَثِيرًا مِّنَ ٱلنَّاسِ لَفَـٰسِقُونَ ﴿٤٩﴾ ﴾

"For some sins of theirs. And truly, most of them are Fāsiqūn (rebellious and disobedient to Allāh)." [*Sūrah al-Mā'idah* 5:49]

Some of the Salaf, if they missed the night prayer, would conclude that it must have been because of a sin and then they would seek repentance. They knew that reluctance from doing good deeds or sinning are only a result of previous sins. It is obvious that if a person is close to Allah, Allah will protect him against sins and bring him even closer to Him.

All of them, without a doubt, are evil caused by the soul. The evil of the soul is a result of two components: intention and determination. Wrongs one commits are actions that, definitely, incur an unfavorable reaction. Allāh says,

﴿ ظَهَرَ ٱلْفَسَادُ فِى ٱلْبَرِّ وَٱلْبَحْرِ بِمَا كَسَبَتْ أَيْدِى ٱلنَّاسِ ﴾

"Evil (sins and disobedience of Allah, etc.) has appeared on land and sea because of what the hands of men have earned." [*Sūrah ar-Rum* 30:41]

And,

﴿ وَمَآ أَصَـٰبَكُم مِّن مُّصِيبَةٍ فَبِمَا كَسَبَتْ أَيْدِيكُمْ ﴾

"And whatever of misfortune befalls you, it is because of what your hands have earned." [*Sūrah Ash-Shura* 42:30]

مَنْ يَهْدِهِ اللهُ فَلَا مُضِلَّ لَهُ

"Whomsoever Allāh guides will never be led astray." When Allāh wants to guide someone, no one can lead him astray. For example, consider someone who committed all kinds of unimaginable sins, yet Allāh wants to guide him, he will be inclined to go on the straight path in spite of the bad friends who want to lead him astray. They tell him why do you go in such way? But they cannot lead him astray because Allāh wants to guide him.

وَمَنْ يُضْلِلْ فَلَا هَادِيَ لَهُ

"**And whomsoever is led astray, no one can guide.**" So, whomsoever is led astray, no one can guide. For example, consider Abu Talib, the Prophet's uncle, who strongly defended the Prophet (ﷺ), yet the Prophet could not guide him. The Prophet (ﷺ) told him before death,

قُلْ : لَا إِلَهَ إِلَّا اللهُ ، كَلِمَةً أُحَاجُّ لَكَ بِهَا عِنْدَ اللهِ

> **"Say 'La ilāha ill Allāh, a word with which I will be able to defend you before Allāh.'"**[33]

But because Allāh wanted to lead him astray, he did not utter it.

One may argue that these two sentences may indicate losing hope of calling the astray to guidance and one may argue that those whom Allāh wants to lead astray, how can they be guided?

We answer that it is not good to think like this. Rather, if you want to guide or be guided, you can beseech Allāh only. And if you do what you have to, but the one you want to guide does not accept your Da'wah, you should leave it all to Allah.

وَأَشْهَدُ أَنْ لاَ إِلَهَ إِلاَّ اللَّهُ وَأَشْهَدُ أَنَّ مُحَمَّدًا عَبْدُهُ وَرَسُولُهُ

"**I bear witness that none has the right to be worshiped but Allāh.**" Testimony is originally used for what a person physically witnessed. Sometimes, however, it is used to refer

---

[33] Related by al-Bukhārī (1360), and Muslim (24) on the authority of Al-Mosaib Ibn Hazn (رَضِيَ اللَّهُ عَنْهُ), Tuhfat Al-Ashraf (11281).

to certainties as if they are perceptive. Based on this, when one says, "I bear witness that none has the right to be worshiped but Allāh," it means, "I certainly testify as if I see with my eyes that none has the right to be worshiped but Allāh." If we say, **"La ilaha illa Allāh,"** it asserts that none has the right to be worshiped but Allāh.

The word "*Ilah*" refers to who is loved and dignified by hearts out of awe. Someone may claim that this testimony is, in fact, a mere lie, because there are gods worshipped along with Allāh, such as al-Lāt, al-Uzza, Manat and Hubal. There are people who worship cows and consider its urine and feces a blessing. In addition, there are people who worship the sun and the moon. Thus, how can we say that "*La ilaha Illa Allāh*" means "None has the right to be worshipped but Allāh"?

The answer: Allāh indicates that these gods are false deities. They are mere names.

﴿ مَا تَعْبُدُونَ مِن دُونِهِۦٓ إِلَّآ أَسْمَآءً سَمَّيْتُمُوهَآ ﴾

"You do not worship besides Him but only names which you have named (forged)." [*Sūrah Yūsuf* 12:40]

So, *al-Lāt* is not a god, but they claimed it to be one. It is not a god, because it cannot create, provide, benefit or harm. Ibrahīm said to his father:

﴿ يَـٰٓأَبَتِ لِمَ تَعْبُدُ مَا لَا يَسْمَعُ وَلَا يُبْصِرُ وَلَا يُغْنِى عَنكَ شَيْـًٔا ﴿٤٢﴾ ﴾

> **"O' my father! Why do you worship that which hears not, sees not and cannot avail you in anything?"** [*Sūrah Maryam* 19:42]

So, this negation denotes that none has the right to be worshipped but Allāh. If anyone claimed otherwise, we would tell him that these other gods are false deities:

وَ أَشْهَدُ أَنَّ مُحَمَّداً

"**And that Muhammad** (ﷺ)" Who is Muhammad? He is Muhammad Ibn Abdullāh Ibn Abdul-Muttalib Al-Qurashi Al-Hashemi.

عَبْدُهُ وَ رَسُولُهُ

"**His servant and His Messenger.**" He is the Servant of Allāh and the Messenger of Allāh, so it is not allowed to worship him. He is just a Messenger. The Prophet (ﷺ) denounced a person's statement, "Whatever Allāh wills, you will." He (ﷺ) responded,

أَ جَعَلْتَنِي لله نِدًّا ؟!

"You have made me an equal with Allāh?"[34]

---

[34] Related by An-Nassai in Assunan Al-Kubra (10824) on the authority of Jaber (رضي الله عنه), and related by Ahmad in Al-Musnad (1/214) on the authority of Ibn 'Abbās (رضي الله عنهما) with a Sahih narration.

He (ﷺ) is a servant of Allāh, and he is unarguably the best representation of servitude to Allāh. The Prophet (ﷺ) said,

إِنِّي لَأَعْلَمُكُمْ بِاللهِ وَ أَتْقَاكُمْ لَهُ

"No one is more Allāh-fearing than me and no one is more knowledgeable of Allāh than me."

He is a servant of Allāh, which would consequently rule out any description of a god.

وَ رَسُولُهُ

"**And His Messenger**" to the creation, both humans and jinn. He is not a liar. he is to worship and never be worshipped and he is a Messenger who cannot be accused of lying.

وَ يَقْرَأُ ثَلَاثَ آيَاتٍ

"Then to recite three verses," meaning one should recite these three verses after he reaches "**His servant and His Messenger.**" He should recite the following three verses:

﴿ يَٰٓأَيُّهَا ٱلَّذِينَ ءَامَنُواْ ٱتَّقُواْ ٱللَّهَ حَقَّ تُقَاتِهِۦ وَلَا تَمُوتُنَّ إِلَّا وَأَنتُم مُّسۡلِمُونَ ١٠٢ ﴾

"O' you who believe! Fear Allāh (by doing all that He has ordered and by abstaining from all that He has forbidden) as He should be feared. (Obey Him, be thankful to Him and remember Him always) and die

not except in a state of Islam (as Muslims with complete submission to Allāh).” [*Sūrah Ali ʻImrān* 3: 102]

And,

﴿ يَٰٓأَيُّهَا ٱلنَّاسُ ٱتَّقُواْ رَبَّكُمُ ٱلَّذِي خَلَقَكُم مِّن نَّفۡسٖ وَٰحِدَةٖ وَخَلَقَ مِنۡهَا زَوۡجَهَا وَبَثَّ مِنۡهُمَا رِجَالٗا كَثِيرٗا وَنِسَآءٗۚ وَٱتَّقُواْ ٱللَّهَ ٱلَّذِي تَسَآءَلُونَ بِهِۦ وَٱلۡأَرۡحَامَۚ إِنَّ ٱللَّهَ كَانَ عَلَيۡكُمۡ رَقِيبٗا ١ ﴾

“O mankind! Be dutiful to your Lord, Who created you from a single person (Adam), and from him (Adam) He created his wife, Hawwa (Eve), and from them both, He created many men and women. And fear Allāh through Whom you demand (your mutual rights), and (do not cut the relations of) the wombs (kinship). Surely, Allāh is Ever an All-Watcher over you.” [*Sūrah an-Nisā’* 4:1]

And,

﴿ يَٰٓأَيُّهَا ٱلَّذِينَ ءَامَنُواْ ٱتَّقُواْ ٱللَّهَ وَقُولُواْ قَوۡلٗا سَدِيدٗا ٧٠ يُصۡلِحۡ لَكُمۡ أَعۡمَٰلَكُمۡ وَيَغۡفِرۡ لَكُمۡ ذُنُوبَكُمۡۗ وَمَن يُطِعِ ٱللَّهَ وَرَسُولَهُۥ فَقَدۡ فَازَ فَوۡزًا عَظِيمًا ٧١ ﴾

“O’ you who believe! Keep your duty to Allāh and fear Him, and speak (always) the truth. He will direct you to do righteous good deeds and will forgive you your sins. And whosoever obeys Allāh and His Messenger (ﷺ), he has indeed achieved a great

> **achievement (i.e. he will be saved from the Hell-fire and will be admitted to Paradise)."** [*Sūrah al-Ahzāb* 33:70-71]

Then, he should address the subject matter of the speech.

The first verse:

﴿ يَٰٓأَيُّهَا ٱلَّذِينَ ءَامَنُوا۟ ٱتَّقُوا۟ ٱللَّهَ حَقَّ تُقَاتِهِۦ ﴾

> **"O' you who believe! Fear Allāh (by doing all that He has ordered and by abstaining from all that He has forbidden) as He should be feared."** [*Sūrah Ali-'Imrān* 3: 102]

In this verse, Allāh urges the believers to duly fear Allāh. The due piety is based on faithfulness, not hypocrisy. Some people seem to be pious for the purpose of building a reputation, but privately they commit sins. Allāh also warns man to die only in a state of Islam,

﴿ يَٰٓأَيُّهَا ٱلَّذِينَ ءَامَنُوا۟ ٱتَّقُوا۟ ٱللَّهَ حَقَّ تُقَاتِهِۦ ﴾

> **"And die not except in a state of Islam (as Muslims) with complete submission to Allāh."** [*Sūrah Ali-'Imrān* 3: 102]

If anyone argues that this is impossible, because one cannot die but as a Muslim? How can it be?

Answer: Allāh (سُبۡحَانَهُۥوَتَعَالَىٰ) would not forbid something impossible to abandon, and would not order something impossible to do. How can a man die but a Muslim? One can die as a Muslim by doing good deeds in his life. Allāh (سُبْحَانَهُ وَتَعَالَىٰ) is Most Generous so much so that He cannot forsake the one who spent his life in doing acts of worship. If anyone worships Allāh, Allāh will make his ending good, and make him die in a state of Islām.

It is known that man cannot die but in a state of Islām, but he can do righteous good deeds that make his ending good. This is not opposed to what is mentioned in the *Ḥadīth* of Ibn Mas'ūd (رَضِيَ ٱللَّهُ عَنْهُ),

وَإِنَّ الرَّجُلَ لَيَعْمَلُ بِعَمَلِ أَهْلِ الْجَنَّةِ، حَتَّى مَا يَكُونُ بَيْنَهُ وَبَيْنَهَا غَيْرُ ذِرَاعٍ أَوْ ذِرَاعَيْنِ، فَيَسْبِقُ عَلَيْهِ الْكِتَابُ، فَيَعْمَلُ بِعَمَلِ أَهْلِ النَّارِ، فَيَدْخُلُهَا

> **"Similarly, a person may do the deeds of the people of Paradise, so much so that there is only the distance of a cubit between him and it, and then what has been written (by the angel) surpasses and he starts doing deeds of the people of the (Hell) Fire and enters the (Hell) Fire."**

This does not contradict with what we said, because Ibn Mas'ūd's *Ḥadīth* is made clearer by what is narrated in Sahīh al-Bukhārī[35]:

[35] Related by Bukhārī (3208), and Muslim (2643) on the authority of Ibn Mas'ūd (رَضِيَ ٱللَّهُ عَنْهُ), Tuhfat Al-Ashraf (9228).

إِنَّ الرَّجُلَ لَيَعْمَلُ بِعَمَلِ أَهْلِ الْـجَنَّةِ ، فِيمَا يَبْدُو لِلنَّاسِ ، وَ هُوَ مِنْ أَهْلِ النَّارِ

"A person performs deeds like the deeds of the people of Paradise apparently before people and he would be amongst the dwellers of Hell, while a person acts apparently like the people of Hell, but (in fact) he would be among the dwellers of Paradise."

All praise and thanks are due to Allāh. One cannot be let down if he is truthful, because Allāh is More Generous than His servant.

﴿ وَٱتَّقُواْ ٱللَّهَ وَٱعْلَمُوٓاْ أَنَّكُم مُّلَٰقُوهُۗ وَبَشِّرِ ٱلْمُؤْمِنِينَ ﴿٢٢٣﴾ ﴾

"And fear Allāh and know that you are to meet Him (in the Hereafter) and give good tidings to the believers (O' Muhammad ﷺ)." [*Sūrah al-Baqarah* 2:223]

Provided that you are a believer, good tidings are given to you before meeting Allāh.

<u>The second verse:</u>

﴿ يَٰٓأَيُّهَا ٱلنَّاسُ ٱتَّقُواْ رَبَّكُمُ ٱلَّذِى خَلَقَكُم مِّن نَّفْسٍ وَٰحِدَةٍ وَخَلَقَ مِنْهَا زَوْجَهَا وَبَثَّ مِنْهُمَا رِجَالًا كَثِيرًا وَنِسَآءًۚ وَٱتَّقُواْ ٱللَّهَ ٱلَّذِى تَسَآءَلُونَ بِهِۦ وَٱلْأَرْحَامَۚ إِنَّ ٱللَّهَ كَانَ عَلَيْكُمْ رَقِيبًا ﴿١﴾ ﴾

""O mankind! Be dutiful to your Lord, Who created you from a single person (Adam), and from him (Adam) He created his wife, Hawwa (Eve), and from them both, He created many men and women. And fear Allāh through Whom you demand (your mutual rights), and (do not cut the relations of) the wombs (kinship). Surely, Allāh is Ever an All-Watcher over you." [*Sūrah an-Nisā'* 4:1]

﴿ خَلَقَكُم مِّن نَّفْسٍ وَاحِدَةٍ ﴾

", Who created you from a single person"

Meaning, Which is Adam.

﴿ وَبَثَّ مِنْهُمَا ﴾

"**And from them both He created.**" Meaning from Adam and Hawwa'.

﴿ رِجَالًا كَثِيرًا وَنِسَاءً ﴾

"**Many men and women**." Which are greater in number: men or women"? In reality, women are greater in number than men. Sheikh Al-Islam Ibn Taymiyyah (رَحِمَهُ ٱللَّهُ) proved this by what the Prophet (صَلَّى ٱللَّهُ عَلَيْهِ وَسَلَّمَ) told women, "**You are the majority of the inhabitants of the Fire,**" and the dwellers of Hell constitute nine hundred ninety-nine out of every thousand.

So, he said that women are greater in number. But the word "many" in the verse qualifies the word "men," Why is this? It is because men are direly needed and women add more responsibility and are too emotional. One can notice this when hard times strike, who can stand there? Men. Women only slap their cheeks, tear their clothes and pull their hair out. Thus, Allāh described men as 'many' because they are beneficial when they are more in number.

﴿ وَٱتَّقُوا۟ ٱللَّهَ ٱلَّذِى تَسَآءَلُونَ بِهِۦ وَٱلْأَرْحَامَ ۚ إِنَّ ٱللَّهَ كَانَ عَلَيْكُمْ رَقِيبًا ۝١ ﴾

"And fear Allāh through Whom you demand (your mutual rights), and (do not cut the relations of) the wombs (kinship)..." [*Sūrah an-Nisā'* 4:1]

Fear Allāh through obeying His orders. Fear the wombs by avoiding the cutting off of the relations. This urges contact with the kinship. What is kinship? They are one's relatives. Allāh (سُبْحَانَهُ وَتَعَالَىٰ) said,

﴿ وَأُو۟لُوا۟ ٱلْأَرْحَامِ بَعْضُهُمْ أَوْلَىٰ بِبَعْضٍ ﴾

"But kindred by blood are nearer to one another (regarding inheritance)" [*Sūrah al-Anfāl* 8:75]

The kindred by blood are not forged by marital relationships as laymen think. The kindred by blood are the relatives of the husband and wife. But in Arabic they are called marital relationships (*ashar*):

﴿ إِنَّ ٱللَّهَ كَانَ عَلَيْكُمْ رَقِيبًا ۝١ ﴾

" Surely, Allāh is Ever an All-Watcher over you."

Allāh is an All-Watcher whenever and wherever. You should always be fully aware of this fact. If you do not fear Allāh, know that He is watching you.

The third verse:

﴿ يَٰٓأَيُّهَا ٱلَّذِينَ ءَامَنُواْ ٱتَّقُواْ ٱللَّهَ وَقُولُواْ قَوۡلٗا سَدِيدٗا ٧٠ ﴾

"O' you who believe! Keep your duty to Allāh and fear Him and speak (always) the truth. He will direct you ...."

In this verse, Allāh urges the believers to fear Allāh and to speak the truth to make things right. What is truth? It is any statement that accrues worldly and religious interest. This is similar to what the Prophet (ﷺ) said,

مَنْ كَانَ يُؤْمِنُ بِاللهِ وَ الْيَوْمِ الْآخِرِ فَلْيَقُلْ خَيْرًا أَوْ لِيَصْمُتْ

"And he who believes in Allāh and the Last Day, let him speak good or remain silent."[36]

Allāh ordered doing two things and then mentioned two rewards,

﴿ ٱتَّقُواْ ٱللَّهَ وَقُولُواْ قَوۡلٗا سَدِيدٗا ٧٠ ﴾

[36] It is mentioned above.

"Keep your duty to Allāh and fear Him and speak (always) the truth."

This is what has been ordered. And the reward,

﴿ يُصۡلِحۡ لَكُمۡ أَعۡمَٰلَكُمۡ وَيَغۡفِرۡ لَكُمۡ ذُنُوبَكُمۡۗ ﴾

"He will direct you to do righteous good deeds and will forgive your sins."

He will set right your worldly and religious deeds in this life if you fear Him and speak the truth.

He forgives the sins you commit because you fear Him and speak the truth. Then he said a general sentence that reads,

﴿ وَمَن يُطِعِ ٱللَّهَ وَرَسُولَهُۥ فَقَدۡ فَازَ ﴾

"And whosoever obeys Allāh and His Messenger (صَلَّىٱللَّهُعَلَيۡهِوَسَلَّمَ), he has indeed achieved a great achievement (i.e. he will be saved from the Hell-fire and will be admitted to Paradise)." [*Sūrah al-Ahzāb* 33:71]

Achievement means to acquire what you want and to be saved from what you fear. Allāh (سُبۡحَانَهُۥوَتَعَالَىٰ) said,

﴿ فَمَن زُحۡزِحَ عَنِ ٱلنَّارِ وَأُدۡخِلَ ٱلۡجَنَّةَ فَقَدۡ فَازَ ﴾

"And whoever is removed away from the Fire and admitted to Paradise, he indeed is successful." [*Sūrah* Ali 'Imran 3:185]

By turning away from the Fire, you are saved from what you fear and by being admitted to Paradise, you acquire what you want. This is the genuine success.

﴿ فَوۡزًا عَظِيمًا ٧١ ﴾

"He has indeed achieved a great achievement"

On the contrary, whoever disobeys Allāh and His Messenger will lose. Allāh said in the same *Sūra*h,

﴿ وَمَن يَعۡصِ ٱللَّهَ وَرَسُولَهُۥ فَقَدۡ ضَلَّ ضَلَٰلٗا مُّبِينٗا ٣٦ ﴾

"And whosoever disobeys Allāh and His Messenger (صَلَّاَللَّهُعَلَيْهِوَسَلَّمَ), he has indeed strayed into a plain error." [*Sūrah al-Ahzāb* 33:36]

The disobedient has strayed in plain error while the obedient obtains great success. Which one do you want to be? Obedience to Allāh is the way to success in this life and the life to come.

Interestingly, there is a switch in pronouns in the following, "**We praise Him and we seek His help,**" while in testimony, it says, "**I bear witness**" instead of "**we.**" Is this just a linguistic diversity and a rhetorical point or does it have another meaning? We say the meaning is different because seeking help and forgiveness is for the Ummah in general. One can ask forgiveness for himself and others. Allāh (سُبْحَانَهُوَتَعَالَىٰ) said about the *Tabi'een*,

﴿ وَٱلَّذِينَ جَآءُو مِنۢ بَعۡدِهِمۡ يَقُولُونَ رَبَّنَا ٱغۡفِرۡ لَنَا وَلِإِخۡوَٰنِنَا ٱلَّذِينَ سَبَقُونَا بِٱلۡإِيمَٰنِ ﴾

"And those who came after them say, 'Our Lord! Forgive us and our brethren who have preceded us in Faith.'" [*Sūrah al-Hashr* 59:10]

They used the plural "we" in cases of asking for forgiveness and seeking help. As for testimony, it is considered telling what is in one's inner self, where nobody shares it.

In this Ḥadīth, there are some benefits:

1. **The Prophet (ﷺ) was keen to convey his Message and guide the Ummah**. This is taken from the phrase, **"taught us."**

2. **Choosing the most suitable name.** He named this speech *at-Tashahhud*.

3. **It is desirable to use this Khutbah in important situations by virtue of its title, "Khutbah of need."** Some scholars believe it is obligatory to say it during the marriage contract because the Prophet (ﷺ) taught them to say it and this reflects its importance. However, the right opinion is that it is desirable. As a proof, the Prophet did not use this Khutbah in the occasion where he (ﷺ) delivered the speech on the marriage between the man who asked him to marry the woman who offered herself in marriage to the Messenger (ﷺ). But he said,

زَوَّجْتُكَ بِمَا مَعَكَ مِنَ الْقُرْآنِ

"I will marry you to her on the basis of what you have memorized of the Qur'ān."

4. **Stating that Allāh is praiseworthy. All praise is exclusive to Him as He deserves it all**.

5. **It is a must to seek forgiveness and help from Allāh Alone**. He said,

وَ نَسْتَعِينُهُ وَ نَسْتَغْفِرُهُ

"And we seek His help and forgiveness."

If one argues, "Can anyone ask help from other than Allāh?"

The answer: Yes, if this one is able to provide help. The Prophet (صَلَّى ٱللَّهُ عَلَيْهِ وَسَلَّمَ) said, "

وَ اللّٰهُ فِي عَوْنِ الْعَبْدِ ، مَا كَانَ الْعَبْدُ فِي عَوْنِ أَخِيهِ

"Allāh helps His servant as long as he helps his brother." [37]

And he said,

---

[37] Related by Muslim (699) on the authority of Abu Hurairah (رَضِيَ ٱللَّهُ عَنْهُ), Tuhfat Al-Ashraf (14700).

وَ تُعِينُ الرَّجُلَ فِي دَابَّتِهِ فَتَحْمِلُهُ عَلَيْهَا أَوْ تَرْفَعُ لَهُ عَلَيْهَا مَتَاعَهُ صَدَقَةٌ.

> **"To help a man with his mount, lifting him onto it or hoisting up his belongings onto it, is a charity."**[38]

On the other hand, it is not allowed to ask the help of a dead person because he is powerless. If anyone believes that this dead person has a secret power, this is major Shirk.

Is it allowed to ask forgiveness from other than Allāh? Is it allowed to say, "O' forgive me, young man?" You can ask forgiveness from such person for the offenses you committed against him. Allāh (سُبْحَانَهُ وَتَعَالَىٰ) said,

﴿ وَإِن تَعْفُوا۟ وَتَصْفَحُوا۟ وَتَغْفِرُوا۟ فَإِنَّ ٱللَّهَ غَفُورٌ رَّحِيمٌ ﴾ ﴿١٤﴾

> **"But if you pardon (them) and overlook and forgive (their faults), then verily Allāh is Oft-Forgiving, Most Merciful."** [*Sūrah at-Taghābūn* 64:14]

But seeking forgiveness from someone concerning Allāh's right is not allowed. Allāh (سُبْحَانَهُ وَتَعَالَىٰ) said,

[38] It is previously related

﴿ وَمَن يَغْفِرُ ٱلذُّنُوبَ إِلَّا ٱللَّهُ ﴾

"And none can forgive sins but Allāh." [*Sūrah Ali 'Imrān* 3:135]

6. **Seeking refuge is with Allāh**.

وَ نَعُوذُ بِاللهِ مِنْ شُرُورِ أَنْفُسِنَا

"We seek refuge with Allāh from the evil of our own souls."

Is it allowed to seek refuge with other than Allāh? It is allowed in something he is able to do? The Prophet (ﷺ) said, after addressing trials,

فَمَنْ وَجَدَ مَعَاذاً ، فَلْيَعُذْ بِهِ

"So whoever can find a place of protection or refuge from them, should take shelter in it."[39]

Many Aḥ*adīth* are mentioned concerning seeking refuge with the human beings in matters they are capable to deliver.

7. **Allāh is so much more Merciful than our souls** that he said,

وَ نَعُوذُ بِاللهِ مِنْ شُرُورِ أَنْفُسِنَا

[39] Related by Bukhārī (3601) and Muslim (2886) on the authority of Abū Hurairah (رَضِيَ ٱللَّهُ عَنْهُ), Tuhfat al-Ashraf (13179).

"From the evil of our own souls."

We sought refuge from our souls. There are many other evidences. For example, Allāh (سُبْحَانَهُوَتَعَالَىٰ) said,

﴿ وَلَا تَقْتُلُوٓا۟ أَنفُسَكُمْ ۚ إِنَّ ٱللَّهَ كَانَ بِكُمْ رَحِيمًا ﴿٢٩﴾ ﴾

"And do not kill yourselves (nor kill one another). Surely, Allāh is Most Merciful to you." [*Sūrah an-Nisā'* 4:29]

Thus, Allāh has forbidden killing ourselves.

8. **There are evils inside our souls** as the Prophet (صَلَّىٰٱللَّهُعَلَيْهِوَسَلَّمَ) said,

وَ نَعُوذُ بِاللهِ مِنْ شُرُورِ أَنْفُسِنَا

"From the evil of our own souls."

9. **Whomsoever Allāh decrees His guidance for, no one can lead him astray**. The Prophet (صَلَّىٰٱللَّهُعَلَيْهِوَسَلَّمَ) said,

مَنْ يَهْدِهِ اللهُ فَلَا مُضِلَّ لَهُ

"Whomsoever Allāh guides will never be led astray."

10. **It indicates that one ought to resort to Allah to guide him, not to someone else**. He said,

مَنْ يَهْدِهِ اللّٰهُ

"**Whomsoever Allāh guides.**" So, ask Allāh to guide you. This matter can be deduced from a different angle. Consider the following,

وَ مَنْ يُضْلِل فَلَا هَادِيَ لَهُ

> "**And whomsoever is led astray, no one can guide.**"
>
> It means that "I am afraid to be led astray, so I beseech Allāh to guide me."

11. **A Muslim must say publicly what he believes concerning the monotheism of Allāh**, and that Muhammad (صَلَّى ٱللَّهُ عَلَيْهِ وَسَلَّمَ) is His servant and Messenger. The Prophet (صَلَّى ٱللَّهُ عَلَيْهِ وَسَلَّمَ) said,

وَ أَشْهَدُ أَنْ لَا إِلَهَ إِلَّا اللهُ ، وَ أَشْهَدُ أَنَّ مُحَمَّدًا عَبْدُهُ وَ رَسُولُهُ

> "**I bear witness...**" Mere belief in the heart is not enough, but it is obligatory to say it publicly. The Prophet (صَلَّى ٱللَّهُ عَلَيْهِ وَسَلَّمَ) said,

أُمِرْتُ أَنْ أُقَاتِلَ النَّاسَ حَتَّى يَشْهَدُوا أَنْ لَا إِلَهَ إِلَّا اللهُ

> **"I have been commanded (by Allāh) to fight people until they testify that there is no true god except Allāh,"**

and he (ﷺ) also said,

يَا أَيُّهَا النَّاسُ قُولُوا : لَا إِلَهَ إِلَّا اللهُ تُفْلِحُوا

> **"O people! Say, 'La ilaha illa Allāh' and you shall succeed."**

He used the word, **"Aay."** It is advisable to say what you believe.

12. **<u>None has the right to be worshipped but Allāh.</u>** Thus, everything else is falsely worshipped.

13. **<u>The Prophet (ﷺ) is His servant</u>**. He said,

عَبْدُهُ

"His servant." This is a refutation of those who say that the Prophet should be worshiped or he is a Lord that can relieve pains or answer prayers. We witnessed some incidents proving this. Some laymen approach the Prophet's grave making *Qiblah* on their right side when they want to supplicate. Whether they ask Allāh in front of the grave or ask the buried Prophet (ﷺ) therein, it is an extremism on both cases.

Certainly, Muhammad (صَلَّى ٱللَّهُ عَلَيْهِ وَسَلَّمَ) is a Messenger. He said,

وَ رَسُولُهُ

"And His Messenger."

14. **It is honorable to describe Muhammad (صَلَّى ٱللَّهُ عَلَيْهِ وَسَلَّمَ)** as being a Messenger and servant to Allāh.

15. **Allāh is Most Merciful to human beings** because He sent them a Messenger from human beings, not angels. If Allāh had sent an angel to people on earth, He would have made him a human being because people do not naturally feel comfortable with what is from a different nature than theirs. And the same goes for him. Allāh (سُبْحَانَهُ وَتَعَالَىٰ) said,

﴿ وَقَالُواْ لَوْلَآ أُنزِلَ عَلَيْهِ مَلَكٌ ۖ وَلَوْ أَنزَلْنَا مَلَكًا لَّقُضِيَ ٱلْأَمْرُ ثُمَّ لَا يُنظَرُونَ ٨ وَلَوْ جَعَلْنَٰهُ مَلَكًا لَّجَعَلْنَٰهُ رَجُلًا وَلَلَبَسْنَا عَلَيْهِم مَّا يَلْبِسُونَ ٩ ﴾

"And they say, "Why has not an angel been sent down to him?" Had We sent down an angel, the matter would have been judged at once and no respite would be granted to them. And had We appointed him an angel, We indeed would have made him a man and We would have certainly confused them in a matter which they have already covered with

confusion (i.e. the Message of the Prophet Muhammad (صَلَّىٱللَّهُعَلَيۡهِوَسَلَّمَ))." [*Sūrah al-An'am* 6:8-9]

Meaning they will reject the one sent to them based on their claim "as he will be an angel looking as human". The Prophet sent by Allāh from the human beings cannot be confused, as Allāh gives Him signs proving he is truthful. Allāh (سُبۡحَانَهُۥوَتَعَالَىٰ) would not send a messenger asking people to believe in him, or otherwise he would take their lives and their possessions. He rather sends a messenger and support him with signs by which humans will believe.

THE ETIQUETTES OF PROPOSAL: THE RULE OF LOOKING AT THE FIANCÉE

930- On the authority of Jābir (رَضِيَ اللَّهُ عَنْهُ), the Prophet (صَلَّى اللَّهُ عَلَيْهِ وَسَلَّمَ) said,

عَنْ جَابِرِ بْنِ عَبْدِ اللَّهِ، قَالَ قَالَ رَسُولُ اللَّهِ صلى الله عليه وسلم " إِذَا خَطَبَ أَحَدُكُمُ الْمَرْأَةَ فَإِنِ اسْتَطَاعَ أَنْ يَنْظُرَ إِلَى مَا يَدْعُوهُ إِلَى نِكَاحِهَا فَلْيَفْعَلْ

"When one of you proposes to a woman, if he is able to look at what will induce him to marry her, he should do so."[40] Related by Ahmad, Abu Dawud, its narrators are in Sahīh, and it is graded as Sahih by al-Hākim.

Explanation

إِذَا خَطَبَ أَحَدُكُمْ

40 Al-Musnad (3/334), Abu Dawud (2082), Alhakim (2/179) and he said it is on the condition of Muslim. It is authenticated by Ibn Hazm in Al-Muhalla (10/31); it is graded as Hassan by the author of Fath Al-Bari (9/181). It is graded as weak by Ibn Al-Qattan, see Nasb Arrayah (4/240).

"When one of you proposes to a woman": In another narration mentioned by Ahmad, the Prophet (صَلَّى ٱللَّهُ عَلَيْهِ وَسَلَّمَ) said,

إِذَا أَلْقَى اللّٰهُ فِي قَلْبِ امْرِئٍ خِطْبَةَ امْرَأَةٍ، فَلَا بَأْسَ أَنْ يَنْظُرَ إِلَيْهَا

"When Allāh causes a man to propose to a woman, there is nothing wrong with him looking at her."[41]

If a man wants to propose to a woman, he is allowed to look at her. In the text of Qur'ān and the Sunnah, there are numerous occasions where the desire to do something is expressed as if one does it or did it already. Allāh (سُبْحَانَهُ وَتَعَالَى) said,

﴿ فَإِذَا قَرَأْتَ ٱلْقُرْءَانَ فَٱسْتَعِذْ بِٱللَّهِ ﴾

"So, when you recite the Qur'ān, seek refuge with Allāh from Shaytān (Satan)" [*Sūrah* an-Nahl 16:98]

"So, when you recite," means when you want to recite. In the Sunnah, "Whenever the Prophet (صَلَّى ٱللَّهُ عَلَيْهِ وَسَلَّمَ) went to the bathroom, he used to say,

أَعُوذُ بِاللّٰهِ مِنَ الْـخُبْثِ وَ الْـخَبَائِثِ

"Allāhumma Inni a`udhu bika minalkhubthi Wal khuba'ith,"

[41] It is the hadith of Muhammad Ibn Maslamah, it will be mentioned later but with another narration.

"I seek refuge in Allah from male and female devils."

This means when he **wants** to go to the bathroom. This usage is only applied when it is a decisive will followed by the action itself. When you want to recite the Qur'ān, seek refuge. Decisive will is needed. Recitation shall follow the decisive will. But when one wants to recite the Qur'ān after Al-Asr prayer, for example, one should not express the recitation done in the morning, as there is a time gap between will and action.

إِذَا خَطَبَ أَحَدُكُمُ الْمَرْأَةَ

"If a man wants to propose to a woman." Proposal is originally to ask a woman for marriage. There are many ways to do so and it depends on the traditions in a given place. A suitor could introduce himself to the woman's family for the sake of proposal. One can go to the *Wali* (guardian) of the woman. Or one can also send a mediator.

Or he can send a message. The method depends on the habits and traditions of society.

فَإِنْ اسْتَطَاعَ

He said, **"If he is able,"** because virgin women cannot be always seen, but when he is able to look at her, he should. In the past, they would hide to look at the women for marriage.

مَا يَدْعُوهُ إِلَى نِكَاحِهَا فَلْيَفْعَلْ

"At what will induce him to marry her, he should do so." What will induce him? Her face is the most important part. Having a beautiful face may make him propose to her. It is clear that the Prophet (صَلَّى ٱللَّهُ عَلَيْهِ وَسَلَّمَ) did not want him to look at her belly or her back, but he means what is allowed to be seen in the presence of her prohibited-to-marry relatives.

فَلْيَفْعَلْ

"He should do so." Scholars have different opinions about this. Some scholars believe it expresses permissibility, because it is generally prohibited to look at a woman. If one argues that the order here is intended for permissibility. Allāh (سُبْحَانَهُۥ وَتَعَالَىٰ) said,

﴿ وَإِذَا حَلَلْتُمْ فَٱصْطَادُوا۟ ﴾

> **"But when you finish the *Ihram* (of Hajj or Umrah), you may hunt."** [*Sūrah al-Mā'idah* 5:2]

The order here is intended for permissibility, as hunting was prohibited before. But some scholars said that order is intended for desirability. I don't know of anyone who said it is obligatory. So, there are two points of view. The first is it is permissible. And the second is that it is desirable as it has many benefits. For example, it makes them closer to each other. And based on that look he can decide either to propose to her if he likes her or to not propose because he does not like her.

No one can blame him if he did not accept her for some reasons. But if he proposes and then unreasonably disengages, he is to be blamed.

There are some benefits in this *Hadīth*:

1. **It is desirable to look at the fiancée on the basis of desirability**. One should look at his fiancée but not beyond the limits.

   Those limits are:

   First: It is prohibited to sit with her in private, the Prophet (صَلَّى ٱللَّهُ عَلَيْهِ وَسَلَّمَ) said,

   لَا يَخْلُوَنَّ رَجُلٌ بِامْرَأَةٍ وَلَا تُسَافِرِ إِلَّا وَمَعَهَا ذُو مَحْرَمٍ

   "No person (man) should be alone with a woman except when there is a Mahram with her."

   Second: To propose to her seriously. But if one is not taking the matter seriously, he should not look at her because this is originally prohibited.

   Third: To have a valid prediction that he would be accepted. If he thinks he would be rejected, he should not look at her because looking, at that time, is useless.

   For example, it is well known that the tribes, especially the nomadic ones, cannot accept any one outside the tribe. Thus, if anyone outside the tribe wants to propose to their daughters, he shall not look at her, why? He will probably not be accepted.

Another example is the one who claims to have kinship with the Prophet (ﷺ), they do not accept anyone out of their family. But this is wrong, they are ignorant. However, it is not allowed to look at their daughters because it is probable that they will not accept.

Fourth: He should not enjoy looking at her. Thus, looking depends on necessity. When he is convinced, he shall stop looking. So, it depends on necessity. Also, the enjoyment out of looking will drive him to continue the unlawful looking.

Fifth: He should be sure that his sexual desire will not be aroused. If he is not sure, he should not look at her. But this opinion is to be reconsidered because no one can be sure about that. So, if he feels himself sexually aroused, he should stop looking at her for the fear of fitnah.

Is it necessary for the woman to know of the presence of her fiancée? There is no problem in that if he wants to look at her unexpectedly. But if she knows, is it allowed to come intentionally? In the past, it was not possible because thc Prophet (ﷺ) said,

فَإِنْ اسْتَطَاعَ أَنْ يَنْظُرَ مِنْهَا إِلَى مَا يَدْعُوهُ إِلَى نِكَاحِهَا

"If he is able to look at what will induce him to marry her."

This is allowed[42] in shaa Allāh.

But, is it allowed to speak with her for a long time? Basically, it is not allowed because he wants only to know her and she is still not his wife. He can speak with her for a short time which allows him to know her voice. This is enough. He should not also speak with her on the phone because there will definitely be enjoyment, either sexual or just talking.

A lot of young men speak with their fiancées all night. He does this because his heart is so attached to her and he is really enjoying the conversation as well.

So, the right way is to stop. You proposed to her and she accepted. Speaking is unnecessary. If he says he cannot stand not speaking with her and he cannot sleep, then we advise him to conclude a marriage contract which enables him to speak with her all night.

---

[42] The Shaykh added, "Is she allowed to beautify herself? No, she is not allowed to intentionally wear attractive dress, and she is not allowed to wear kohl or makeup, why? She is not his wife. And there is another problem, if she is beautified at that time but after marriage she is not, what can he be like? There will be a reaction. There is another problem during the wedding party that the man sits with the unveiled women. In addition to being prohibited, this is bad for the bridegroom, because there may be more beautiful woman which may cause him to be unhappy with this marriage.

The fiancée is like any other woman whom he is not allowed to speak with.

Other benefits of the Ḥadīth:

2. **Islāmic Sharia is highly prestigious** because man cannot engage into something without prior knowledge.

3. **One cannot get worried. According to Islam, man should not open doors of sorrow on himself** because it may cause him to lose his faith or worry about his life. The Prophet (ﷺ) said about the one who is inflicted after taking all possible means,

لَا تَقُلْ : لَوْ .... فَإِنَّ لَوْ تَفْتَحُ عَمَلَ الشَّيْطَانِ

"And beware of (saying) 'If only,' because 'If only' opens the door to Satan."[43]

This *Ḥadīth* indicates that man should not be sorry. If he proposes to her and looks at her, no sorrow will be caused.

4. **It is not allowed to look at women** as the Prophet (ﷺ) said,

إِذَا خَطَبَ أَحَدُكُمْ امْرَأَةً

[43] Related by Muslim on the authority of Abū Hurairah (رضي الله عنه) (2664).

"When one of you asks a woman in marriage."

Had looking at women been made allowable and it was a habit of the Companions' wives, it would have been easy for someone to look at women whether he is engaged or not. So, it is obligatory for the woman to wear a veil in the presence of other men.

ḤADĪTH 977 AND 978

977- There is a relevant *Ḥadīth* related by Al-Tirmidhi and An-Nassai on the authority of Al-Moghira (رَضِيَ ٱللَّهُ عَنْهُ).[44] And it is related by Ibn Majah and Ibn Hibban on the authority of Muḥammad Ibn Maslamah (رَضِيَ ٱللَّهُ عَنْهُ).[45]

978- Related by Muslim on the authority of Abu Huraira (رَضِيَ ٱللَّهُ عَنْهُ) who said,

وَلِمُسْلِمٍ عَنْ أَبِي هُرَيْرَةَ – رَضِيَ اللهُ عَنْهُ – أَنَّ النَّبِيَّ قَالَ لِرَجُلٍ تَزَوَّجَ اِمْرَأَةً : أَنْظَرْتَ إِلَيْهَا ؟ قَالَ : لَا . قَالَ : اِذْهَبْ فَانْظُرْ إِلَيْهَا .

"The Prophet (صَلَّى ٱللَّهُ عَلَيْهِ وَسَلَّمَ) said to a man who proposed to a woman, 'Did you look at her?' He (صَلَّى ٱللَّهُ عَلَيْهِ وَسَلَّمَ) said, 'No.' The Prophet instructed him, 'Go and look at her.'"[46]

Explanation

[44] Related by Tirmidhi (1087), An-Nassai (6/69). It is authenticated by Ibn Hibban (4043), Al-Hakim (2/179) who said on the condition of Bukhari and Muslim, this hadith depends on Bakr Ibn Abullah Al-Mozani, and Al-Daraqutni mentioned it in Al-Ilal that it is related by Al-Moghira.

[45] Ibn Majah (1864), Ahmad (4/226), Ibn Hibban (4042), Al-Baihaqi (7/85) who said that the chain of narration of this hadith is different. It is based on the narration of Al-Hajjaj Ibn Artaa, and graded as gharib by Al-Hakim (3/492).

[46] Related by Muslim (1424).

تَزَوَّجَ

"Proposed" asserts his desire to marry. Had he married her, looking at her would have been unnecessary.

When he said,

أَنْظَرْتَ إِلَيْهَا

"Did you look at her?" he answered, **"No."** The response was,

اِذْهَبْ فَانْظُرْ إِلَيْهَا

"Go and look at her." This refers to the desirability which we preferred in the previous Ḥadīth. The individual should look at the woman he wants to marry, particularly if her family line is not known to feature beauty or has defects in their eyes, noses or mouths.

In this case, there is even more reason to look at the woman.

If one asks, "If I cannot look at her, can someone else look at her instead?

The answer: Yes, we can say if you cannot look at her yourself, you can ask someone like her brother, or someone else who is close to her, look at her and tell you about her features. You can also send one of the women you trust to look at her and tell you about her. However, some women are not trustworthy. If the fianceé is not beautiful, she may say, "I have seen a very beautiful woman who is like the moon," though she is not!

Once, a kind-hearted individual told us he proposed to a woman, but when they got married she didn't turn out as he had expected. One time, he entered the Masjid, preaching to the people. He warned people against those matchmakers who lie about the real features of the women. In short, you should send a trustworthy woman.

One can claim that even if he sent a trustworthy matchmaker, people have various opinions and views about beauty. The woman may be beautiful in one person's opinion and ugly in another person's opinion.

We say this is right. Everyone has his own opinion, but anyone is better than none. Anyway, this *Ḥadīth* supports the previous one.[47]

---

[47] The Sheikh was asked about sending her photo to the fiancé, is this enough? No. this fiancé may enjoy looking at the photo before marriage. In addition, he can show his friends the photo and ask what they think of this woman, so that his friends speak ill of her or make fun of her. Moreover, the photo may be unreal, as woman may take a photo which causes the fiancé to accept her while the photo is doctored. So, it is not allowed.

ḤADĪTH 979: A MUSLIM SHOULD NOT PROPOSE TO AN ENGAGED WOMAN

979- Ibn Umar (رَضِيَ ٱللَّهُ عَنْهُ) narrated, the Prophet (صَلَّى ٱللَّهُ عَلَيْهِ وَسَلَّمَ) said,

وَ عَنْ اِبْنِ عُمَرَ – رَضِيَ اللهُ عَنْهُمَا – قَالَ : قَالَ رَسُولُ اللهِ صَلَّى اللهُ عَلَيْهِ وَ سَلَّمَ : لَا يَخْطُبُ بَعْضُكُمْ عَلَى خِطْبَةِ أَخِيهِ ، حَتَّى يَتْرُكَ الْـخَاطِبُ قَبْلَهُ ، أَوْ يَأْذَنَ لَهُ الْـخَاطِبُ . مُتَّفَقٌ عَلَيْهِ ، وَ اللَّفْظُ لِلْبُخَارِي .

"The Muslim should not propose to somone who is already engaged to his Muslim brother, unless the first suitor gives her up or allows him to propose to her." Related by Bukhārī and Muslim, but this wording is related by Bukhārī.

Explanation

There are two different opinions on the way this sentence should be structured. One that says,

لَا يَخْطُبُ

"A Muslim is not to propose," while the other says, **"A Muslim should not propose."**

Scholars have said that choosing the statement structure that is found in the first opinion in place of the request which is found in the second is more eloquent than a mere request, as if he assumes this matter is out of question. Why is a statement in the place of request more eloquent than a mere request?

The answer: A request implies there is a choice, whereas a statement leaves choice out of the picture. For instance, the statement in which Allāh (سُبْحَانَهُ وَتَعَالَىٰ) said,

﴿ وَٱلْمُطَلَّقَٰتُ يَتَرَبَّصْنَ ﴾

> **"And divorced women shall wait (as regards their marriage),"** [*Sūrah al-Baqarah* 2:228]

This is more eloquent than the request as statements imply inevitability. In other words, those divorced women have to wait. It is not their choice.

أَخِيهِ

"Brother" here indicates the Muslim brother. Allāh (سُبْحَانَهُ وَتَعَالَىٰ) said,

﴿ إِنَّمَا ٱلْمُؤْمِنُونَ إِخْوَةٌ ﴾

> **"The believers are nothing else than brothers (in Islamic religion)."** [*Sūrah Al-Hujurāt* 48:10]

He said **"His Muslim brother"** instead of just "a man" to urge him not to propose. This is because they are brothers and they should not violate each other's rights.

حَتَّى يَتْرُكَ الْـخَاطِبُ

"**Gives her up**" indicates that he does not want to marry her and he should tell her family about this or some friends of his.

أَوْ يَأْذَنَ لَهُ

"Or allows him to propose to her." It means allowing whoever announces his desire to become engaged to such-and-such woman to whom the former is engaged to. Then he would allow him, in clear words, to propose to her.

This phrase also indicates that seeking permission from the fiancé is necessary. It would be invalid to take permission from someone else. The fiancé may give up the engagement for a specific individual and not for someone else. He may regard a particular person more beneficial owing to his wealth, knowledge or other reason. It is invalid to give a general permission for anyone to propose. It must be a specific person.

<u>There are some benefits in this *Ḥadīth*:</u>

1. **Sharia is concerned with the brotherhood between Muslims**. Proposing to an engaged woman causes hatred and enmity. So, many Islamic texts implant friendliness and love between the believers.

   Similarly, conducting a business transaction by a Muslim individual who is already agreed upon is prohibited. Thus, Islamic Sharia caters to brotherhood and friendliness between Muslims.

2. **It is prohibited to propose to an engaged woman** as the Prophet (صَلَّى ٱللَّهُ عَلَيْهِ وَسَلَّمَ) said,

   لَا يَخْطُبُ

   "A man should not propose to a woman who is already engaged."

   This indicates prohibition. Prohibition indicates that this proposal is regarded as hostility against the Muslim brother.

   One may ask, "Is the woman allowed to propose to someone who is already engaged?

   The answer: By analogy, it is not allowed for the same reasons.

   One may ask, "What can you say about the *Ḥadīth*[48] of Fatimāh Bint Qais (رَضِيَ ٱللَّهُ عَنْهَا) who was engaged to

[48] Related by Muslim (1480).

Mua'wiyya, Abu Jahm and Usāma ibn Zaid (رَضِيَ اللَّهُ عَنْهُمْ) at the same time? She consulted the Prophet (صَلَّى اللَّهُ عَلَيْهِ وَسَلَّمَ) who told her that Mua'wiyya (رَضِيَ اللَّهُ عَنْهُ) is moneyless, Abu Jahm (رَضِيَ اللَّهُ عَنْهُ) habitually beats women and finally, he said,

اِنْكِحِي أُسَامَةَ

"Marry Usāma."

What can you say?

The answer: None of them knew of the other two proposals. It is to be interpreted on par with the Sharia guidelines, which suggests, in such cases, that none of them knew of the other two proposals.

3. **The Muslim is allowed to propose to a woman engaged to a *Dhimmi* (Christian or Jewish) or to a non-Muslim fighter.** But how can a Muslim do that given that those two kinds of people are not allowed to marry a Muslim woman? The Muslim is allowed to marry a Christian or Jewish woman. If a Muslim wants to propose to a Jewish woman engaged to a Jewish man, the literal interpretation of the Ḥadīth allows it, because the Jewish man is not a fellow Muslim. And the same applies to Christians[49].

---

[49] Imam Ahmad (رَحِمَهُ اللَّهُ) says, "If the first suitor is a *Dhimmi*, it is not prohibited to engage his fiancée. He also said this Hadīth under study is concerned with the Muslims. So proposing to a girl engaged to a Jewish

Some scholars said it is prohibited to do that with the Christians and Jews in case there is a covenant of protection. But if they are fighters, they have no rights. And there are many *aḥadīth* that prohibit violating the rights of non-Muslims in the Muslim countries.

One can ask, "Why does it specify in the *Ḥadīth,* "the Muslim brother"?

<u>The answer</u>: Such phrasing follows the common usage in Ḥadith phraseology[50] and therefore it carries no reasonable justification to scholars. A similar example is when Allāh addressed the matter of prohibited-to-marry women,

﴿ وَرَبَٰٓئِبُكُمُ ٱلَّٰتِي فِي حُجُورِكُم مِّن نِّسَآئِكُمُ ٱلَّٰتِي دَخَلۡتُم بِهِنَّ ﴾

> **"Your step-daughters under your guardianship, born of your wives to whom you have consummated the marriage with."** [*Sūrah an-Nisā'* 4:23]

He says,

---

or a Christian, or cancelling their bargains is allowed because they are not Muslims.

50 - Editor's note: This terms means a particular mode of expression, especially one characteristic of a particular speaker or subject area. In this case, the particular speaker is the Prophet, and the subject area is Hadīth.

﴿ فَإِن لَّمْ تَكُونُوا۟ دَخَلْتُم بِهِنَّ فَلَا جُنَاحَ عَلَيْكُمْ ﴾

"but there is no sin on you if you have not gone in them (to marry their daughters)"

Despite the restriction expressed by the phrase, "**Under your guardianship,**" the step-daughters not under guardianship are prohibited as well according to most of the scholars. The above restriction follows the common usage, as step-daughters are most likely to stay with their step-father. Therefore, textual proofs that follow this manner do not have a reasonable justification of why they were used in such wording.

According to this point of view, the Muslim is not allowed to propose to a woman engaged to a Jew, a Christian or a non-Muslim. This is a valid and well-reasoned opinion. The non-Muslims may reject Islam when their rights are violated, particularly when they know that Islam considers such overstepping in engagement as being allowed. However, when they know that Islam respects their rights, they may be inclined to embrace Islam or at least speak good of it.

The individual is not allowed to propose to his brother's (in Islam) fiancée despite not knowing if his brother's proposal was rejected or not. Are you allowed to propose to a woman even if you do not know if she is still engaged or not? According to the *Ḥadīth,* this is prohibited because the Prophet (صَلَّىٰ اللَّهُ عَلَيْهِ وَسَلَّمَ) made the ruling dependent on the engagement.

This issue of engagement has no more than three scenarios:

First: To know that his brother's proposal is rejected, in which case, he is allowed to propose.

Second: To know that his brother's proposal is accepted, in which case, he is not allowed to propose. These two scenarios are not problematic.

Third: To be ignorant regarding whether his brother's proposal was rejected or accepted. This scenario has three more scenarios: (1) to have probable knowledge that the proposal was accepted; (2) to have probable knowledge that the proposal was rejected; (3) to have no hint of whether the proposal was rejected or accepted.

In all of these later scenarios, he is not allowed to propose to the engaged woman of his brother, because the Prophet (ﷺ) hinged the ruling on the engagement, not its acceptance. Nevertheless, some scholars believe that engagement is allowed in the case where the person has no knowledge of acceptance or rejection. They reasoned that there is no legal presence of the engagement in this case. This, however, contradicts the literal interpretation of the *Ḥadīth*. There is a chance the woman or her guardians may have been inclined to accept the first suitor, but this inclination may be spoiled by the second proposal, which would be considered a violation of the first suitor's rights.

Similarly, the Prophet (صَلَّى ٱللَّهُ عَلَيْهِ وَسَلَّمَ) prohibited cancelling a transaction made by a Muslim brother that is already agreed upon though there is no sale contract yet. It is not allowed, even if the seller wants to buy from the other buyer. In short, it is not allowed to propose to a woman until there is a certain knowledge of the first suitor's acceptance or rejection.

"Unless the first suitor gives her up." This is the second case, in which he changes his mind, but how is it possible to find out? Either the suitor announces he will not go through with the engagement or it is known through a trustworthy man. In this case, a proposal is allowed.

أَوْ يَأْذَنَ لَهُ

In the third case, "**Or allows him to propose to her,**" when he knows there is someone who expressed a desire to propose to his fiancée. In this case, a proposal is allowed. Thus, the proposal is allowed in the three cases illustrated above.

THE ḤADĪTH OF THE WOMAN WHO OFFERED HERSELF FOR MARRIAGE

980- Sahl b. Sa'd al-Sa'idi (رَضِيَ ٱللَّهُ عَنْهُ) reported,

عَنْ سَهْلِ بْنِ سَعْدٍ، السَّاعِدِيِّ قَالَ جَاءَتِ امْرَأَةٌ إِلَى رَسُولِ اللَّهِ صلى الله عليه وسلم فَقَالَتْ يَا رَسُولَ اللَّهِ جِئْتُ أَهَبُ لَكَ نَفْسِي . فَنَظَرَ إِلَيْهَا رَسُولُ اللَّهِ صلى الله عليه وسلم فَصَعَّدَ النَّظَرَ فِيهَا وَصَوَّبَهُ ثُمَّ طَأْطَأَ رَسُولُ اللَّهِ صلى الله عليه وسلم رَأْسَهُ فَلَمَّا رَأَتِ الْمَرْأَةُ أَنَّهُ لَمْ يَقْضِ فِيهَا شَيْئًا جَلَسَتْ فَقَامَ رَجُلٌ مِنْ أَصْحَابِهِ فَقَالَ يَا رَسُولَ اللَّهِ إِنْ لَمْ يَكُنْ لَكَ بِهَا حَاجَةٌ فَزَوِّجْنِيهَا . فَقَالَ " فَهَلْ عِنْدَكَ مِنْ شَىْءٍ " . فَقَالَ لاَ وَاللَّهِ يَا رَسُولَ اللَّهِ . فَقَالَ " اذْهَبْ إِلَى أَهْلِكَ فَانْظُرْ هَلْ تَجِدُ شَيْئًا " . فَذَهَبَ ثُمَّ رَجَعَ فَقَالَ لاَ وَاللَّهِ مَا وَجَدْتُ شَيْئًا . فَقَالَ رَسُولُ اللَّهِ صلى الله عليه وسلم " انْظُرْ وَلَوْ خَاتِمًا مِنْ حَدِيدٍ " . فَذَهَبَ ثُمَّ رَجَعَ . فَقَالَ لاَ وَاللَّهِ يَا رَسُولَ اللَّهِ وَلاَ خَاتِمًا مِنْ حَدِيدٍ . وَلَكِنْ هَذَا إِزَارِي - قَالَ سَهْلٌ مَا لَهُ رِدَاءٌ - فَلَهَا نِصْفُهُ . فَقَالَ رَسُولُ اللَّهِ صلى الله عليه وسلم " مَا تَصْنَعُ بِإِزَارِكَ إِنْ لَبِسْتَهُ لَمْ يَكُنْ عَلَيْهَا مِنْهُ شَىْءٌ وَإِنْ لَبِسَتْهُ لَمْ يَكُنْ عَلَيْكَ مِنْهُ شَىْءٌ " . فَجَلَسَ الرَّجُلُ حَتَّى إِذَا طَالَ مَجْلِسُهُ قَامَ فَرَآهُ رَسُولُ اللَّهِ صلى الله عليه وسلم مُوَلِّيًا فَأَمَرَ بِهِ فَدُعِيَ فَلَمَّا جَاءَ قَالَ " مَاذَا مَعَكَ مِنَ الْقُرْآنِ " . قَالَ مَعِي سُورَةُ كَذَا

وَسُورَةُ كَذَا - عَدَّدَهَا . فَقَالَ " تَقْرَؤُهُنَّ عَنْ ظَهْرِ قَلْبِكَ " . قَالَ نَعَمْ . قَالَ " اذْهَبْ فَقَدْ مَلَّكْتُكَهَا بِمَا مَعَكَ مِنَ الْقُرْآنِ

A woman came to Allāh's Messenger (ﷺ) and said, "Messenger of Allāh, I have come to you to offer myself to you (that you may marry me)." Allāh's Messenger (ﷺ) saw her and cast a glance at her from head to foot. Allāh's Messenger (ﷺ) then lowered his head. When the woman saw that he had made no decision, she sat down.

There stood up a person from amongst his Companions and said, "Messenger of Allāh, marry her to me if you have no interest in her." He (the Prophet (ﷺ)) said, "Is there anything with you (which you can give as a dowry)?" He said, "No, Messenger of Allāh, by Allāh, I have nothing." Thereupon Allāh's Messenger (ﷺ) said, "Go to your people (family) and see if you can find something." He returned and said, "I have found nothing." The Messenger of Allāh (ﷺ) said, "See even if it is an iron ring." He went and returned and said, "No, by Allāh, not even an iron ring, but only this lower garment of mine (Sahl (رَضِيَ اللَّهُ عَنْهُ) said that he had no upper garment), half of which (I am prepared to part with) for her." Thereupon Allāh's Messenger (ﷺ) said, "How can your lower garment serve your purpose, for if you wear it, she would not be able to make any use of it, and if she wears it there would not be anything on you?" The man sat down, and as the sitting prolonged he stood up (in disappointment)

and as he was leaving." Allāh's Messenger (صَلَّىٱللَّهُعَلَيۡهِوَسَلَّمَ) sent someone to call him back, and as he came, he said to him, "Have you memorized any part of the Qur'ān?" He said, "I have memorized such-and-such *Sūrah*s (and he counted them), whereupon he (صَلَّىٱللَّهُعَلَيۡهِوَسَلَّمَ) said, "Can you recite them from heart (from your memory)?" He said, "Yes," whereupon, he (Allāh's Messenger (صَلَّىٱللَّهُعَلَيۡهِوَسَلَّمَ)) said, "Go, I have given her to you in marriage for the part of the Qur'ān which you know." Related by Bukhari and Muslim, but this is the narration of Muslim.

Explanation

اِمْرَأَةٌ

"**A woman**." It is indefinite who the woman was. It is, however, unnecessary because legal rulings are general for everybody. Yet, we sometimess find someone who unduly searches for that specific unnamed person. This endeavor is unnecessary unless naming that specific individual bears a legal value, which makes his identification necessary.

جِئْتُ أَهَبُ لَكَ نَفْسِي

"**To offer**" is to give without expecting any return. Here it means that a woman offers herself for marriage, which is a privilege of the Prophet (صَلَّىٱللَّهُعَلَيۡهِوَسَلَّمَ). Allāh says,

﴿ إِن وَهَبَتْ نَفْسَهَا لِلنَّبِيِّ إِنْ أَرَادَ ٱلنَّبِيُّ أَن يَسْتَنكِحَهَا خَالِصَةً لَّكَ مِن دُونِ ٱلْمُؤْمِنِينَ ﴾

"And a believing woman, if she offers herself to the Prophet, and the Prophet wishes to marry her - a privilege for you only, not for the (rest of) the believers." [*Sūrah al-Ahzāb* 33:50]

فَصَعَّدَ النَّظَرَ فِيهَا ، وَ صَوَّبَهُ

"Allāh's Messenger (ﷺ) saw her and cast a glance at her from head to foot." He (ﷺ) raised his eyes to see her and then he lowered his eyes.

"Saw her and cast a glance at her from head to foot." He looked at her, as he is considered a suitor who is allowed to look at his fiancée. Many scholars mentioned that the Prophet (ﷺ) had some privileges concerning looking at women and privacy with them. This is because the Prophet (ﷺ) can never be seduced, given that looking at women is fundamentally prohibited for fear of temptation. Thus, privacy with women and looking at them is prohibited. So, he (ﷺ) is allowed to look at women or meet them in private. Also, the proposal is another reason for looking.

فَلَمَّا رَأَتْ الْمَرْأَةُ أَنَّهُ لَمْ يَقْضِ فِيهَا شَيْئاً جَلَسَتْ

"When the woman saw that he had made no decision, she sat down."

This indicates how the Prophet (ﷺ) was polite enough not to say no to someone to his/her face. Had he said he had no desire to marry her, she would have been shocked. Instead, he lowered his head and kept silent. But the woman understood the hint and sat down without leaving.

فَقَامَ رَجُلٌ مِنْ أَصْحَابِهِ . فَقَالَ : يَا رَسُولَ اللَّهِ إِنْ لَمْ يَكُنْ لَكَ بِهَا حَاجَةٌ فَزَوِّجْنِيهَا

"There stood up a person from amongst his Companions and said, 'Messenger of Allāh, marry her to me if you have no need of her.'"

This is a request not a command, because the Companion cannot command the Prophet (ﷺ). He asked him to marry her. The Prophet (ﷺ) said,

فَهَلْ عِنْدَكَ مِنْ شَيْءٍ ؟

"Is there anything with you (which you can give as a dowry)?"

This indefinite pronoun (anything) does not specify any amount as long as it qualifies as a dowry. It cannot be a barleyy grain as *ad-Dhahriyah*[51] believed, why? Because the dowry must be money or something equivalent. Allāh said,

---

51 - Editor's note: It is a legal school calling for adopting the literal interpretation of the religious texts from Quran and Sunnah, while disregarding their implications.

﴿ وَأُحِلَّ لَكُم مَّا وَرَآءَ ذَٰلِكُمْ أَن تَبْتَغُوا۟ بِأَمْوَٰلِكُم ﴾

"All others are lawful, provided you seek (them in marriage) with Mahr (dowry)." [*Sūrah An-Nisā'*: 4:24]

قَالَ : لَا وَ اللهِ يَا رَسُولَ اللهِ

"**He said, "No, Messenger of Allāh, by Allāh, I have nothing."** The man swore that he had nothing that fits as a dowry for her. And he (ﷺ) said,

فَقَالَ : اِذْهَبْ إِلَى أَهْلِكَ ، فَانْظُرْ هَلْ تَجِدُ شَيْئًا

"Thereupon Allāh's Messenger (ﷺ) said, 'Go to your people (family) and see if you can find something.'"

One may ask, How dif the Prophet command him to go to his family when he swore that he had nothing?

<u>The answer:</u> A person may swear that he likely does not have anything. Yet, he may forget that he already has something he wasn't aware of.

فَذَهَبَ ، ثُمَّ رَجَعَ؟ فَقَالَ : مَا وَجَدْتُ شَيْئًا

"He returned and said, 'I have found nothing.'"

He did not find even a cent. This indicates that the Companions lived in extreme poverty.

فَقَالَ رَسُولُ اللهِ صَلَّى اللهُ عَلَيْهِ وَ سَلَّمَ : أُنْظُرْ وَ لَوْ خَاتَمًا مِنْ حَدِيدٍ

"The Messenger of Allāh (صَلَّىٱللَّهُعَلَيْهِوَسَلَّمَ) said, 'See even if it is an iron ring.'"

He did not even have an iron ring? The point is that the marriage would work even with something as insignificant as an iron ring.

فَذَهَبَ ثُمَّ رَجَعَ ، فَقَالَ : لَا وَ اللهِ يَا رَسُولَ اللهِ ، وَ لَا خَاتَمًا مِنْ حَدِيدٍ

"He went and returned and said, 'No, by Allāh, not even an iron ring.'"

Because he was poor.

وَ لَكِنْ هَذَا إِزَارِي

"But only this lower garment of mine." He did not even have an upper garment. He only had a lower garment to cover his private parts. Sahl (رَضِيَٱللَّهُعَنْهُ) said that he had no upper garment.

فَقَالَ سَهْلٌ : مَا لَهُ رِدَاءٌ ، فَلَهَا نِصْفُهُ ، فَقَالَ رَسُولُ اللهِ صَلَّى اللهِ وَ سَلَّمَ :
مَا تَصْنَعُ بِإِزَارِكَ ؟

"'Half of which (I am prepared to part with) for her.' Thereupon Allāh's Messenger (صَلَّىٱللَّهُعَلَيْهِوَسَلَّمَ) said, 'How can your lower garment serve your purpose?'"

Even if he gave her half of it as a dowry, how could she make use of it? He continued,

إِنْ لَبِسْتَهُ لَمْ يَكُنْ عَلَيْهَا مِنْهُ شَيْءٌ وَإِنْ لَبِسَتْهُ لَمْ يَكُنْ عَلَيْكَ مِنْهُ شَيْءٌ

"For if you wear it, she would not be able to make any use of it and, if she wears it, there would not be anything on you?"

He continued,

" مَاذَا مَعَكَ مِنَ الْقُرْآنِ " قَالَ " اذْهَبْ فَقَدْ مَلَّكْتُكَهَا

"'Have you memorized any part of the Qur'ān?' He said, 'Go, I have given her to you in marriage.'"

He married her to the man and then commanded him to go.

اذْهَبْ فَقَدْ مَلَّكْتُكَهَا بِمَا مَعَكَ مِنَ الْقُرْآنِ

"Go, I have given her to you in marriage. For the part of the Qur'ān which you know."

This may refer to two meanings. **First,** the Prophet (صَلَّى اللَّهُ عَلَيْهِ وَسَلَّمَ) considered that the memorization of this part of the Qur'ān a dowry, which could be beneficial for the woman. **Second**, it would benefit her in the sense that he would teach her the part of the Qur'ān he memorized. The second meaning is the right one for two reasons:

First:

Allāh (سُبْحَانَهُ وَتَعَالَىٰ) says,

﴿ وَأُحِلَّ لَكُم مَّا وَرَآءَ ذَٰلِكُمْ أَن تَبْتَغُوا۟ بِأَمْوَٰلِكُم ﴾

"All others are lawful, provided you seek (them in marriage) with Mahr (bridal money given by the husband to his wife at the time of marriage) from your property. [*Sūrah An-Nisā'* 4:24}

Second: There are other narrations of this *Ḥadīth* that read, **"to teach her."**

"For the part of the Qur'ān which you know." Is this part of the Qur'ān unknown? No, because he said at first, "I can recite such-and-such *Sūrah*." This is the narration of Muslim.

In another narration, he said,

اِنْطَلِقْ ، فَقَدْ زَوَّجْتُكَهَا ، فَعَلِّمْهَا مِنَ الْقُرْآنِ

"Go, I have given her to you in marriage, so teach her the Qur'ān."

There are different narrations of this particular *Ḥadīth*. Do these different narrations render this a *Ḥadīth Mudtarib*[52] and therefore weak? No. Why? That's because the narrations are not contradictory. The *Mudtarib Ḥadīth* requires that the narrations must be contradictory, irreconcilable and that there be no preponderant narration. It is better if there is a

52 - Editor's note: This refers to the type of Ḥadīth where there are several narrations of the same Ḥadīth with different wording.

chance that they are reconcilable or that there is a narration authentic enough to take preference. Otherwise, the *Ḥadīth* would be considered Mudtarib should those steps be unattainable. And the Mudtarib type of *Ḥadīth* is one of the reasons for criticizing the authenticity of the *Ḥadīth*.

Not all scholars are upon the same levels in understanding the *Ḥadīth*. Some scholars are skilled enough to extract more than forty benefits. Other scholars fall short and extract twenty benefits. Whereas some scholars can only extract six or seven benefits.

Ali Ibn Abi Talib (رَضِيَ ٱللَّهُ عَنْهُ) was asked, "Did the Prophet (صَلَّى ٱللَّهُ عَلَيْهِ وَسَلَّمَ) impart upon you (i.e. Companions) any extra knowledge?" Alī said, "No. By Him Who made the grain split (germinate) and created the soul, we have nothing besides the Qur'ān, except the gift of understanding the Qur'ān, which Allāh gives a man, in addition to what is written in this manuscript." He was asked (رَضِيَ ٱللَّهُ عَنْهُ), "What is in this manuscript?" Alī said, "The regulations of Diyah (Blood money), the ransom for captives and the ruling that no Muslim should be killed in *Qisas* for killing a disbeliever."

Thus, some people extract out of one text many benefits while others cannot.

<u>There are many benefits in this *Ḥadīth*:</u>

1. **<u>It is permissible to speak about unknown person in case his/her identification is not necessary</u>**, as the Prophet (صَلَّى ٱللَّهُ عَلَيْهِ وَسَلَّمَ) said,

جَاءَتْ اِمْرَأَةٌ

"A woman came."

2. **A woman is allowed to offer herself in marriage to the Prophet (ﷺ), not in exchange for dowry**. She said,

يَا رَسُولَ اللهِ : جِئْتُ أَهَبُ لَكَ نَفْسِي

"Messenger of Allāh. I have come to you to offer myself to you."

Can anyone else be the same as the Prophet (ﷺ)? No. No woman is allowed to offer herself with no dowry. Allāh (سُبْحَانَهُ وَتَعَالَىٰ) said,

﴿ يَٰٓأَيُّهَا ٱلنَّبِيُّ إِنَّآ أَحۡلَلۡنَا لَكَ أَزۡوَٰجَكَ ٱلَّٰتِيٓ ءَاتَيۡتَ أُجُورَهُنَّ وَمَا مَلَكَتۡ يَمِينُكَ مِمَّآ أَفَآءَ ٱللَّهُ عَلَيۡكَ وَبَنَاتِ عَمِّكَ وَبَنَاتِ عَمَّٰتِكَ وَبَنَاتِ خَالِكَ وَبَنَاتِ خَٰلَٰتِكَ ٱلَّٰتِي هَاجَرۡنَ مَعَكَ وَٱمۡرَأَةً مُّؤۡمِنَةً إِن وَهَبَتۡ نَفۡسَهَا لِلنَّبِيِّ إِنۡ أَرَادَ ٱلنَّبِيُّ أَن يَسۡتَنكِحَهَا خَالِصَةً لَّكَ مِن دُونِ ٱلۡمُؤۡمِنِينَۗ ﴾

"O Prophet (Muḥammad ﷺ)! Verily, We have made lawful to you your wives, to whom you have paid their *Mahr* (bridal money given

> **by the husband to his wife at the time of marriage), and those (captives or slaves) whom your right hand possesses - whom Allah has given to you, and the daughters of your '*Amm* (paternal uncles) and the daughters of your '*Ammah* (paternal aunts) and the daughters of your *Khal* (maternal uncles) and the daughters of your *Khalah* (maternal aunts) who migrated (from Makkah) with you, and a believing woman if she offers herself to the Prophet, and the Prophet wishes to marry her; a privilege for you only, not for the (rest of) the believers. "** [*Sūrah Al-Ahzāb* 33:50]

So, if a woman married herself with no dowry, the marriage (nikāh) will be lawful, but the husband would have to give her a dowry similar to that of her peers.

Let us categorize this issue:

First: A fixed amount of dowry is set for marriage. For example, the woman's guardian would say, "I married my daughter to you for a dowry in the amount of ten thousand. This is allowed according to the *Ḥadīth,*

زَوَّجْتُكَهَا بِمَا مَعَكَ مِنَ الْقُرْآنِ

> **"I have given her to you in marriage for the part of the Qur'ān which you know."**

Second: A fixed amount of dowry is set for marriage, but the amount is unknown. For example, the guardian would say, "I marry her to you for a dowry of the amount you have with you. This is also allowed because the marriage contract is not like the disputable compensation contracts in which all the parties seek gains. The marriage contract is considered a contract for pleasure regardless of compensation.

Third: There is no mention of the dowry. For example, the guardian would say, "I marry you to my daughter," and he would answer, "I accept." No dowry is mentioned. In this case, the marriage is also lawful and she is given the dowry similar to that of her peers.

Fourth: Stipulating there is no dowry. For example, the husband would say, "I accept marriage, but I stipulate that I will not give a dowry." There are two opinions concerning this:

First Opinion: According to Shaykh Al-Islam Ibn Taymīyah (رَحِمَهُ ٱللَّهُ), the marriage is not lawful because Allāh stipulates giving a dowry for marriage. Allāh (سُبْحَانَهُ وَتَعَالَىٰ) said,

﴿ أَن تَبْتَغُواْ بِأَمْوَٰلِكُم ﴾

"Provided you seek (them in marriage) with Mahr (bridal money given by the husband to

> **his wife at the time of marriage) from your property."** [*Surah an-Nisā' 4:24]*

The marriage is unlawful and this man will be just a fiancé. If he proposes again and the proposal is accepted, he must provide a dowry.

Second Opinion: By analogy, marriage is lawful, but she must be given a dowry similar to that of her peers, just as in the case of the unspecified amount for dowry. Yet, there is a significant difference between both cases here. The marriage with an unspecified dowry is made lawful in Qur'ān and Sunnah. Allāh (سُبْحَانَهُ وَتَعَالَىٰ) says,

﴿ لَّا جُنَاحَ عَلَيْكُمْ إِن طَلَّقْتُمُ ٱلنِّسَآءَ مَا لَمْ تَمَسُّوهُنَّ أَوْ تَفْرِضُوا۟ لَهُنَّ فَرِيضَةً ﴾

> **"There is no sin on you, if you divorce women while yet you have not touched them, nor appointed to them their Mahr."** [*Sūrah al-Baqarah* 2:236]

It is obvious that divorce would not be effective unless the original marriage contract was valid. This verse indicates that the husband can divorce his wife without giving a specified dowry. As for the Sunnah, the *Ḥadīth* where Ibn Mas'ūd (رَضِيَ ٱللَّهُ عَنْهُ) indicated that if a woman is married to a man who died later without a specified dowry, then she will have to take the dowry similar to that of her peers.

At that time, a man declared that the Prophet (صَلَّىٱللَّهُعَلَيْهِوَسَلَّمَ) decreed the same ruling. This *Ḥadīth*, however, is not fit for analogy in the case where there is a stipulation of no dowry, because such stipulation completely contradicts the literal meaning of the Qur'ānic verse,

﴿ وَأُحِلَّ لَكُم مَّا وَرَآءَ ذَٰلِكُمْ أَن تَبْتَغُوا۟ بِأَمْوَٰلِكُم ﴾

"All others are lawful, provided you seek (them in marriage) with Mahr (bridal money given by the husband to his wife at the time of marriage) from your property." [*Surah an-Nisā' 4:24*]

So, the right opinion is that of Shaykh Al-Islam Ibn Taymīyah (رَحِمَهُٱللَّهُ). Also, stipulating no dowry for marriage is the very definition of a the situation where a woman is given in marriage for free, which Allāh (سُبْحَانَهُوَتَعَالَىٰ) says that is a privilege of the Prophet (صَلَّىٱللَّهُعَلَيْهِوَسَلَّمَ).

3. **It is allowed for the fiancé to look at the fiancée**, according to what was said regarding the Prophet (صَلَّىٱللَّهُعَلَيْهِوَسَلَّمَ),

فَصَعَّدَ فِيهَا النَّظَرَ

"Allāh's Messenger (صَلَّىٱللَّهُعَلَيْهِوَسَلَّمَ) saw her and cast a glance at her from head to foot."

If one argues that the Prophet (صَلَّىٰ ٱللَّٰهُ عَلَيْهِ وَسَلَّمَ) did not propose, we can say that the woman offered herself for marriage. Even so, if looking by the one who proposes is lawful, then there is more reason for looking to be lawful for the one who is proposed to.

4. **It is allowed to look at the fiancée thoroughly**. It was said regarding the Prophet (صَلَّىٰ ٱللَّٰهُ عَلَيْهِ وَسَلَّمَ),

صَعَّدَ وَ صَوَّبَ

"Allāh's Messenger (صَلَّىٰ ٱللَّٰهُ عَلَيْهِ وَسَلَّمَ) saw her and cast a glance at her from head to foot"

Looking for one time does not allow the man to have a thorough look as long as the conditions for looking are applied.

5. **According to some scholars, the woman is not obliged to cover her face in the presence of the other men**, as the Prophet (صَلَّىٰ ٱللَّٰهُ عَلَيْهِ وَسَلَّمَ) cast a glance at her from head to foot. So, this *Ḥadīth* indicates that the woman is allowed to uncover her face in the presence of men.

In reality, this *Ḥadīth* is not considered evidence, because there is a model answer to every *Ḥadīth* indicating that the woman is allowed to uncover her face in the presence of men.

The model answer is: There are two cases regarding the uncovering of the face: (1) being allowed, and (2) not being allowed. In early Islam, it was allowed to uncover the face as the veil was not made obligatory until the fifth or sixth year. So, every *Ḥadīth* indicating that the woman is allowed to uncover her face may have taken place before the obligation of the veil. Therefore, this is not evidence.

The scholars use a fixed rule for deduction which maintains, "Probability does not constitute a proof, because it implies two possible and competing interpretations. This means that choosing one of the two meanings without a [supporting] proof is in need of a proof itself. This is why the scholars said that if probability is found, evidence is nullified.

So, according to this *Ḥadīth*, uncovering the face may have happened before the obligation of the veil. Regardless, I do not believe that this *Ḥadīth* indicates that the woman is allowed to uncover her face, because looking at the woman does not necessarily indicate that the woman is uncovering her face.

Man can know briefly about a woman's beauty without seeing her face. So, this is not clear evidence that she uncovered her face. Thus, the texts indicating that the woman is obliged to cover her face are so clear with no competing evidence suggesting otherwise.

6. **The good morals of the Prophet (صَلَّىٰ اللَّهُ عَلَيْهِ وَسَلَّمَ).** It was said,

ثُمَّ طَأْطَأَ رَسُولُ اللَّهِ صلى الله عليه وسلم رَأْسَهُ

"Allāh's Messenger (صَلَّىٰ اللَّهُ عَلَيْهِ وَسَلَّمَ) then lowered his head."

He (صَلَّىٰ اللَّهُ عَلَيْهِ وَسَلَّمَ) did not say, "I have no desire of you." He lowered his head and kept silent."

7. **This woman was so polite** and so patient that she sat down and kept silent so that the Prophet (صَلَّىٰ اللَّهُ عَلَيْهِ وَسَلَّمَ) may accept.

8. **The Companions (رَضِيَ اللَّهُ عَنْهُمْ) were so polite when addressing the Prophet (صَلَّىٰ اللَّهُ عَلَيْهِ وَسَلَّمَ).** The Companion said,

يَا رَسُولَ اللَّهِ إِنْ لَمْ يَكُنْ لَكَ بِهَا حَاجَةٌ فَزَوِّجْنِيهَا

"Messenger of Allāh, marry her to me if you have no need of her."

Also, what has happened when the Prophet (صَلَّىٰ اللَّهُ عَلَيْهِ وَسَلَّمَ) was told that he prayed two rak'ahs in Al-Asr or Dhuhr prayers. The Prophet (صَلَّىٰ اللَّهُ عَلَيْهِ وَسَلَّمَ) was so prestigious that that his closest Companions, like Abu Bakr and Umar (رَضِيَ اللَّهُ عَنْهُمْ), hesitated to ask the Prophet about that. However, a big-handed man whom the

Prophet (ﷺ) called Dhul- Yadain (out of jesting with him (رَضِيَ ٱللَّهُ عَنْهُ)), asked the Prophet (ﷺ),

يَا رَسُولَ اللهِ : أَ نَسِيتَ أَمْ قَصُرَتِ الصَّلاَةُ ؟

> **"O Allāh's Messenger (ﷺ)! Have you forgotten or has the prayer been reduced?"**

The Prophet (ﷺ) replied,

لَمْ أَنْسَ ، وَلَمْ تقصر

> **"I have neither forgotten nor has the prayer been reduced."**

The people who were in haste left the masjid through its gates. They wondered whether the prayer was reduced. This man asked the Prophet (ﷺ) if he had forgotten or the prayer was reduced. There may be three probabilities:

1. The Prophet (ﷺ) forgot;
2. The prayer was reduced;
3. The Prophet (ﷺ) intentionally saluted before completing the prayer, but this is not right.

The Prophet (ﷺ) said,

لَمْ أَنْسَ ، وَلَمْ تقصر

"I have neither forgotten nor has the prayer been reduced."

One of these probabilities is not right and this begs the question: Are any of the Prophet's sayings not right? No, but the Prophet (صَلَّى ٱللَّهُ عَلَيْهِ وَسَلَّمَ) believed he completed the prayer. So, we can say that there is a great benefit in this. If anyone told what he believed to be true, but, in reality, it is not true, it cannot be said he told a lie. Even if he swore, he would not be called a liar. The Prophet (صَلَّى ٱللَّهُ عَلَيْهِ وَسَلَّمَ) said,

لَمْ أَنْسَ ، وَلَمْ تقصر

"I have neither forgotten nor has the prayer been reduced."

In this case, there are two possible scenarios. One of them can happen and the other cannot happen. The probable thing is that the prayer is reduced even though the Prophet (صَلَّى ٱللَّهُ عَلَيْهِ وَسَلَّمَ) said it has not been reduced. So, the second probability shall be true that the Prophet (صَلَّى ٱللَّهُ عَلَيْهِ وَسَلَّمَ) said,

لَمْ أَنْسَ

"No, I have forgotten."

So, there is a discrepancy between what the Prophet (صَلَّى ٱللَّهُ عَلَيْهِ وَسَلَّمَ) thought and what Dhul- Yadain (رَضِيَ ٱللَّهُ عَنْهُ)

thought, as the Prophet (ﷺ) thought that he completed the prayer and Dhul-Yadain (رَضِيَ ٱللَّهُ عَنْهُ) knew it was not. What was the solution?

The Prophet (ﷺ) asked the Companions,

أَ حَقٌّ مَا يَقُولُ ذُو الْيَدَيْنِ ؟

"Is what Dhul-Yadain says true?" They said, **"Yes."** Then the Prophet (ﷺ) completed praying. I can say that the Companions (رَضِيَ ٱللَّهُ عَنْهُمْ) are the politest ever because the Companion politely told the Prophet (ﷺ),

يَا رَسُولَ اللَّهِ إِنْ لَمْ يَكُنْ لَكَ بِهَا حَاجَةٌ فَزَوِّجْنِيهَا

> **"Messenger of Allāh, marry her to me if you have no need of her."**

9. **<u>The Prophet (ﷺ) could marry a woman without her guardian</u>**, as he (ﷺ) did not ask her where your wali is when the woman said,

أَهَبُ لَكَ نَفْسِي

"I offer myself to you for marriage."

The Prophet (ﷺ) could also marry without a dowry or wali. He has been given many privileges regarding marriage. This is very important. Every woman married to the Prophet (صَلَّى ٱللَّٰهُ عَلَيْهِ وَسَلَّمَ) will narrate to us many of the Prophet's private life affairs, which we otherwise would not have access to. That's why he was allowed to marry whenever he wanted until Allāh revealed,

﴿ لَّا يَحِلُّ لَكَ ٱلنِّسَآءُ مِنۢ بَعْدُ ﴾

"It is not lawful for you (to marry other) women after this." [*Sūrah al-Ahzāb* 33:52]

10. **The Prophet (صَلَّى ٱللَّٰهُ عَلَيْهِ وَسَلَّمَ) was allowed to give a woman in marriage to anyone without the permission of her guardian.** When the man said, **"Marry her to me,"** he did not say, "I am not her guardian," nor did he ask for her guardian. Allāh (سُبْحَانَهُۥ وَتَعَالَىٰ) says,

﴿ ٱلنَّبِيُّ أَوْلَىٰ بِٱلْمُؤْمِنِينَ مِنْ أَنفُسِهِمْ ﴾

"The Prophet is closer to the believers than their ownselves." [*Sūrah al-Ahzāb* 33:6]

So, he is closer to this woman than her guardian.

11. **It is allowed to pay little or much as dowry**, because the Prophet (صَلَّى ٱللَّٰهُ عَلَيْهِ وَسَلَّمَ) said, **"anything,"** which indicates generalization. Does this include everything, even if it is not money? According to *ad-Dhariyah*, **"yes,"** even if the dowry was an eggshell or a seed of

barley. However, this is a very weak opinion because what cannot be spent is not considered a 'thing'. Allāh says,

﴿ وَأُحِلَّ لَكُم مَّا وَرَآءَ ذَٰلِكُمْ أَن تَبْتَغُواْ بِأَمْوَٰلِكُم ﴾

"Provided you seek (them in marriage) with Mahr."

There is another evidence where Allāh says,

﴿ وَإِن طَلَّقْتُمُوهُنَّ مِن قَبْلِ أَن تَمَسُّوهُنَّ وَقَدْ فَرَضْتُمْ لَهُنَّ فَرِيضَةً فَنِصْفُ مَا فَرَضْتُمْ ﴾

"And you have appointed to them the Mahr (bridal money given by the husband to the wife at the time of marriage), then (pay) half of that Mahr." [*Sūrah al-Baqarah 2:237*]

The seed of barley cannot be divided into two parts. So, it is wrong to take one piece of evidence in consideration without considering the other relevant evidence. It is important to be well-learned if you want to give an opinion. Some people, especially the young people, may give an opinion without having enough knowledge on the matter. All the evidence in the subject must be taken into account. They must not be pieced off. It is obvious that no one would know everything. However, in the least, there must be a strong background.

12. **It is allowed to swear even though you do not need to swear**. The man said to the Prophet (ﷺ),

لَا وَ اللهِ يَا رَسُولَ اللهِ

"**No, Messenger of Allāh, by Allāh, I have nothing**." Though the Prophet (ﷺ) did not ask him to swear, it was necessary to make an assurance in this situation.

13. **It is allowed to answer with "no" to the high prestigious ones**. When the Prophet (ﷺ) said to Jabir ibn Abdullah (رَضِيَ ٱللَّهُ عَنْهُمْ),

بِعْنِيهِ

"Can you sell it (the camel)," Jabir answered with **"no."** People now consider it impolite to answer with **"no,"** to people of high prestige. However, the Companions (رَضِيَ ٱللَّهُ عَنْهُمْ) were politer than we are and they answered the Prophet (ﷺ) with "no." That's why we shall not replace it with any other word.

14. **The Prophet (ﷺ) was so wise that he told him**,

اِذْهَبْ إِلَى أَهْلِكِ ، فَانْظُرْ هَلْ تَجِدُ شَيْئًا

"Go to your people (family) and see if you can find something."

The Prophet (صَلَّى ٱللَّهُ عَلَيْهِ وَسَلَّمَ) said that because the man may find something in his house that he does not know about. This may happen often. There may be something in your house, but you forget about it or do not know about it. Thus, the Prophet (صَلَّى ٱللَّهُ عَلَيْهِ وَسَلَّمَ) was wise when interacting with the Companions.

15. **The Companions (رَضِيَ ٱللَّهُ عَنْهُمْ) were so polite when speaking with the Prophet (صَلَّى ٱللَّهُ عَلَيْهِ وَسَلَّمَ).** When the Prophet (صَلَّى ٱللَّهُ عَلَيْهِ وَسَلَّمَ) said to the man,

اِذْهَبْ ، فَانْظُرْ هَلْ تَجِدُ شَيْئًا ؟

"Go to your people (family) and see if you can find something"

He went, though he said at first,

لَا وَ اللهِ يَا رَسُولَ اللهِ

"No, Messenger of Allāh, by Allāh, I have nothing."

So, he obeyed the Prophet's command. Or he thought that the Prophet (صَلَّى ٱللَّهُ عَلَيْهِ وَسَلَّمَ) may have known that he had something in his house by means of Revelation.

Anyway, this Companion was so polite that he went without any other question.

16. **<u>It is allowed to wear an iron ring</u>**[53] as the Prophet (صَلَّى ٱللَّهُ عَلَيْهِ وَسَلَّمَ):

أُنْظُرْ وَلَوْ خَاتَمًا مِنْ حَدِيدٍ

"See even if it is an iron ring."

The iron ring is intended to be worn. One may argue that it can be sold, but this is a disputable matter. Some scholars said it is not allowed to wear the iron ring, but they depended on a weak *Ḥadīth*, where the Prophet (صَلَّى ٱللَّهُ عَلَيْهِ وَسَلَّمَ) was reported to have said,

إِنَّهُ حِلْيَةُ أَهْلِ النَّارِ

"Jewelry of the people of the Fire."[54]

---

[53] The Shaykh said, it is not allowed to wear it as kind of imitation of the disbelievers. However, when it is widespread, it can no longer be described as imitation of the disbelievers.

[54] Related by Abu Dawud (4223), Tirmidhi (1785), An-Nassai (8/172) on the authority of the father of Abdullah Ibn Buraidah (رَضِيَ ٱللَّهُ عَنْهُ). In the chain of narrators Abdullah Ibn Muslim Al-Marwazi – Abu Taibah- Abu Hatim said, "His narrations are to be taken into account but they are not to be considered for argumentation." Ibn Hibban said, "He habitually makes

This indicates disapproval. Nevertheless, it is allowed on the basis of an authentic *Ḥadīth* related by Bukhari and Muslim, which is more authentic than the above *Ḥadīth.* When it says in the *Ḥadīth,* "**Jewelry of the people of the Fire,**" this may indicate that the disbelievers at that time used to wear it. That would be enough to make the Prophet (ﷺ) declare such statement, in order that there would be no imitation of the disbelievers, not because the iron ring itself is undesirable.

But Allāh is the Ever-Knower. Thus, the *Ḥadīth* related by Bukhari and Muslim takes overriding priority. Can this be likened to the watch bracelet? Some scholars believe that it can be likened to the iron ring. So, one is not allowed to wear these kinds of bracelets in case it is undesirable or Haram. However, this is a disputable matter because these bracelets are used for keeping the watch steady, regardless of being jewelry, even though some people choose a particular bracelet. So, if we said that wearing rings is lawful, then the iron ring will be consequently allowed.

17. **It is lawful that the dowry may be paid as little or much** because the Prophet (ﷺ) said,

أُنْظُرْ وَلَوْ خَاتَمًا مِنْ حَدِيدٍ

---

mistakes and his narrations are mostly inconsistent with other narrator's reports."

"See even if it is an iron ring."

And dowry may be a property. This sentence indicates that it is allowed to wear an iron ring. In this case, one should reconcile between this ruling and considering the iron ring as the jewelry of the people of Fire. Reconciliation between texts is needed when two *Ḥadīths* need to be compared for preference. However, reconciliation is not possible when one of the two *Ḥadīths* is authentic whereas the other one is weak.

18. **The Companions were so poor** that the man did not find clothing to wear. He (رَضِيَ ٱللَّهُ عَنْهُ) said,

وَ لَا خَاتَمًا مِنْ حَدِيدٍ ، وَ لَكِنْ هَذَا إِزَارِي

"Not even an iron ring, but only this lower garment of mine."

19. **It is not obligatory to cover the upper part of the body** because this man had no upper garment **(Sahl (رَضِيَ ٱللَّهُ عَنْهُ) said that he had no upper garment)**.

Jabir Ibn Abdullāh (رَضِيَ ٱللَّهُ عَنْهُمْ) narrated that the Prophet (صَلَّى ٱللَّهُ عَلَيْهِ وَسَلَّمَ) said about the garment,

إِنْ كَانَ وَاسِعًا فَالْتَحِفْ بِهِ ، وَ إِنْ كَانَ ضَيِّقًا فَاتَزِرْ بِهِ

> **"If the garment is large enough, wrap it round the body (covering the shoulders) and if it is tight (too short) then use it as an Izār (tie it around your waist only)."** [55]

Jabir (رَضِيَٱللَّهُعَنْهُمْ) himself had worn an Izār during prayers though he had a garment.

20. **<u>One is not allowed to give the others what he direly needs</u>**, as the Prophet (صَلَّىٱللَّهُعَلَيْهِوَسَلَّمَ) said,

وَ إِنْ لَبِسَتْهُ لَمْ يَكُنْ عَلَيْكَ مِنْهُ شَيْءٌ

> **"And if she wears it, there would not be anything on you."**

It is apparent that this sentence is problematic as he (صَلَّىٱللَّهُعَلَيْهِوَسَلَّمَ) said, "**And if she wears it,**" because the Izār worn by men is not like that of women. So, it may be an imitation of men which is considered a greater sin, because the Prophet (صَلَّىٱللَّهُعَلَيْهِوَسَلَّمَ) cursed women who imitate men.

But what about the literal meaning of the *Ḥadīth*? It indicates that she can use it either to wear it like men or to use it as an under-garment. When Anas Ibn Malik (رَضِيَٱللَّهُعَنْهُ) mentioned the Prophet's visit to him, his mother and his grandmother Mulaikah (رَضِيَٱللَّهُعَنْهُمْ), he

[55] It is related before.

said that he took a mat, whose color turned black because of its overuse. Obviously, a mat cannot be worn but it is used. So, according to the literal meaning of the *Ḥadīth,* the woman could wear the Izār of a man in a way that does not resemble that of men, in order to avoid committing the detestable sin of imitation.

21. **If one is patient, he will win**. The man in this *Ḥadīth,* kept silent and stayed a long time but when he stood up, Allāh gave him a way out. He said,

فَجَلَسَ الرَّجُلُ ، حَتَّى إِذَا طَالَ مَجْلِسهُ قَامَ

> **"The man sat down and, as the sitting prolonged he stood up."**

22. **It is allowed to use the property as a dowry**. He said,

مَلَّكْتُكَهَا بِمَا مَعَكَ مِنَ الْقُرْآنِ

> **"I have given her to you in marriage for the part of the Qur'ān which you know."**

So, dowry is allowed to be a utility. This can be supported by what happened to Musa (عَلَيْهِ الصَّلَاةُ وَالسَّلَامُ) when the dowry of one of the two girls was to raise goats for eight or ten years[56].

23. **It is allowed to take a wage in exchange for teaching the Qur'ān** because marriage, in this *Ḥadīth,* was in

56 - Editor's note: The author refers to the story mentioned in full in Sūrah al-Qasas.

effect by the dowry, which was Qur'ān. In other words, this marriage would not have been in effect had there been no wage in exchange for teaching the Qur'ān to the wife. Allāh (سُبْحَانَهُ وَتَعَالَى) says,

﴿ وَأُحِلَّ لَكُم مَّا وَرَآءَ ذَٰلِكُمْ أَن تَبْتَغُواْ بِأَمْوَٰلِكُم ﴾

"Provided you seek (them in marriage) with Mahr (bridal money given by the husband to the wife at the time of marriage) from your property." [*Surah an-Nisā'* 4:24]

24. **The permissibility of making the actual teaching of the Qur'ān itself as a wage**. Is there any difference between this benefit and the previous one? Yes. For example, I asked a person who has a house to rent me his house in exchange for me teaching him the Qur'ān. Here, teaching the Qur'ān is considered itself a wage. We consider that the one who teaches the Qur'ān shall take a wage. Some scholars believe that it is not allowed to consider teaching the Qur'ān as a dowry on the basis of a weak *Ḥadīth*, where the Prophet (صَلَّى اللَّهُ عَلَيْهِ وَسَلَّمَ) said,

لَنْ تَكُونَ لِمَنْ بَعْدَكَ مَهْرًا

"She can no longer be a dowry."[57] This is a weak *Ḥadīth*. However, if we assume it is authentic, **"no longer be"** can be explained as being another case, as we said concerning *Ḥadīth* of Burda Ibn Nyar (رَضِيَ ٱللَّهُ عَنْهُ) when the Prophet (صَلَّى ٱللَّهُ عَلَيْهِ وَسَلَّمَ) said to him about a young female-goat:

إِنَّهَا لَنْ تُجْزِئَ عَنْ أَحَدٍ بَعْدَكَ

"Yes, and it is better and it will suffice for you, but a Jadha' will not be accepted after you."[58],

Shaykh Al-Islam Ibn Taymiyyah (رَحِمَهُ ٱللَّهُ) said that the phrase, "Will not be accepted after you," is not about time. Rather, it is about every she-kid of that description. Generally speaking, the Islamic Shariah does not particularly address a specific individual with a ruling. Rather, it addresses the surrounding circumstances which required the revelation of that ruling in the first place. For example, the Prophet's unique characteristics are not endowed by merit of their ownselves. There are many clear signs given to

[57] Related by Said Ibn Mansour (642). It is a Mursal hadith. The author said in Al-fath (9/212), "In addition, its chain of narration includes an anonymous narrator." Ibn Hazm said, "It is a fabricated hadith in which there are three faults; it is incompletely transmitted hadith and therefore cannot be used for argument; second: Abu Arfaga Al-Fashi (a narrator in the chain) is anonymous; third: Abu El-No'aman Al-Azdi is also anonymous. Al-Mohalla (9/499).

[58] Related before.

the Prophet (صَلَّىٰاللَّهُعَلَيْهِوَسَلَّمَ) by merit of being a Messenger, not because he is Muhammad Ibn Abdullāh (صَلَّىٰاللَّهُعَلَيْهِوَسَلَّمَ). Ibn Taimyyah's opinion (رَحِمَهُٱللَّهُ) is the right one.

25. **<u>The *Ḥadīth* may indicate that the ability to give the dowry is stipulated</u>**, as the Prophet (صَلَّىٰاللَّهُعَلَيْهِوَسَلَّمَ) said,

تَقْرَؤُهُنَّ عَنْ ظَهْرِ قَلْبٍ

"Can you recite them from heart?"

Because the one who cannot recite the Qur'ān by heart cannot get a copy of the Qur'ān, particularly at the time of the Prophet (صَلَّىٰاللَّهُعَلَيْهِوَسَلَّمَ). Whereas, the one who memorizes the Qur'ān by heart is able to teach it without needing a copy of the Qur'ān.

26. **<u>Marriage can be concluded with words expressing it</u>**, as the Prophet (صَلَّىٰاللَّهُعَلَيْهِوَسَلَّمَ) said,

مَلَّكْتُكَهَا ، زَوَّجْتُكَهَا ، أَمْكَنَاكَهَا

"I have given her to you in marriage for the part of the Qur'an which you know."

Words like **"give"** and **"marry."** Scholars have different opinions about this matter. Can marriage be concluded by any word expressing it? Or is it necessary to use particular words? The Hanbali's opinion is that particular words which refer to marriage are a must. Concerning the bondmaid, her master may say, "I have set you free and made your freedom your dowry," as the Prophet (صَلَّى ٱللَّهُ عَلَيْهِ وَسَلَّمَ) did with Safia Bnt Huauy (رَضِيَ ٱللَّهُ عَنْهَا). The Prophet (صَلَّى ٱللَّهُ عَلَيْهِ وَسَلَّمَ) set her free and made this her dowry. What is their evidence? They said, "This is the word mentioned in the Qur'ān. Allāh (سُبْحَانَهُ وَتَعَالَىٰ) says,

﴿ يَٰٓأَيُّهَا ٱلَّذِينَ ءَامَنُوٓاْ إِذَا نَكَحۡتُمُ ﴾

"O' you who believe! When you marry believing women" [*Sūrah al-Ahzāb* 33:49]

And says,

﴿ وَلَا تُنكِحُواْ ٱلۡمُشۡرِكِينَ ﴾

"And give not (your daughters) in marriage to Al-Mushrikun [*Sūrah al-Baqarah* 2:221]

And says,

﴿ وَأَنكِحُواْ ٱلۡأَيَٰمَىٰ مِنكُمۡ ﴾

"And marry those among you who are single (i.e. a man who has no wife and the woman who has no husband)." [*Sūrah an-Nūr* 24:32]

"Marry" is the word mentioned in the Qur'ān, and therefore, it has to be used. One may argue that Allāh does not mean the word itself but its meaning is what is intended. Following the same way (in deduction), one would have to say that transactions cannot be concluded except with "I sell you so and so," because this is the word that is mentioned in the Qur'ān.

So, the word of marriage is used to refer to its meaning and not this word in particular. Generally speaking, any act of worship that does not have a fixed formula (in terms of what is to be said in it) by the Sharia, then its formula is to be dependent on tradition. So, language of contracts is originally determined by tradition.

Accordingly, the marriage contract, like any contract, may be concluded by any term such as "marry you, nikāh, I set you free," or "I give you my daughter," or any term by which the nikāh can be concluded.

27. **The husband has to deliver the dowry** to whoever in charge[59], as he (صَلَّى ٱللَّهُ عَلَيْهِ وَسَلَّمَ) said,

فَعَلِّمْهَا

[59] Shaykh was asked if Qur'ān fits as a dowry nowadays? He said, "Teaching [Qur'ān] is considered a type of work that entails payment. He is like someone hired for a job and he will be paid."

"You teach her something of the Qur'ān."

ḤADĪTH 981

981- Related by Abu Dawud on the authority of Abu Hurairah (رَضِيَٱللَّهُعَنْهُ), the Prophet (صَلَّىٱللَّهُعَلَيْهِوَسَلَّمَ) said,

مَا تَحْفَظُ مِنَ الْقُرْآنِ " . قَالَ سُورَةَ الْبَقَرَةِ أَوِ الَّتِي تَلِيهَا . قَالَ " فَقُمْ فَعَلِّمْهَا عِشْرِينَ آيَةً وَهِيَ امْرَأَتُكَ

> **"How much have you memorized from Qur'ān? He (رَضِيَٱللَّهُعَنْهُ) said, Sūrah al-Baqarah and the one that follows it. He (صَلَّىٱللَّهُعَلَيْهِوَسَلَّمَ) said, "Teach her twenty verses. She is your wife."**[60]

Explanation

This narration related by Abu Dawud contradicts the narration related by Bukhari and Muslim. According to the literal meaning of the narration of Bukhari and Muslim, it indicates that the woman is married in exchange for all of what he memorized from the Qur'ān. Whereas this narration says, **"Teach her twenty verses."** It seems that this narration is not memorized.

---

[60] Related by Abu Dawud (2112), An-Nassai in "As-Sunan Al-Kobra" (5506), but it is weak; see "At-Talkhis" (3/60).

PUBLICIZING THE NIKĀH

936- On the authority of Amir Ibn Abdullāh Ibn Az-Zubair from his father (رَضِيَٱللَّهُعَنْهُمْ) that the Prophet (صَلَّىٱللَّهُعَلَيْهِوَسَلَّمَ) said,

أَعْلِنُوا النِّكَاحَ

"Publicize the marriage."[61]

Explanation

أَعْلِنُوا

"Publicize." This speech addresses the Ummah. Publicizing marriage includes publicizing the contract and consummation. The Prophet (صَلَّىٱللَّهُعَلَيْهِوَسَلَّمَ) commanded publicizing marriage for the benefits included.

61 Al-Musnad (4/5), Al-Bazzar (2214), Ibn Hibban (4066), Al-Haithami (4/289) said, the narrators in Al-Musnad are trustworthy. It is also authenticated by Al-Hakim (2/200).

One of the benefits of publicizing marriage is to differentiate between it and fornication. Fornication is made in secret, but marriage is made in public.

1. Publicizing marriage is something required by nature and Sharia.
2. It urges following the steps of the one who is married, so that people would marry.
3. Assuming the husband and the wife are foster brothers, publicizing the marriage would push people with knowledge of such matter to disclose it.

These are the benefits of the publicizing of the marriage that is commanded by the Prophet (صَلَّىٱللَّهُعَلَيْهِوَسَلَّمَ).

أَعْلِنُوا

"Publicize" is an order which indicates obligation. However, not one of the scholars maintained this opinion and, hence, it is desirable.

Pay heed that marriage is perfect when it is publicized along with witnesses [to the contract]. If there are witnesses, but it is not publicized[62], then the scholars have different opinions about that. Some scholars believe it is lawful. Others express no opinion because if there are witnesses but the marriage is not publicized, then this will not be beneficial.

---

62 The Sheikh said that car horns are considered one of the ways of publicizing marriage provided that it causes no disturbance.

Another case is if the marriage is publicized without the presence of witnesses to the contract. For example, in a situation where a man married in the presence of the guardian who said, “I marry you to my daughter,” and the other replied, “I accept.” And then he publicizes this marriage.

There are different opinions on this regard. The right of which is that of Sheikh Al-Islam Ibn Taimyyah (رَحِمَهُ ٱللَّهُ) who said publicizing marriage is more beneficial than only having the contract witnessed.

Also, the issue of witnessing is included when the marriage is publicized because everyone would know. But if there is no publicizing or witnessing, the marriage will be unlawful because it lacks the element of witnessing that certifies the marriage or the issue of making it public. [63]

---

[63] The Shaykh was asked about a man visiting his friend who has a young girl. This man said in the presence of two other men about this young girl that she is beautiful. At that time her father assumingly said, “I have given her to you in marriage.” All the people who were present have gone and time passed. What is the ruling here? He said (رَحِمَهُ ٱللَّهُ), “The marriage is unlawful because the man had not accepted. But if the man said, “Give her to me in marriage,” and the father replied, “I have given her to you in marriage.” In this situation, if we say that the father has the right to force his daughter to marry the man, this contract is lawful but I have no opinion about that, because the father may believe that it is beneficial for his daughter to marry that man. People must be careful. If the man said, “I have given her to you,” is this a lawful contract? No. This is just a promise according to the traditions.

THE CONDITION OF A WALI (GUARDIAN)

937- On the authority of Bordah Ibn Abu Musa on the authority of his father (رَضِيَٱللَّهُعَنْهُمْ) who said that the Prophet (صَلَّىٱللَّهُعَلَيْهِوَسَلَّمَ) said,

لَا نِكَاحَ إِلَّا بِوَلِيٍّ

"There is no marriage except with a guardian."[64] Related by Ahmad and the four Imams, graded as Sahih by Ibn Al-Madini, At-Tirmidhi, Ibn Hibban who maintained that it has the defect of *Irsal* (a missing Companion between the *Tabi'ee* and the Prophet (صَلَّىٱللَّهُعَلَيْهِوَسَلَّمَ) in the chain of narration).

Explanation

لَا نِكَاحَ إِلَّا بِوَلِيٍّ

"There is no marriage except with a guardian." The negative word 'no' addresses the validity of the marriage without the

[64] Al-Musnad (4/413), Abu Dawud (2085), At-Tirmidhi (1101), Ibn Majah (1881), Ibn Hibban (4077), At-Tirmidhi said in Al-Elal (p. 155), "I think that the hadith of Abu Burdah (رَضِيَٱللَّهُعَنْهُمْ) is sahih." And Al-Baihaqi (7/108) narrated through Ibrahim Ibn Jabalah said, I heard Ali Ibn Al-Madidni said, the hadith of "There is no marriage except with a guardian," is Sahih.

presence of the guardian. The guardian must be one of the blood relatives from the paternal kinsmen. The maternal kinsman or maternal brothers shall not be guardians.

لَا نِكَاحَ إِلَّا بِوَلِيٍّ

"There is no marriage except with a guardian." The guardian is often more knowledgeable and far-sighted compared to the woman. He is also considerably more cautious than the woman. The woman, in contrast, is near-sighted and easily deceived by the appearance, gentle words and so on. So, Allāh is so Merciful that He (سُبْحَانَهُ وَتَعَالَىٰ) made her unable to marry herself except with a guardian.

Ḥadīth **benefits:**

1. **Nikāh is not lawful without a guardian**. The presence of the guardian must be stipulated for the lawfulness of nikāh, as Allāh (سُبْحَانَهُ وَتَعَالَىٰ) said,

﴿ وَلَا تُنكِحُوا۟ ٱلْمُشْرِكِينَ حَتَّىٰ يُؤْمِنُوا۟ ﴾

"And give not (your daughters) in marriage to Al-Mushrikun till they believe (in Allāh Alone)." [*Sūrah al-Baqarah* 2:221]

﴿ وَلَا تَنكِحُوا۟ ٱلْمُشْرِكَٰتِ حَتَّىٰ يُؤْمِنَّ ﴾

"And give not (your daughters) in marriage." Allāh uses this verb because the man can marry himself, but the woman cannot. Thus, Allāh said,

﴿ وَلَا تُنكِحُوا۟ ﴾

"And give not (your daughters) in marriage."

Allāh also says,

﴿ وَأَنكِحُوا۟ ٱلْأَيَـٰمَىٰ ﴾

"And marry those among you who are single." [*Sūrah an-Nūr* 24:32]

'**Single**' refers to the woman who has no husband and the man who has no wife.

﴿ وَٱلصَّـٰلِحِينَ مِنْ عِبَادِكُمْ وَإِمَآئِكُمْ ﴾

"And (also marry) the Salihun (pious, fit and capable ones) of your male slaves and maid-servants (female slaves)." *[Sūrah an-Nūr* 24:32]

The male and female slaves are to be married by their master. Here, Allāh ascribed the marriage to the unmarried. So, there must be a guardian.

Allāh (سُبۡحَانَهُۥ وَتَعَالَىٰ) says,

﴿ فَلَا تَعۡضُلُوهُنَّ أَن يَنكِحۡنَ أَزۡوَٰجَهُنَّ ﴾

"Do not prevent them from marrying their (former) husbands." [*Sūrah al-Baqarah* 2:232]

Thus, had there been no stipulated guardian, there would not have been any act of prevention that would warrant the command in the verse. These are three verses, in addition to the above *Ḥadīth*. The wisdom behind the stipulation of the guardian is that the woman is near-sighted so she wouldn't be able to bear a serious responsibility such as concluding this contract for life by herself without a guardian.

إِلَّا بِوَلِيٍّ

"Except with a guardian" indicates that the guardian must be perceptive. The *Ḥadīth* indicates that the woman cannot get any benefit if the guardian is not perceptive.

2. **<u>The guardian must be one of the blood relatives of the woman</u>**. A disbeliever cannot act as a guardian for a Muslim woman, even if he is her father. Therefore, if her father does not perform salāt, but her uncle does, then her uncle will replace him as the guardian. The father cannot be a guardian because he is a disbeliever.

3. **If there are two more guardians, the closest will be chosen**. Thus, if there is an uncle and a brother, who is responsible for concluding the marriage? Her bother must be her guardian, because he is closer than her uncle. So, how are the guardians arranged? They are arranged according to their order of inheritance except in the presence of the father of the woman and her son.

   The father takes precedence for two reasons. First, it is necessary for a virgin because she does not have a son to begin with. Second, if she is a widow with sons and a father, her father is entitled to be her guardian because he has more experience than the son and he is probably more merciful than the son. Thus, the father is worthier when it comes to marriage, though the son is worthier when it comes to inheritance.

   Suppose one died and left a father or a son? We say, "The father will take the sixth and the son will take the remaining inheritance."

   But if the closest guardian is not worthy or he prevents his daughter from marriage, then we move to the closest one after him. If the father prevents his daughters, who are teachers, from marriage in order to take their salaries, can their uncle be allowed to marry them if one proposes? Yes, or the closest one like the brother[65].

---

[65] Sheikh was asked if there are two guardians of the same level, is the eldest, the most learnt or the most religious responsible for marriage? He

HADITH 983

983- Imām Ahmad narrated on the authority of 'Imran Ibn Al-Husain (رَضِيَ ٱللَّهُ عَنْهُمْ), the Prophet (صَلَّى ٱللَّهُ عَلَيْهِ وَسَلَّمَ) said,

لَا نِكَاحَ إِلَّا بِوَلِيٍّ ، وَ شَاهِدَيْنِ

"There is no marriage except with a guardian and two witnesses."[66]

The narration with the addition of the two witnesses is a weak one. However, the first narration, "**There is no marriage except with a guardian,**" is Sahih and it has a supporting narration from the *Ḥadīth* of Abu Musa (رَضِيَ ٱللَّهُ عَنْهُ).

---

answered: There is no doubt that the one who knows what is more beneficial for the women and the most perceptive must be chosen. Though, if the lesser one marries her to someone, the marriage will be lawful. This is like the order of the right and left hand in Wudu (ablution). If one washes the left hand before the right one, his Wudu will be correct, but it is desirable to wash the right hand first.

[66] I did not find ḥadīth of Imran in Al-Musnad. It is related by Abdul-razzaq (10473), and from this way it is related by At-Tabarani in Al-Kabir (18/142/299). Al-Haithami (4/287) commented on this chain of narration, "There is 'Abdullāh Ibn Mihrez who is a abandoned narrator."

MARRIAGE WITHOUT THE GUARDIAN'S PERMISSION

938- On the authority of 'Aishah (رَضِيَ اللَّهُ عَنْهَا), the Messenger of Allāh (صَلَّى اللَّهُ عَلَيْهِ وَسَلَّمَ) said,

أَيُّمَا امْرَأَةٍ نُكِحَتْ بِغَيْرِ إِذْنِ وَلِيِّهَا فَنِكَاحُهَا بَاطِلٌ فَنِكَاحُهَا بَاطِلٌ فَنِكَاحُهَا بَاطِلٌ فَإِنْ دَخَلَ بِهَا فَلَهَا الْمَهْرُ بِمَا اسْتَحَلَّ مِنْ فَرْجِهَا فَإِنِ اشْتَجَرُوا فَالسُّلْطَانُ وَلِيُّ مَنْ لاَ وَلِيَّ لَهُ

"Whichever woman marries without the permission of her guardian, her marriage is (*Batil*) invalid. If he had sexual intercourse with her, then the dowry is for her in lieu of that sexual intercourse. If they (guardians) disagree, then the Sultan is the guardian for the one who has no guardian."[67] Related by the four Imams except An-Nassa'i, and graded as Sahih by Abu 'Awana, Ibn Hibban and Al-Hakim.

---

[67] Related by Ahmad (6/47), Abu Dawud (2083), At-Tirmidhi (1102), Ibn Majah (1879), Ibn Hibban (4074), Al-Hakim (2/182), it is also authenticated by the author in Al-Fath (9/494).

Explanation

اِمْرَأَةٍ

"Woman" is an indefinite noun that includes the virgin and the previously-married woman.

بِغَيْرِ إِذْنِ وَلِيِّهَا

"**Without the permission of her guardian her,**" He did not say, "Without a guardian," because he may allow marriage by way of authorizing someone else. However, if he is present, the need for permission is less significant in this case. And if one asks, "What if her guardian allowed her to marry herself?"

The answer: This is unlawful, because had she been allowed to conclude the marriage by herself with the permission of her guardian, she could have done that herself without his permission in the first place.

So, we say, "Whoever is not entitled to do something, he does not have the right to be authorized in that thing." Therefore, this *Ḥadīth* cannot be evidence that if the guardian gives the woman permission to conclude the marriage herself that the marriage will be lawful.

فَنِكَاحُهَا بَاطِلٌ

"**Her marriage is invalid.**" Meaning ineffective. A valid marriage, however, entails lawful sexual intercourse, ascribing the children to the husband and that the expenses are obligatory in addition to many rulings. All these rulings will not be effective if marriage is invalid. So, whoever is married without the permission of her guardian, her marriage will be invalid.

فَإِنْ دَخَلَ بِهَا

"**If he had sexual intercourse with her.**"[68] Allāh (سُبْحَانَهُ وَتَعَالَىٰ) says,

﴿ وَرَبَٰٓئِبُكُمُ ٱلَّٰتِي فِي حُجُورِكُم مِّن نِّسَآئِكُمُ ٱلَّٰتِي دَخَلْتُم بِهِنَّ ﴾

> "**Born of your wives with whom you had sexual intercourse.**" [*Sūrah an-Nisā'* 4:23]

فَلَهَا الْمَهْرُ بِمَا اسْتَحَلَّ مِنْ فَرْجِهَا

> "**Then the dowry is for her in lieu of that sexual intercourse.**"

The married woman is entitled to take the dowry in lieu of the sexual intercourse. He did not say, "If he had sexual intercourse with her, she is his wife." He said, "**The dowry is for her.**" She is unlawful, but, as he enjoyed having sexual intercourse with her through this invalid contract, she is

---

68 Sheikh was asked if a woman married herself without the permission of the guardian, and then the husband had intercourse with her, shall he be flogged? No, he shall not be flogged, because there is a chance of a suspicion here, and the prescribed punishment is averted if there is a chance of suspicion.

entitled to be given dowry. Dowry is defined as "a permanent compensation for the woman documented in the marriage contract and what is included."

The pronoun "they" in "**if they disagree**" refers to the guardians. One may argue, "How does one know?"

The answer: It is known from the context because he said, "**Without the permission of her guardian. If they disagree.**"

فَالسُّلْطَانُ وَلِيُّ مَنْ لاَ وَلِيَّ لَهُ

"**Then the Sultan is the guardian for the one who has no guardian.**" How can they disagree? The father says, "My daughter will not be married to this man." Her uncle will say, "I will do it myself." Her father will say, "If you do so, I will shoot ten bullets in your head."

This happens a lot between the nomads. Thus, if a dispute arises between the father and the uncle or someone else from the guardians, he (صَلَّىٰٱللَّهُعَلَيۡهِوَسَلَّمَ) said,

فَالسُّلْطَانُ وَلِيُّ مَنْ لاَ وَلِيَّ لَهُ

"**Then the Sultan is the guardian for the one who has no guardian.**" The Prophet (صَلَّىٰٱللَّهُعَلَيۡهِوَسَلَّمَ) did not say, "The Sultan is entitled to conclude the marriage contract for her." Instead, he made a general rule:

فَالسُّلْطَانُ وَلِيُّ مَنْ لاَ وَلِيَّ لَهُ

"**The Sultan is the guardian for the one who has no guardian,**" Who is the Sultan? The Sultan is the one who has the authority in the place of the contract. If they are in a country in which there is a superior Sultan, the superior Sultan or his representative will be the guardian. If they are in a country without a superior Sultan, like a non-Muslim country in which the Sultan has no power over Muslims, her guardian will be the leader of that particular community.

There are some benefits in this *Ḥadīth*:

1. **The woman is not allowed to marry herself without the permission of her guardian**, as he (صَلَّى ٱللَّهُ عَلَيْهِ وَسَلَّمَ) said,

    فَنِكَاحُهَا بَاطِلٌ

    "**Her marriage is invalid.**"

2. **If she allowed any other one to marry her, her marriage is also invalid**, as he (صَلَّى ٱللَّهُ عَلَيْهِ وَسَلَّمَ) said,

    بِغَيْرِ إِذْنِ وَلِيِّهَا

    "**Without the permission of her guardian.**"

3. **If the guardian allowed a man to marry her**, her marriage will be lawful as it was concluded with the permission of her guardian.

4. **<u>There is no difference between *batil* and *fasid*</u>**[69] as he (صَلَّى ٱللَّهُ عَلَيْهِ وَسَلَّمَ) said,

فَنِكَاحُهَا بَاطِلٌ

"**Her marriage is invalid (*batil*)**."

In legislative terminology, there is no difference between both terms. *Fasid* and *batil* have the same meaning. Howver, Jurists (رحمهم الله)have different opinions. According to Abu Hanifa (رَحِمَهُ ٱللَّهُ), *batil* is that which is prohibited due to its base and the *fasid* is what is prohibited due to its description. For example, selling the swine is batil while selling a measure of barley in lieu of two measures of barley is *fasid*.

According to Ibn Hanbal[70] (رَحِمَهُ ٱللَّهُ), there is no difference between *batil* and *fasid* except regarding two sections of Fiqh. The first is Hajj and the second is marriage. In Hajj, if one consummated the marriage before the first removal of *Ihram*, this would be *fasid*. However, one must complete this unlawful Hajj and make up for it in the following year. For example, a man had sexual intercourse with his wife on the night of the Day of Sacrifice in Muzdalifah, before the first removal of *Ihram*, the Hajj is consequently unlawful and he has to

[69] - Editor's note: Both words, when translated, mean the same thing. The only difference, as the sheikh explains it in the following lines is merely in legislative implication according to specific schools of Fiqh.
[70] Al-Mobdi' (3/162), Al-Kafi in the Fiqh of Ibn Hanbal (رَحِمَهُ ٱللَّهُ) (1/418), Al-Moghni (3/160).

complete all the pillars and perform Hajj in the following year.

Batil happens when one apostates from the religion during the performance of the Hajj rituals. His Hajj will be *fasid,* and he shall not complete it. Allāh (سُبْحَانَهُۥوَتَعَالَىٰ) says,

﴿ وَمَن يَرْتَدِدْ مِنكُمْ عَن دِينِهِۦ فَيَمُتْ وَهُوَ كَافِرٌ فَأُوْلَـٰٓئِكَ حَبِطَتْ أَعْمَـٰلُهُمْ ﴾

"And whosoever of you turns back from his religion and dies as a disbeliever, then his deeds will be lost in this life and in the Hereafter." [*Sūrah al-Baqarah* 2:217]

The scholars have said, "Apostasy makes all deeds invalid." Concerning marriage, *batil* is what the scholars have agreed upon as being unlawful, while *fasid* is what they disagree upon.

Example of *batil*: Allāh (سُبْحَانَهُۥوَتَعَالَىٰ) says,

﴿ وَلَا تَعْزِمُوا۟ عُقْدَةَ ٱلنِّكَاحِ حَتَّىٰ يَبْلُغَ ٱلْكِتَـٰبُ أَجَلَهُۥ ﴾

"And do not consummate the marriage until the term is fulfilled." [*Sūrah al-Baqarah* 2:235]

Example of *fasid*: A woman married without any witnesses, this is fasid. There are many similar examples. A woman married with no witnesses, with no guardian. To marry a woman whom her mother breastfed him once or thrice, this is *fasid* (unlawful) marriage, because the scholars have different opinions about the number of times of breastfeeding that prohibits a marriage. So, everything the scholars have different opinions about is considered *fasid* marriage.

Anyway, according to the Hanbali school, it is known that there is no difference between *fasid* and *batil* except in marriage and Hajj. The *Ḥadīth* indicates that *fasid* is called *batil* also. If this above-mentioned situation has happened, then there are different opinions about the lawfulness of the contract. According to Jurists (رحمهم الله), it is *fasid,* whereas the Prophet (صَلَّى ٱللَّهُ عَلَيْهِ وَسَلَّمَ) called it *batil*. So, there is no difference between *fasid* and *batil* in their legislative meaning.

5. **If one divorced a woman that he has married without a guardian before consummation, she deserves no dowry or she, at the least, is not entitled to take a full dowry**, as he (صَلَّى ٱللَّهُ عَلَيْهِ وَسَلَّمَ) said,

فَإِنْ دَخَلَ بِهَا فَلَهَا الْمَهْر

"If he consummated the marriage, she has all the dowry",

This denotes that if he does not consummate the marriage, she is not entitled to take the dowry. Does she deserve half of the dowry because of privacy with her, even without consummation? We say that scholars have different opinions about that. Some scholars said she deserves half of the dowry because of the suspicion (of consummation). Other scholars said she is not entitled to have the dowry. So, in this situation, should judgment be measured in accordance with one's thoughts or reality?

If we say that thoughts are the measure of judgment, she will deserve half of the dowry, because the husband and the wife herein believed that the contract was valid. If we say reality is the measure of judgment, she is not entitled to take the dowry, because this contract is in reality invalid. Thus, no inheritance will be resulted.

But if one consummates the marriage, she deserves all the dowry, as mentioned in the *Ḥadīth,* because he consummated the marriage believing she is his lawful wife. The Prophet (صَلَّىٰ ٱللَّهُ عَلَيْهِ وَسَلَّمَ) said:

فَلَهَا الْمَهْرُ بِمَا اسْتَحَلَّ مِنْ فَرْجِهَا

"Then the dowry is for her in lieu of what he enjoyed from her private part."

The right opinion is that if he has privacy with her, she is entitled to half of the dowry because he enjoyed from her what is enjoyed only by the husband, on the basis that they believed in the validity of the contract.

6. **<u>If any dispute arises between the guardians, the Sultan will be her guardian</u>** as the Prophet (صَلَّى ٱللَّهُ عَلَيْهِ وَسَلَّمَ) said,

فَإِنِ اشْتَجَرُوا فَالسُّلْطَانُ وَلِيُّ مَنْ لاَ وَلِيَّ لَهُ

"If they disagree, then the Sultan is the guardian for the one who has no guardian."

Shall he conclude the contract himself or enforce one of the guardians? The first opinion is right; he shall be the guardian and settle the dispute[71].

If none of them want to marry her, the Sultan will be the guardian. An example of the situation about settling the dispute between the guardians is an incompetent man who will pay a lot of money proposed to a woman and her father approves of him, but her guardians refuse and a dispute arose.

They must refer to the Sultan, who, in this case, will decree that no marriage will be concluded or vice versa. If the suitor is competent and one of the guardians accepted, but the others rejected, then the Sultan will give permission to the one who accepted. So, if all of them prevented her from marriage, in the

71 Sheikh was asked if the husband is a righteous man, the woman's acceptance is a must even if the guardian is the Sultan. He said, "The problem is that if she chooses a bad man whom her guardians prevent her from as he is a bad man, then the Sultan is not entitled to marry her because they are right.

case of the competent suitor, the Sultan would be entitled to marry her.

7. **The Muslim Ummah cannot stay without a Sultan**. He (صَلَّى ٱللَّهُ عَلَيْهِ وَسَلَّمَ) said,

فَالسُّلْطَانُ وَلِيُّ مَنْ لاَ وَلِيَّ لَهُ

"Then the Sultan is the guardian for the one who has no guardian."

The reason is that there are not enough guardians for every woman and disputes will inevitably arise. If disputes arises when there is no guardian, the Sultan is the one who will be responsible for settling all the disputes. Thus, the scholars said that appointing the Imam is a collective obligation and the Ummah shall not stay without a Sultan[72]. In addition, the Prophet (صَلَّى ٱللَّهُ عَلَيْهِ وَسَلَّمَ) said,

مَنْ مَاتَ وَ لَيْسَ فِي عُنُقِهِ بَيْعَةٌ مَاتَ مَيْتَةً جَاهِلِيَّةً

"And one who dies without having bound himself by an oath of allegiance (to an Amir) will die the death of one belonging to the days of Jahillyya [pre-Islāmic era]."

In another narration:

[72] See a detailed account of this point in the Sheikh's explanation of the book *'Assiyasa Ash-Shar'iya'* by Ibn Taymiaa.

فَقَدْ خَلَعَ رِبْقَةَ الْإِسْلَامِ مِنْ عُنُقِهِ

"The yoke of Islām is cast off from his neck."

And some people, out of jealousy and narrow-mindedness, take off the yoke of Islām from their neck. They say, "I do not acknowledge this Sultan or this president."[73] Then they die the death of Jahillyya or take off the yoke of Islām from their neck. In addition, they meet Allāh having no yoke on their neck as they parted the Islāmic community. Whoever deviates, he deviates to the Fire.

---

[73] Sheikh was asked if there is an evident disbelief [of the ruler] upon which there is a clear proof from Allah. He said, one must believe that he shall be bound by an oath of a Muslim ruler. We say evident disbelief because those who do not judge by what Allah has revealed may have misconceptions. But if he prays but mocks the prayers and says publically that Islam is a backwardness religion, he is undoubtedly a disbeliever.

THE CONDITION OF THE WIFE'S APPROVAL

985- Abu Hurairah (رَضِيَ اللَّهُ عَنْهُ) reported Allāh's Messenger (صَلَّى اللَّهُ عَلَيْهِ وَسَلَّمَ) as having said,

لاَ تُنْكَحُ الأَيِّمُ حَتَّى تُسْتَأْمَرَ وَلاَ تُنْكَحُ الْبِكْرُ حَتَّى تُسْتَأْذَنَ ". قَالُوا يَا رَسُولَ اللَّهِ وَكَيْفَ إِذْنُهَا قَالَ " أَنْ تَسْكُتَ

A woman without a husband (or divorced or a widow) must not be married until she is consulted, and a virgin must not be married until her permission is sought. They asked the Prophet of Allāh (صَلَّى اللَّهُ عَلَيْهِ وَسَلَّمَ), "How her (virgin's) consent can be solicited?" He (صَلَّى اللَّهُ عَلَيْهِ وَسَلَّمَ) said, "That she keeps silent."[74] Related by Bukhārī and Muslim.

986- Ibn 'Abbās (رَضِيَ اللَّهُ عَنْهُ) reported Allāh's Messenger (صَلَّى اللَّهُ عَلَيْهِ وَسَلَّمَ) as saying,

الثَّيِّبُ أَحَقُّ بِنَفْسِهَا مِنْ وَلِيِّهَا وَالْبِكْرُ تُسْتَأْمَرُ وَإِذْنُهَا سُكُوتُهَا

"A woman who has been previously married (Thayyib) has more right to her person than her

[74] Related by Bukhari (5136), Muslim (1419), Tuhfat Al-Ashraf (15425).

guardian. And a virgin should also be consulted, and her silence implies her consent."[75]Related by Muslim.

In another narration,

لَيْسَ لِلْوَلِيِّ مَعَ الثَّيِّبِ أَمْرٌ وَالْيَتِيمَةُ تُسْتَأْمَرُ

"A guardian has no command over a woman previously married and who has no husband; and an orphan girl (i.e. virgin) must be consulted." Related by Abu Dawud, An-Nassai, and graded as Sahih by Ibn Hibban[76].

987- It was narrated from Abu Hurairah (رَضِيَ اللَّهُ عَنْهُ) that the Messenger of Allāh (صَلَّى اللَّهُ عَلَيْهِ وَسَلَّمَ) said,

لاَ تُزَوِّجُ الْمَرْأَةُ الْمَرْأَةَ وَلاَ تُزَوِّجُ الْمَرْأَةُ نَفْسَهَا فَإِنَّ الزَّانِيَةَ هِيَ الَّتِي تُزَوِّجُ نَفْسَهَا

"No woman should arrange the marriage of another woman and no woman should arrange her own marriage. The adulteress is the one who arranges her

75 Related by Muslim (1421).

76 Related by Abu Dawud (2100), An-Nassai (6/85), Ibn Hibban (4089), Al-Baihaqi mentioned in Al-khilafiat:, "Its narrators are trustworthy." The author of Iqtrah said, "In accordance with the conditions of both al-Bukhari and Muslim." Khulasat Al-badr Al-moneer: (2/188).

own marriage."[77] Related by Ibn Majah and Ad-Daraqotni. Its narrators are trustworthy.

Explanation

All these *aḥadīth* tackle the wife's approval and clarify if it is a condition or not. In the Ḥ*adīth* of Abu Hurairah (رَضِيَ ٱللَّهُ عَنْهُ), the Prophet (صَلَّى ٱللَّهُ عَلَيْهِ وَسَلَّمَ) said,

لاَ تُنْكَحُ الأَيِّمُ حَتَّى تُسْتَأْمَرَ

"A woman without a husband (or divorced or a widow) must not be married until she is consulted."

She must not be married until she is consulted. The widow is the woman who lost her husband. In the second *Ḥadīth,* she is called *Thayyib,* because she lost her virginity by the former husband.

حَتَّى تُسْتَأْمَرَ

"Until she is consulted." This means until expresses her approval, "Yes, marry me to this man." In the case of the virgin,

---

77 Related by Ibn Majah (1882), Ad-Darakotni (3/227) in the chain of narrators there is Mohamed ibn Marwan, Ibn Adyy said, "It is clear that his narrations are weak", Al-Kamil (6/263).

وَلاَ تُنْكَحُ الْبِكْرُ حَتَّى تُسْتَأْذَنَ

"A virgin must not be married until her permission is sought." We can say, "We will marry you to this man?" We should not say, "Do you want to marry this man? Do you agree? What is your opinion?" The Companions (رَضِيَ اللَّهُ عَنْهُمْ) wanted to know how she can give permission? He (صَلَّى اللَّهُ عَلَيْهِ وَسَلَّمَ) says,

أَنْ تَسْكُتَ

"To keep silent." They asked this question because the virgin is often shy regarding the marriage matters.

The benefits of the *Ḥadīth*:

1. **It is prohibited to marry the *Thayyib* until she is consulted** as he (صَلَّى اللَّهُ عَلَيْهِ وَسَلَّمَ) said,

   لَا تُنْكَحُ

   "Must not be married." This indicates the prohibition of proceeding without asking her permission.

2. **The Sharia is so wise** regarding differentiation between the *Thayyib* and the virgin woman.

3. **Observing the reasons and the meanings in legislated rulings** in the sense that there is a difference between the virgin and *Thayyib*. The virgin is often shy and cannot be consulted, so her permission is sought.

4. **Stipulating the wife's approval** even if her father is the one who concludes her marriage, because the father is not excluded. So, the rule is fundamentally general. The father or the guardian must not marry his daughter without her permission, and and it is the same with the *Thayyib*.[78]

5. **By means of analogy, the husband's approval is a must**. If the husband is married by force, the marriage will be unlawful. Can one be married by force? Yes, because some people force their sons to marry their nieces. In this case, the marriage is unlawful.

   What do you say if a man consulted his virgin daughter saying, "A man proposed to you. Do you want to marry him?" She responded, "Yes, this man is suitable for me." Can he marry her to this man?

[78] Shaykh was asked if the woman became *Thayyib* by means of adultery, is she regarded *Thayyib* or supposedly a virgin? He said, "She is considered *Thayyib* because if the woman has intercourse, she is no longer shy.

The answer: Yes, preferably. But *ad-Dhahriyah* said, "She must not be married." Why? Because the Messenger of Allāh (صَلَّى ٱللَّٰهُ عَلَيْهِ وَسَلَّمَ) said,

أَنْ تَسْكُتَ

"That she keeps silent." Whereas, this woman did not keep silent. She said, "Marry me," while another kept silent. Which one is to be married? The former is to be married. What if her father consulted her but she laughed or cried? scholars have different opinions. Some scholars maintained that laughing cannot be considered a permission. She may laugh out of surprise or her laugh may be out of disapproval. Others said this is considered a permission, because laughing indicates happiness and delight. It is more expressive than silence.[79]

What about the one who cried? Is this considered disapproval or permission? What is apparent is that it is more of a disapproval, though the Jurists (رَحِمَهُمُ ٱللَّٰهُ) maintained that if she cried or laughed, this would be considered an approval. However, it seems that if she cried, it means she does not want to marry. Crying may be out of happiness, but it is not an approval. But if the

[79] Al-Mobdi' (7/27), Al-Moharrar (2/15).

> guardian said, "Do not cry, what do you say?" If she kept silent, this is an approval.[80]

In the second *Ḥadīth*, of Ibn 'Abbās (رَضِيَ ٱللَّهُ عَنْهُ), the Prophet (صَلَّى ٱللَّهُ عَلَيْهِ وَسَلَّمَ) said,

الثَّيِّبُ أَحَقُّ بِنَفْسِهَا مِنْ وَلِيِّهَا

> **"A woman who has been previously married (*Thayyib*) has more right to her person than her guardian"**

She must be consulted concerning marriage. It is not enough to say, "A man has proposed to you. Do you agree?" She must be consulted and everything must be clarified. We shall say, "He is young or old, knowledgeable or ignorant, rich or poor, noble or otherwise."

Everything must be clear, because she has more right to her person. And the virgin must be asked permission and **"Her silence implies her consent."** So, he (صَلَّى ٱللَّهُ عَلَيْهِ وَسَلَّمَ) did not say, "Her order is her consent." This explanation indicates that the meaning of **"consulted"** is to ask permission. Her silence implies her consent. Her father or the guardian is the one who shall ask her permission. Concerning the virgin, it is enough to say, "A good man proposed to you. Do you agree?" If she

[80] Al-Mardawi said, "If she cried out of reluctance, this is disapproval unless she is forced. Crying may be either out of happiness or out of anger or dissatisfaction. If this is unclear, we look at her tears, if they are cold, she is happy but if hot, she is unhappy. This is mentioned in Al-Insaf (8/65), and it is ascribed to Al-Baghawi's Tafsir by some scholars when interpreting the ayah: ﴿and be glad﴾.

said, "Yes." Her permission is valid, because the Prophet (صَلَّى ٱللَّهُ عَلَيْهِ وَسَلَّمَ) ordered them to ask her permission. On the basis of this *Ḥadīth,* some scholars said that the *Thayyib* can marry herself, as the Prophet (صَلَّى ٱللَّهُ عَلَيْهِ وَسَلَّمَ) said,

أَحَقُّ بِنَفْسِهَا مِنْ وَلِيِّهَا

"She has more right to her person than her guardian."

However, there is no evidence for this because **"She has more right to her person than her guardian,"** indicates that everything must be crystal clear and then she must either give permission or not. This interpretation, despite being inconsistent with the literal meaning of the *Ḥadīth,* is the only way to understand this *Ḥadīth* when combined with the other previous aḥadīth that stipulate the approval of the guardian. In another narration,

لَيْسَ لِلْوَلِيِّ مَعَ الثَّيِّبِ أَمْرٌ

"A guardian has no command over a woman previously married and who has no husband."

A guardian has no command in her marriage. It is her business to give permission and allow her guardian to either conclude the contract or not.

وَالْيَتِيمَةُ تُسْتَأْمَرُ

"And an orphan girl (i.e. virgin) must be consulted."

The orphan is the one whose father died before the age of puberty. However, what is meant by the orphan here? Is she the one who is really an orphan or the who has not married and she reached puberty recently? It is the latter one because the one who has not reached puberty must not be married by any guardian. Why? Because her permission is not considered according to many scholars. Although, some scholars say, "Permission is considered from the ninth year", most of the scholars disagree.

So, the orphan is the one who has recently reached puberty and her permission is legally considered. Before puberty, her permission is not considered as she knows nothing about marriage matters. Anyway, all these *aḥadīths* indicate that the wife must be asked for permission regarding her marriage.[81]

Then he (صَلَّىٰ اللَّهُ عَلَيْهِ وَسَلَّمَ) said,

لاَ تُزَوِّجُ الْمَرْأَةُ الْمَرْأَةَ

> **"No woman should arrange the marriage of another woman..."**

Even in the case of her daughter. Even if she is an adult. If another woman authorized her by saying, "I authorize you to conclude the marriage contract for me," and she did, the marriage is unlawful. Primarily, this is because it is impermissible for her to conclude the marriage contract for herself, so that is even more reason for her not being allowed to conclude the marriage contract for someone else. This

[81] Al-Forou' (5/125).

Ḥadīth is joined with the previous one because the guardian is necessary in marriage. Both Qur'ān and Sunnah indicate the stipulation of the guardian.

The benefits of the *Ḥadīth* of Abu Hurairah (رَضِيَ ٱللَّهُ عَنْهُ) are mentioned above.

The benefits of Ibn 'Abbās' *Ḥadīth* (رَضِيَ ٱللَّهُ عَنْهُ) are almost the same as those of the first *Ḥadīth*:

1. ***The Thayyib* must be consulted in a way that clarifies everything**, because she has more right to her person.

2. **The orphan (i.e. the unmarried woman) must be consulted**.

3. **The wisdom of the Islamic Sharia**, in that it suits every condition.

The benefits of all the *Aḥadīths*:

1. **Unlike in Jāhiliyyah, when they used to force their daughters to marry whoever they wanted, women's rights are regarded in Islam**.

2. **Considering the eligibility of the guardian**, no one can assume charge unless he is eligible.

3. **It indicates that a woman is like a minor**, because she cannot be a guardian for herself regarding marriage. She should not be appointed as a ruler, Emir or a judge. However, she is allowed to settle disputes between women or she can be a principal of a girls' schools. However, a woman is not allowed to be a general ruler.

THE RULING OF *ASH-SHIGHAR*

988- Narrated Ibn `Umar and Nafi' (رَضِيَ اللَّهُ عَنْهُمَا),

نَهَى رَسُولُ اللَّهِ صلى الله عليه وسلم عَنِ الشِّغَارِ، وَالشِّغَارُ أَنْ يُزَوِّجَ الرَّجُلُ ابْنَتَهُ عَلَى أَنْ يُزَوِّجَهُ الآخَرُ ابْنَتَهُ، لَيْسَ بَيْنَهُمَا صَدَاقٌ

"Allāh's Messenger (صَلَّى اللَّهُ عَلَيْهِ وَسَلَّمَ) forbade *Ash-Shighar*, which means that somebody marries his daughter to somebody else, and the latter marries his daughter to the former without paying dowry."[82] Related by al-Bukhārī and Muslim.

In another narration, they agreed that Nafi' (رَضِيَ اللَّهُ عَنْهُ) is the one who explained *Ash-Shighar*.

Explanation

Ibn 'Umar (رَضِيَ اللَّهُ عَنْهُمْ) says:

[82] Related by Bukhari (5112), Muslim (1415), Tuhfat Al-Ashraf (8323).

نَهَى رَسُولُ اللهِ صَلَّى اللهُ عَلَيْهِ وَ سَلَّمَ عَنِ الشِّغَارِ

"Allāh's Messenger (صَلَّىٰٱللَّهُعَلَيۡهِوَسَلَّمَ) forbade Ash-Shighar."

"Forbidding" is the asking of one to stop doing something by a superior person. Here, doing here is not the opposite of saying. Rather, it covers all actions including saying. "Superior person" indicates that he is superior to the one who is addressed, even if he is actually lower than him in reality.

نَهَى رَسُولُ اللهِ صَلَّى اللهُ عَلَيْهِ وَ سَلَّمَ

"Allāh's Messenger (صَلَّىٰٱللَّهُعَلَيۡهِوَسَلَّمَ) forbade." There is no doubt that the Prophet (صَلَّىٰٱللَّهُعَلَيۡهِوَسَلَّمَ) is superior enough to forbid the Ummah from doing something. The scholars have different opinions about the phrase, **"The Prophet (صَلَّىٰٱللَّهُعَلَيۡهِوَسَلَّمَ) forbade something."** They wondered if the Companion's expression, "The Prophet (صَلَّىٰٱللَّهُعَلَيۡهِوَسَلَّمَ) forbade," is like "The Prophet (صَلَّىٰٱللَّهُعَلَيۡهِوَسَلَّمَ) said, 'Do not do such-and-such!'" They said that the former expression is weaker than the latter one, because "do not do" is clearer.

However, **"Forbade"** is what the Companion (رَضِيَٱللَّهُعَنۡهُ) understood. There is no doubt that it has the same ruling as the straight form of forbiddance for two reasons.

First: Certainly, the Companions (رَضِيَٱللَّهُعَنۡهُمۡ) know what is meant by forbidding. They are not non-Arabs who do not know the difference in the composition between a forbiddance and a statement.

Second: They are so pious that they would not say, "The Prophet (صَلَّى ٱللَّهُ عَلَيْهِ وَسَلَّمَ) forbade," when he did not. So, stating that it does not refer to forbiddance because of the way it is phrased is considered a weak opinion. Thus, **"forbade"** is as if the Prophet (صَلَّى ٱللَّهُ عَلَيْهِ وَسَلَّمَ) said,

لَا تَفْعَلُوا

"Do not marry in the way of *Shighar*."

"Allāh's Messenger (صَلَّى ٱللَّهُ عَلَيْهِ وَسَلَّمَ) forbade *Ash-Shighar*."

What is the definition of *Shighar*? It is explained by the narrator:

وَالشِّغَارُ أَنْ يُزَوِّجَ الرَّجُلُ ابْنَتَهُ عَلَى أَنْ يُزَوِّجَهُ الآخَرُ ابْنَتَهُ

"Ash-Shighar, which means that somebody marries his daughter to somebody else, and the latter marries his daughter to the former."

This may be Ibn Umar's explanation or Nafi's or Malik's (رَضِيَ ٱللَّهُ عَنْهُمْ), but it is not ascribed to the Prophet (صَلَّى ٱللَّهُ عَلَيْهِ وَسَلَّمَ).

These three narrations are said by Ibn Umar, Nafi and Mālik (رَضِيَ ٱللَّهُ عَنْهُمْ) and there is no contradiction. How? Ibn Umar (رَضِيَ ٱللَّهُ عَنْهُمْ) may have explained it, and Nafi' (رَضِيَ ٱللَّهُ عَنْهُ) narrated it without ascribing the explanation to Ibn Umar (رَضِيَ ٱللَّهُ عَنْهُمْ), and so did Mālik (رَضِيَ ٱللَّهُ عَنْهُ).

For example, you tell someone, "Do not intend to do bad deeds, for deeds are judged upon their intentions." In reality, this is the Prophet's saying.

If Ibn 'Umar (رَضِيَٱللَّهُعَنْهُمَ) had explained it and Nafi' (رَضِيَٱللَّهُعَنْهُ) narrated this explanation and ascribed it to Ibn 'Umar (رَضِيَٱللَّهُعَنْهُمَ), then no one can say, "This is not what Ibn 'Umar (رَضِيَٱللَّهُعَنْهُمَ) said," Since Nafi' (رَضِيَٱللَّهُعَنْهُ) may have narrated it without ascribing it to Ibn 'Umar (رَضِيَٱللَّهُعَنْهُمَ), a listener may hear it and think that it is Nafi's explanation and thinks the explanation is by Nafi' (رَضِيَٱللَّهُعَنْهُ). Anyway, there is no narration indicating that the Prophet (صَلَّىٱللَّهُعَلَيْهِوَسَلَّمَ) explained *Shighar*.

<u>But we can say:</u> It is explained by a Companion (رَضِيَٱللَّهُعَنْهُ) who knew what the Prophet (صَلَّىٱللَّهُعَلَيْهِوَسَلَّمَ) meant because he was living with him and understood what he said, especially Ibn 'Umar (رَضِيَٱللَّهُعَنْهُمَ), who was so concerned with the Prophet's *Ḥadīth*. Thus, the closest Companions of the Prophet were the ones who knew him best.

Therefore, if this was Ibn 'Umar's explanation, it must be ascribed to him, because Ibn 'Umar (رَضِيَٱللَّهُعَنْهُمَ) was a Companion. Also, the Companions knew best what the Prophet (صَلَّىٱللَّهُعَلَيْهِوَسَلَّمَ) meant.

وَالشِّغَارُ أَنْ يُزَوِّجَ الرَّجُلُ ابْنَتَهُ عَلَى أَنْ يُزَوِّجَهُ الآخَرُ ابْنَتَهُ

> **"That somebody marries his daughter to somebody else, and the latter marries his daughter to the former."**

This indicates that the second marriage is a condition for the first marriage.

ابْنَتَهُ

"His daughter." It is not just about the daughter in particular, she is merely an example. If somebody marries his sister to somebody else and the latter marries his sister to the former, this is *Shighar*. Or somebody marries his sister to somebody else and the latter marries his daughter to the former, these are just examples.

Thus, jurists used the term "guardianship", which is rather applicable for a sister or a daughter. Guardianship is more general than daughter. Daughter is clearer while guardianship is ambiguous. Usually, one finds the Salaf's expressions are easier and more understandable and the expressions of the later scholars are more complicated, in spite of being comprehensive.

لَيْسَ بَيْنَهُمَا صَدَاقٌ

"Without paying dowry." Dowry is called *Sadaq,* because it indicates the truthfulness the suitor displayed in paying money. Obviously, money is loved by people. So, they pay to get what they like, not what they hate. No one can give what he likes in return for what he dislikes. And no one can give what he likes to get the same thing, this is absurd. But one only gives what he likes to get the best thing.

Thus, it is called *'sadaq'* as it indicates the truthfulness of the suitor, like the *'sadaqah'* (i.e., charity) which indicates the sincerity of the giver. *Shighar* involves no dowry. Allāh (سُبْحَانَهُ وَتَعَالَى) says,

﴿ وَأُحِلَّ لَكُم مَّا وَرَآءَ ذَٰلِكُمْ أَن تَبْتَغُوا۟ بِأَمْوَٰلِكُم ﴾

"All others are lawful, provided you seek (them in marriage) with Mahr (bridal money given by the husband to his wife at the time of marriage) from your property." [*Sūrah an-Nisā'* 4:24]

First: The woman's honor is not considered money. However, these two persons conducted this marriage exchanging the honor of their respective women as dowry for each other. This is unlawful.

Second: Assuming it is allowed, it would be a betrayal of trust by the guardian. It could happen that the guardian marries his daughter to an unsuited man, just because that other man will marry him his daughter in return. This is a betrayal of trust.

Third: It may lead to forcing the woman to marry if the guardian wants to satisfy his desire regardless of her approval or disapproval.

Fourth: It often causes endless disputes and problems. If one of the two women is divorced, that divorced man will try to sabotage the other marriage. This happens a lot. These are four demerits which indicate that *Shighar* is unlawful.

The *Hadīth* indicates that *Shighar* is based on two conditions:

First: To be based on the first marriage as he (صَلَّىٱللَّهُعَلَيْهِوَسَلَّمَ) said,

عَلَى أَنْ يُزَوِّجَهُ

"On the condition that the other marries him."

Second: No dowry will be paid.

If somebody married his daughter and then the married man married his daughter to the former without a condition, then this is not *Shighar* and it is lawful. But is the dowry obliged for every one or not? Yes, every woman deserves a dowry similar to that of her peers as long as the dowry had not been fixed.

Another point: If somebody married his daughter to a man and the latter married his daughter to the former and each paid a dowry, this is not *Shighar*.

According to the literal meaning of the hadith, it is lawful to pay the lowest dowry. The lowest dowry is what makes the sale contract lawful. Does (an item in exchange for one fourth of a riyal) make the sale contract lawful? Yes,

اِلْتَمِسْ وَلَوْ خَاتَمًا مِنْ حَدِيدٍ

"Try to find something, even if it were an iron ring."

However, according to the Shariah, this is not intended, even if it what is apparent is that it is supported by the *Ḥadīth*. If he gave her one dirham, can this be her actual dowry? Or is her dowry the dirham and the honor of the other woman?

It is the latter because it is much more precious than the dirham. So, the dowry has to be conditioned to the amount similar to the one paid to her peers. Otherwise, it will be unlawful because the honor of each one will be part of the dowry and the honor is not money.

If one of the women is a young virgin while the other is an old *Thayyib*, the dowry will be different. So, whoever married an old *Thayyib*, he would have to pay the dowry of the amount similar to that of her peers and the one who married the young virgin would have to pay the dowry of the amount similar to that of her peers.

In addition, the approval of the two women is a second condition. According to the previous evidence, the two spouses must accept, otherwise the marriage will be unlawful.

Moreover, each one should be suitable to the woman, this must be a third condition. If he is unsuitable, the marriage will be unlawful.

If all these conditions are met, the marriage will be lawful. One may argue that even if all these conditions are met, the guardian may still betray the trust because he will have a wife, what can we do? We can say that as long as the approval of the wife is stipulated, she will accept what she wants.

One may also argue that there is another problem. One of the two wives may not be on good terms with her husband. So, her spouse may also spoil the other marriage. What can we say?

In reality, there is no answer, but to say there should be no such thing. And we cannot consider this answer because we said that it is the reason for forbiddance. Some scholars believe that *Shighar* is unlawful in all cases, even if the two wives accepted it and their spouses are suitable for them and a dowry of a similar amount to that of their peers has been appointed.

This opinion is persuasive due to two evidences:

First: What is related in Sahih Muslim[83] when the Prophet (صَلَّى ٱللَّهُ عَلَيْهِ وَسَلَّمَ) said,

لَا شِغَارَ فِي الْإِسْلَامِ

"There is no *Shighar* in Islam."

This is a general evidence.

Second: Out of precaution, we should be careful in opening this door in our present time Should we open the door to [*Shighar*], they will set an amount for the dowry. One may say, "I will marry you my daughter in exchange for ten thousand riyals on the condition that you marry me your daughter in exchange for ten thousand riyals." When the contract is concluded, he may say, "I am her father and I waive the dowry you must pay" and the other party may do the same thing and consequently no dowry is paid.

---

83 Related by Muslim (1415) on the authority of Ibn Omar (رَضِيَ ٱللَّهُ عَنْهُ).

Thus, it is better to prohibit *Shighar* in our present time, even though what is explained before follows the position of the Hanbali school. Owing to the corruption of people in these times, it is better to close the door. There are some noteworthy situations that did happen with the nomads. They called it "*Al-badal* (exchange) Marriage." It is, nevertheless, made by the approval of the two parties, dowry has been paid and marriage conditions were made. Can we say it is forbidden because of the corruption of people in these times? Or should we say it has already happened and as long as it happened in accordance with the *Ḥadīth*, we should approve it?

I believe that since dowry has already been paid, it is better not to break up the marriage. In addition, one cannot consider their children illegitimate. It is better to consider their marriage lawful as long as they accepted already[84], and that they are both suitable to each other and a lawful dowry is set.

However, if this has not happened yet, we should stop that marriage before anything happens, based on the rule that says, "To break up an ongoing matter is more difficult than breaking up what has not started yet."[85 & 86] This rule has

---

[84] Shaykh was asked if a case of *Shighar* already happened, he said, "They should be separated and then married again with dowry, but their children are legitimate, because this is a suspicious intercourse." He added, "Because all their sons are born of suspicious marriage, they are legitimate children."

[85] - **Editor's note:** In other words, the Shaykh ruled for the legitimacy of the *Shighar* marriage that already took place, and where there is agreement between both parties, dowry has been paid, and marriage conditions were made. He nonetheless ruled against the legitimacy of the *Shighar* marriage that has not been made yet. Simply put, it is harder to break up an ongoing marriage than to break up what hasn't started yet.

[86] Shaykh said, "A Mufti should pay attention to this rule."

many related branches: wearing perfume is forbidden for the *Muhrim* before he starts *Ihram,* but it not forbidden when he is engaged in *Ihram*.

Narrated `Aishah (رَضِيَ اللَّهُ عَنْهَا),

كَأَنِّي أَنْظُرُ إِلَى وَبِيصِ الْمِسْكِ فِي مَفَارِقِ رَسُولِ اللهِ صَلَّى اللهُ عَلَيْهِ وَسَلَّمَ ، وَهُوَ مُحْرِمٌ

"It is just as if I am looking at the glitter of scent in the parting of the Prophet's head hair while he was a Muhrim."

The Benefits of The Hadīth

1. ***Ash-Shighar* is prohibited** on the basis of the Prophet's order against it. Such an order is fundamentally used to indicate prohibition, as Allāh says,

﴿ يَٰٓأَيُّهَا ٱلَّذِينَ ءَامَنُوٓاْ أَطِيعُواْ ٱللَّهَ وَأَطِيعُواْ ٱلرَّسُولَ ﴾

"O' you who believe! Obey Allāh and obey the Messenger (Muḥammad (صَلَّى ٱللَّهُ عَلَيْهِ وَسَلَّمَ))" [*Sūrah an-Nisā'* 4:59]

And,

﴿ يَٰٓأَيُّهَا ٱلَّذِينَ ءَامَنُواْ ٱسۡتَجِيبُواْ لِلَّهِ وَلِلرَّسُولِ إِذَا دَعَاكُمۡ لِمَا يُحۡيِيكُمۡۖ وَٱعۡلَمُوٓاْ أَنَّ ٱللَّهَ يَحُولُ بَيۡنَ ٱلۡمَرۡءِ وَقَلۡبِهِۦ ﴾

"O' you who believe! Answer Allāh (by obeying Him) and (His) Messenger when he (صَلَّى ٱللَّهُ عَلَيْهِ وَسَلَّمَ) calls you to that which will give you life and know that Allāh comes in between a person and his heart (i.e. He prevents an evil person to decide anything)." [*Sūrah al-'Anfāl* 8:24]

2. **If *Ash-Shighar* marriage is concluded, it is unlawful**. Why? Because it is forbidden. If we considered it lawful, we would act against Allāh's will because Allāh wanted us to avoid it and not to conclude it. If one considered it lawful, it would mean it's affirmed by the Prophet, [which is not the correct]. The Prophet (صَلَّى ٱللَّهُ عَلَيْهِ وَسَلَّمَ) said,

مَنْ عَمِلَ عَمَلاً لَيْسَ عَلَيْهِ أَمْرُنَا فَهُوَ رَدٌّ

"He who does an act which we have not commanded, will have it rejected (by Allāh)."

The forbidden act is against the Allah's command and the Prophet's command. Allāh and His Prophet (صَلَّى ٱللَّهُ عَلَيْهِ وَسَلَّمَ) commanded that we should avoid this act which makes it rejected.

3. **Shariah cares for the woman's rights**, lest she becomes a plaything among men. If *Shighar* is lawful, men will play with women and guardians will make their women a means to marry more women. So, *Ash-Shighar* is forbidden.

4. **Shariah averts all that causes disputes** because *Ash-Shighar* is one of the reasons for dispute. For example, if a *Shighar* contract is already concluded and the relations between one of the two spouses was on bad terms, her husband will try to spoil the other marriage and then dispute will arise.

FREEDOM OF CHOICE FOR THE ONE WHO WAS MARRIED AGAINST HER WILL

989- Narrated Abdullāh Ibn 'Abbās (رَضِيَ اللَّهُ عَنْهُ),

أَنَّ جَارِيَةً، بِكْرًا أَتَتِ النَّبِيَّ - صلى الله عليه وسلم - فَذَكَرَتْ لَهُ أَنَّ أَبَاهَا زَوَّجَهَا وَهِيَ كَارِهَةٌ . فَخَيَّرَهَا النَّبِيُّ - صلى الله عليه وسلم - .

"A virgin female came to the Prophet (صَلَّى اللَّهُ عَلَيْهِ وَسَلَّمَ) and mentioned that her father had married her against her will. The Prophet (صَلَّى اللَّهُ عَلَيْهِ وَسَلَّمَ) allowed her to exercise her choice."[87] Related by Ahmad, Abu Dawud, Ibn Majah and it is flagged defective as being in a Mursal form.

Explanation

جَارِيَةً

[87] Related by Ahmad in Al-Musnad (1/273), Abu Dawud (2069), Ibn Majah (1875), and Al-Baihaqi (3/234) who said that this Sahih hadith is in Mursal form. The author said in At-Talkhis (3/161), "Its narrators are trustworthy, but Abu Hatem flagged it as defective because of being Mursal."

"A female" refers to the young female, the female maid and the female in general. However, in most cases, it refers to the young females.

فَخَيَّرَهَا النَّبِيُّ صَلَّى اللهُ عَلَيْهِ وَسَلَّمَ

> **"So the Prophet (صَلَّى اللهُ عَلَيْهِ وَسَلَّمَ) allowed her to exercise her choice."**

She was allowed to stay married or dissolve marriage though she is virgin and her father is her guardian.

This Ḥadīth is narrated through two ways. One of them is connected and the other is incompletely transmitted.

If the narrator of the first narration is trustworthy, the *Mursal* form in the second *Isnad* will not be affected badly. Thus, the weakness here is ineffective, as there are supporting narrations, including what is mentioned in Bukhari and Muslim,

لَا تَنْكَحُ الْبِكْرُ حَتَّى تُسْتَأْذَنَ

> **"And a virgin should not be given in marriage except after her permission."**

And in a clear narration in Muslim,

اَلْبِكْرُ يَسْتَأْذِنُهَا أَبُوهَا

> **"A virgin's father must ask her consent from her."**

So long as the virgin is not to be married except after her permission, marriage will be forbidden if she is married without her consent. If this is forbidden, how shall we give her a choice after the marriage took place? Does not the rule decree that forbidding indicates unlawfulness and if she agreed to the marriage the contract will be renewed?

Forbidding here is not because it is Allāh's right, but it is the human right. If anybody waved his right and concluded the contract, the reason for forbidding will go away. So, the Prophet (صَلَّىٰ ٱللَّٰهُ عَلَيْهِ وَسَلَّمَ) gave her the choice and did not break up the marriage.

The Benefits of The Hadīth:

1. **One is allowed to file a complaint against his father concerning the personal rights**. For example, if a wealthy father refused to marry his poor son, the son will have the right to make a claim against him. These are personal rights. Moreover, if a wealthy father refused to give his poor son his living, the son is entitled to file a complaint against him. If he married him one wife but she did not satisfy his needs, the father is obliged to marry him another. But the other rights such as debts, he should not claim against his father.

   For example, a son lends his father some dirhams but his father refused to give them back, he has no right to file a complaint against him. If he did, the judge would tell him,

أَنْتَ وَمَالُكَ لِأَبِيكَ

"**You and your wealth belong to your father**."

2. **The father must ask his virgin daughter for her permission**, as the Prophet (صَلَّى اللَّهُ عَلَيْهِ وَسَلَّمَ) gave her the choice. If the father had the right to force her, the Prophet (صَلَّى اللَّهُ عَلَيْهِ وَسَلَّمَ) would have said, "You do not have the freedom of choice while your father is alive."

3. **The unauthorized dealer is allowed to make deals**. It indicates that one is allowed to deal in others' rights without their permission. And if he is given permission, his deal will be effective, as the Prophet (صَلَّى اللَّهُ عَلَيْهِ وَسَلَّمَ) allowed the virgin female to accept or dissolve this marriage. So, if she accepted, the marriage would be concluded. But if she rejected, marriage would not be concluded.

   Therefore, if this act is allowed concerning marriage, it will be consequently allowed in other contracts. For example, an unauthorized person sold a car which he knew that the owner wanted to sell. Later, he told the owner who accepted that he sold it. Is this contract lawful? Yes. Does the buyer own the car upon concluding the contract or the permission of the owner? The car is owned upon concluding the contract, which was approved by the owner.

This is, in some respects, similar to the approval of the will by the inheritors or the approval of the beneficiary after the death of the testator. Is the trust owned by the beneficiary upon the death of the testator or the approval of the beneficiary? The scholars have different opinions about this, but the author of "*Zad Al-Mostaqni'*" said that it will be owned upon the death of the testator.

4. **Islāmic Sharīʿah protects the right of the unjustly treated ones even when it is a relative**, as the Prophet (صَلَّى ٱللَّهُ عَلَيْهِ وَسَلَّمَ) gave this woman, who was married by her father against her will, the freedom to choose. It is extremely unfair to marry a woman to a person she dislikes and who will be her life-partner. So, how can a woman be forced to marry a person she does not want?[88] She will get worried and she may go mad. Some women may try to burn or kill themselves because of the oppression. There is no doubt that this is unfair and oppressive. In addition, Islamic Sharia does not approve these acts even by the closest relatives.

---

[88] Shaykh said, "If she claimed that she is forced after the marriage consummation, this could not be approved without producing evidence. But if she claimed that she is forced before consummation, her claim would be acceptable.

WHAT IF A WOMAN WAS MARRIED BY TWO GUARDIANS TO TWO DIFERENT MEN?

990- It was narrated from Sammurah (رَضِيَ اللَّهُ عَنْهُ) that the Messenger of Allāh (صَلَّى اللَّهُ عَلَيْهِ وَسَلَّمَ) said,

أَيُّمَا اِمْرَأَةٍ زَوَّجَهَا وَلِيَّانِ، فَهِيَ لِلْأَوَّلِ مِنْهُمَا

> **"If a woman is married off by two guardians, then the first marriage is the one that counts."**[89] Related by Ahmad, the four Imāms, and graded as Hassan by At-Tirmidhī.

Explanation

فَهِيَ لِلْأَوَّلِ مِنْهُمَا

"The first marriage is the one that counts." This means that the second contract is unlawful because the woman is already

[89] Related by Ahmad (5/8,18), Abu Dawud (2088), At-Tirmidhi (1110), An-Nassai (7/314), Ibn Majah (2190). Ibn Majah related the hadith through Al-Hassan through Samurrah or Uqba Ibn Amer. It is authenticated by Abu Zur'a and Abu Hatem. Related by Al-Hakim (2/41), the author mentioned in At-Talkhis: "This hadith's authenticity is dependent on that Al-Hassan already heard from Samurrah. Its narrators are trustworthy, At-Talkhis (3/165).

married. So, the woman is legally married to the first husband. For example, a woman has two brothers. A suitor proposed to her elder brother who approved her marriage. Simultaneously, her younger brother, who was abroad, accepted a second suitor, to whom does she belong?

She belongs to the first one. It is clear that the second marriage is unlawful because she is already married. But if the first one is a step-brother and the other is a full brother, to whom does she belong? She belongs to the latter because the step-brother has no guardianship in the presence of the full brother and the guardianship of the full brother is stronger.

If they both married her off, both marriages would be unlawful. Why? Because the annulment of one of them is impossible, so both are unlawful.

If the woman was married by one after another but no one knows or remembers which contract was the first, a lot should be drawn because one of them is lawful. So, there are three categories:

1. To know which is the latter marriage, so the former will be lawful.

2. The two marriages happen at the same time, so both are unlawful.

3. To know that one of them happened before the other, but they forgot the order, a lot should be

> drawn. Why? Because one of the two contracts is lawful and no one can say that both are unlawful, so a lot[90] shall be drawn.

A lot is also used for a far superior purpose, as in souls. For example, some people board an overloaded ship at the sea. A number of people must be thrown overboard into the sea, so that the rest can survive. Do we throw them all?

No. Since this leads to killing innocent passengers, whom can we throw? Young people would say, "You shall throw the old people because they will die soon." Is this lawful? No, it is unlawful. The old people would say, You can throw the young people since their mothers can give birth to others" Is this lawful?

The answer: Both suggestions are unlawful. Rather, lots must be drawn. Yūnus (عَلَيْهِ ٱلصَّلَاةُ وَٱلسَّلَامُ) went on an overloaded ship which would sink unless some passengers were thrown away. Yūnus (عَلَيْهِ ٱلصَّلَاةُ وَٱلسَّلَامُ) took part in the drawing of lots and was consequently thrown in the sea. All those who were thrown overboard except Yūnus (عَلَيْهِ ٱلصَّلَاةُ وَٱلسَّلَامُ), who was swallowed alive by a huge whale. Allāh (عَزَّوَجَلَّ) said,

---

[90] Sheikh said in his poem (line 91):
Every suspicious act with no means to find out the truth, only a lot would do. See Sahih Al-Bukhari, chapter of testimonies (unit 30), Alfath (5/293), Almoghni by Ibn Qudamah (10/254), Qurtubi interpretation (6/56), Al-Torok Al-hokmia (p.265), Qawaid Al-Ahkam (p.136), Al-Manthor fil Qawaid (3/62), Qawaid Ibn Rajab (q/160), Qawaid Ibn Saadi (q/25).

﴿ فَلَوْلَآ أَنَّهُۥ كَانَ مِنَ ٱلْمُسَبِّحِينَ ﴿١٤٣﴾ لَلَبِثَ فِى بَطْنِهِۦٓ إِلَىٰ يَوْمِ يُبْعَثُونَ ﴿١٤٤﴾ ﴾

"Had he not been of them who glorify Allāh, he would have indeed remained inside its belly (the fish) till the Day of Resurrection." [*Sūrah as-Saffat* 37:143-144]

So, pay attention to what the Prophet (صَلَّى ٱللَّهُ عَلَيْهِ وَسَلَّمَ) said,

تَعَرَّفْ إِلَى اللهِ فِي الرَّخَاءِ يَعْرِفُكَ فِي الشِّدَّةِ.

"Recognize and acknowledge Allāh in times of ease and prosperity, and He will remember you in times of adversity."[91]

As Yūnus (عَلَيْهِ ٱلصَّلَاةُ وَٱلسَّلَامُ) glorified Allāh, Allāh saved him in times of adversity.

The Benefits of the *Hadīth*:

1. **It is desirable that the guardians should consult each other** in case of marriage so that a scenario of two contracts will not take place.

[91] Related by Imam Ahmad (1/307), At-Tirmidhi (2516), Abu Ya'la (2556). Its different versions of narration are mentioned in Jami' Al-Uloom Wa Al-hikam without authentication.

2. **If one of the guardians concluded the marriage contract before the other, the former one will be lawful** provided it is concluded by a guardian. If the former one is not concluded by a guardian, this contract will not be legally considered, such as when the former contract is concluded by a cousin or a step-brother, while the latter one is concluded by a full brother.

3. **Priority is considered in Islām**, so the Prophet (صَلَّىٰ ٱللَّهُ عَلَيْهِ وَسَلَّمَ) ordered that whoever was invited (for anything) by two persons to answer the first one who proposed an invitation[92]. Priority takes precedence in Islām, but in some other situations, posteriority may be taken into consideration.

[92] It will be narrated in the marriage banquet section.

WHAT IS THE RULING OF A SLAVE'S MARRIAGE WITHOUT THE MASTER'S PERMISSION?

991- Narrated Jabir ibn Abdullah (رَضِيَ اللَّهُ عَنْهُ) that the Prophet (صَلَّى اللَّهُ عَلَيْهِ وَسَلَّمَ) said,

أَيُّمَا عَبْدٍ تَزَوَّجَ بِغَيْرِ إِذْنِ مَوَالِيهِ فَهُوَ عَاهِرٌ

"If any slave marries without the permission of his masters or his family, he is a fornicator."[93] Related by Ahmad, Abu Dawud, graded as Sahih by At-Tirmidhi and Ibn Hibban.

Explanation

بِغَيْرِ إِذْنِ مَوَالِيهِ

"Without the permission of his masters." The masters are those who originally set him free. Here, "masters" indicates

[93] Related by Ahmad (3/300), Abu Dawud (2078), At-Tirmidhi (1112) who graded it as Hassan Sahih, but there are different opinions about the authenticity of Mohamed Ibn Aqil though he is authenticated by Ahmad and Ishaq Ibn Rahoya, while most of the scholars stated he is weak; Allah knows best.

the owner. As long as he was a slave, his master would be responsible for him. Allāh (سُبْحَانَهُ وَتَعَالَىٰ) said,

﴿ وَأَنكِحُوا۟ ٱلْأَيَـٰمَىٰ مِنكُمْ وَٱلصَّـٰلِحِينَ مِنْ عِبَادِكُمْ وَإِمَآئِكُمْ ﴾

"And marry those among you who are single (i.e. a man who has no wife and the woman who has no husband) and (also marry) the Salihun (pious, fit, and capable ones) of your (male) slaves and maid-servants (female slaves)." [*Sūrah an-Nūr* 24:32]

أَوْ أَهْلِهِ

"Or his family." "Or" indicates that the narrator is uncertain whether the *Ḥadīth* related as "his guardians or his family"? They have the same meaning. So, guardians here indicate the owners.

فَهُوَ عَاهِرٌ

"He is a fornicator." Meaning adulterous because his marriage is unlawful. The slave is not entitled to marry himself, as Allāh (سُبْحَانَهُ وَتَعَالَىٰ) said,

﴿ وَأَنكِحُوا۟ ٱلْأَيَـٰمَىٰ مِنكُمْ وَٱلصَّـٰلِحِينَ مِنْ عِبَادِكُمْ وَإِمَآئِكُمْ ﴾

"And marry those among you who are single (i.e. a man who has no wife and the woman who has no husband) and (also marry) the Salihun (pious, fit, and

capable ones) of your (male) slaves and maid-servants (female slaves)." [*Sūrah an-Nūr* 24:32]

﴿ وَأَنكِحُوا۟ ﴾

"And marry" indicates that the slave cannot marry himself. His marriage would be the same as the divorced or widowed female, who cannot be married without a guardian. So, the marriage of the slave, without the permission of his masters, is like that of the woman who married without the permission of her guardian.

The Benefits of the Ḥadīth:

1. **The marriage of the slave is lawful provided that his master gave permission**. If his master gave permission, is the slave allowed to marry himself or must his master marry him? We say: According to the literal meaning of the *Ḥadīth,* if his master gave permission, he could marry on his own. On the contrary, if the woman's guardian gives her permission to marry, she is not allowed to marry herself because she is originally ineligible to conclude contracts. However, the slave is allowed to conclude contracts if he is set free.

   So, the slave is not allowed to marry himself owing to ownership by his master, not because he is ineligible. There are two ways for the master to marry his slave. The first way is when the woman's guardian says, "I marry your slave (his name) to my daughter (her name)." The master then replies, "I accept my slave's marriage." He must add "my slave". The second way is when the master says to his slave, "You are allowed to marry." Then, woman's guardian says to the slave himself, "I marry you to my daughter (her name)," and the slave says, "I agree."

THE RULING OF MARRYING THE WOMAN AND HER PATERNAL AUNT, HER MATERNAL AUNT AND HER SISTER OR THE SAME TIME

992- Abu Huraira (رَضِيَ ٱللَّهُ عَنْهُ) reported Allāh's Messenger (صَلَّى ٱللَّهُ عَلَيْهِ وَسَلَّمَ) having said,

لَا يُـجْمَعُ بَيْنَ الْمَرْأَةِ وَعَمَّتِهَا، وَلَا بَيْنَ الْمَرْأَةِ وَخَالَتِهَا

"One should not combine a woman, her paternal aunt, nor between a woman and her maternal aunt in marriage."[94] Related by Bukhari and Muslim.

Explanation

This indicates the forbiddance of the simultaneous marriage of a woman and her paternal aunt because this woman will be the niece of the other woman, **"nor a woman and her mother's sister in marriage"** because the wife will be the

[94] Related by Bukhari (5109) and Muslim (1408), Tuhfat Al-Ashraf (13812)

niece of her aunt. Thus, it is not allowed to combine them in marriage.

In this case, can we say that the husband is not allowed to marry the wife's maternal aunt and the wife's paternal aunt as well? Some scholars said it is temporarily unlawful. But it is better to say that it is not unlawful unless they are combined in marriage. Thus, the words of the Qur'ān and the Sunnah are to be used. Allāh (سُبْحَانَهُ وَتَعَالَىٰ) said,

﴿ وَأَن تَجْمَعُوا۟ بَيْنَ ٱلْأُخْتَيْنِ ﴾

"And [to combine between] two sisters in wedlock at the same time." [*Sūrah an-Nisā'* 4:23]

Allāh did not say: "Forbidden to you (for marriage) are the sisters of your wives." And in this abovementioned *Hādīth* from the Sunnah, he (صَلَّى ٱللَّهُ عَلَيْهِ وَسَلَّمَ) did not say, "Forbidden to you (for marriage) are the maternal aunts of your wives and the paternal aunts of your wives." Committing to the words mentioned in the Qur'ān and the Sunnah does not cause problems.

But the words of the Jurists (رحمهم الله) are ambiguous which drove some people to think that the sister, maternal aunt and paternal aunt of the wife are unmarriageable (to the husband). The laymen think that they are unmarriageable like the wife's mother.

Thus, the wife's sister is temporarily unmarriageable (to the husband) and so are her paternal and maternal aunt. It is better to phrase it as follows: her sister and her maternal and paternal aunts are not unlawful except in the case of combining them in marriage. Therefore, it is prohibited to combine these three ones (wife's sister, her maternal and paternal aunt) in marriage, as mentioned in both the Qur'ān and the Sunnah.

If one asks, "Does this ruling apply to those ones (i.e. wife's sister, paternal and maternal aunt) related by breastfeeding?

The answer: Yes, the Prophet (صَلَّىٱللَّهُعَلَيْهِوَسَلَّمَ) said,

يَحْرُمُ مِنَ الرَّضَاعِ مَا يَحْرُمُ مِنَ النَّسَبِ

"What is haram by birth is haram by breastfeeding."

So, combining the ones mentioned above in marriage is forbidden. As opposed to Sheikh Al-Islam Ibn Taimyyah (رَحِمَهُٱللَّهُ) who believed that it is not prohibited to combine those related by breastfeeding in marriage.

The Ḥadīth,

يَحْرُمُ مِنَ الرَّضَاعِ مَا يَحْرُمُ مِنَ النَّسَبِ.

"What is haram by birth is haram by breastfeeding," is general and addresses both situations. One other question may be asked. Is anyone allowed to combine in marriage the previous wife of a man and that man's daughter from another woman?

The answer: Yes, because this is not forbidden.

And if they ask, "Is anyone allowed to combine in marriage the woman and her daughter from another husband?" Meaning a man died and left a woman (widow) who was later married to another one who married her daughter from another husband?

The answer: No, it is not allowed because she is the mother of his wife. Allāh (سُبْحَانَهُۥوَتَعَالَىٰ) said, in regards to the permanent unmarriageable women,

"Your wives' mothers."

Thus, combining the previous wife of a man and his daughter (from another wife) is allowed, while combining in marriage the previous wife of a man and her daughter is not allowed. Even if this daughter is divorced or died, he is not allowed to marry her mother because it is eternally forbidden. This is linguistically easier than what the Jurists said.

Of course, words of the Qur'ān and the Sunnah are easier because you say, "It is not allowed to combine in marriage three women in marriage: the woman and her sister, the woman and her maternal aunt and paternal aunt.

One may ask a question, "Is it allowed to combine in marriage a previous wife of a man and his daughter from another woman?"

The answer: Yes. Pay attention that it is better to use the legal words in this regard. For example, the laypeople call the stepmother "aunt"[95] and if you say to the laypeople, "It is

[95] It is a vernacular word in Saudi Arabia.

allowed to combine the daughter of a man and that man's previous wife in marriage," they will say, "How is it allowed to combine them in marriage?" So, words can alter the meaning. If one says, "The father of the wife is her uncle," this will be problematic.

Thus, the Prophet (صَلَّى ٱللَّهُ عَلَيْهِ وَسَلَّمَ) forbade calling 'Isha' prayer *Al'atama*[96] because it is called as such by the nomads. And he (صَلَّى ٱللَّهُ عَلَيْهِ وَسَلَّمَ) said,

فَإِنَّهَا فِي كِتَابِ اللهِ الْعِشَاءُ

"For it is called 'Isha' in the Book of Allāh."[97]

So, it is better to maintain the legal terminology of Sharīʿah.

In a nutshell, this *Ḥadīth* indicates that it is prohibited to combine in marriage the woman and her maternal aunt or paternal aunt. The right opinion indicates that this prohibition extends to those related by breastfeeding. And in the case where the two marriage contracts were concluded, one after another, which one is lawful? The former one is lawful. If the two contracts are concluded at the same time, as in saying, "I married you both of my daughters?" Both are unlawful, because not one of the contracts can be terminated.

---

[96] It is already related in the chapter of Ṣalāh.

[97] Collected by al-Imām Muslim in the book of masājid and the places of prayer (No. 644).

What can you say about the story of the brother of Madyan who said to Mūsā (عَلَيْهِ ٱلصَّلَاةُ وَٱلسَّلَامُ):

﴿ قَالَ إِنِّيٓ أُرِيدُ أَنْ أُنكِحَكَ إِحْدَى ٱبْنَتَيَّ ﴾

"I intend to wed one of these two daughters of mine to you." [*Sūrah al-Qasas* 28:27]

This is not a combination because Allāh (سُبْحَانَهُ وَتَعَالَىٰ) said, **"One of these two daughters,"** and Mūsā (عَلَيْهِ ٱلصَّلَاةُ وَٱلسَّلَامُ) appointed one of them.

THE RULING ON ENGAGMENT AND MARRIAGE OF AL-MUHRIM

993- Uthman b.'Affan (رَضِيَ ٱللَّهُ عَنْهُ) reported Allāh's Messenger (صَلَّى ٱللَّهُ عَلَيْهِ وَسَلَّمَ) as saying,

لَا يَنْكِحُ الْمُحْرِمُ، وَلَا يُنْكَحُ

"A Muhrim must neither marry himself, nor should anyone marry him (while in the state of *Ihram*)."

In a narration of Imam Muslim, **"nor should he make the proposal of marriage."** Ibn Hibban added, **"Nor arrange a marriage for others."**[98]

994- Narrated Ibn `Abbās (رَضِيَ ٱللَّهُ عَنْهُ),

تَزَوَّجَ رَسُولُ اللهِ (صَلَّى اللهُ عَلَيْهِ وَسَلَّمَ) مَيْمُونَةَ وَهُوَ مُـحْرِمٌ

"The Prophet (صَلَّى ٱللَّهُ عَلَيْهِ وَسَلَّمَ) married Maimuna (رَضِيَ ٱللَّهُ عَنْهَا) while he was in the state of lhram."[99] Related by Bukhari and Muslim.

995- Imām Muslim also related,

---

[98] Related by Muslim (1409).

[99] Related by Bukhari (5114), Muslim (1410), Tuhfat Al-Ashraf (5376).

أَنَّ النَبِيَّ (صَلَّى اللهُ عَلَيْهِ وَسَلَّمَ) تَزَوَّجَهَا وَهُوَ حَلَالٌ

"Allāh's Messenger (صَلَّى ٱللَّٰهُ عَلَيْهِ وَسَلَّمَ) married Maimuna (رَضِيَ ٱللَّٰهُ عَنْهَا), not in the state of *Ihram*."[100]

Explanation

These a*ḥādīth* address the marriage of men and women in the state of *Ihram*. The Prophet (صَلَّى ٱللَّٰهُ عَلَيْهِ وَسَلَّمَ) said,

لَا يَنْكَحُ الْمُحْرِمُ

"A Muhrim must neither marry himself" Woman should not be married and men should not marry themselves (in the state of *Ihram*). Anybody married in the state of *Ihram* will be in a hurry to consummate marriage, which would entail the nullification of the Hajj. Allāh (سُبْحَانَهُ وَتَعَالَىٰ) said,

﴿ وَأَتِمُّوا۟ ٱلْحَجَّ وَٱلْعُمْرَةَ لِلَّهِ ﴾

"And perform properly (i.e., all the ceremonies according to the ways of the Prophet Muhammad

100 Related by Muslim (1411).

(صَلَّى ٱللَّهُ عَلَيْهِ وَسَلَّمَ) **the Hajj and Umrah (i.e. the pilgrimage to Makkah) for Allāh."** [*Sūrah al-Baqarah* 2:196]

Or he will be busy thinking of his wife and, hence, he would not be fully focused on the worship. Thus, the Prophet (صَلَّى ٱللَّهُ عَلَيْهِ وَسَلَّمَ) forbade this.

وَلَا يُنْكَحُ

Also, **"nor arrange a marriage for others."** If the guardian (of a woman) was in the state of *Ihram*, he should not marry his daughter to anybody, even if the wife and her would-be husband are not in a state of *Ihram*.

In another narration,

وَلَا يَـخْطُبُ

"Nor should he make the proposal of marriage." And he must not propose to anyone because he would be occupied with this proposal.

وَلَا يُـخْطَبُ عَلَيْهِ

"Nor arrange a marriage for others." A woman in the state of *Ihram* must not be proposed to. Thus, in the state of *Ihram*, the Prophet (صَلَّى ٱللَّهُ عَلَيْهِ وَسَلَّمَ) forbade concluding the marriage contract and its means, which are proposal, nikāh and the contract.

The Benefits of the Ḥadīth:

1. **This *Ḥadīth* indicates forbidding the marriage of the Muhrim** as the Prophet (ﷺ) said,

لَا يَنْكِحُ الْمُحْرِمُ

"A Muhrim should neither marry himself."

According to the literal meaning of the *Ḥadīth*, the nikāh is unlawful as long as the individual is a Muhrim, even if he finished the first removal of *Ihram*. For example, a Hājji has thrown the pebbles at Jamrat-ul 'Aqabah on Eid day, and had his hair cut and completed the first removal of *Ihram*. Is he allowed to marry?

From what is apparent, this is not allowed. However, according to Shaykh Al-Islām Ibn Taymiyyah (رَحِمَهُ ٱللَّهُ), "This is allowed. He added, "The definite article '*Al*' in the word ***'Al-Muhrim'*** refers to the person who is in full *Ihram*." In other words, those who haven't made their first removal of *Ihram*. What is prohibited instead is engaging in sexual intercourse with women after the first removal of *Ihram,* as the *Ḥadīth* indicates:

إِذَا رَمَيْتُمْ وَحَلَقْتُمْ وَذَبَحْتُمْ فَقَدْ حَلَّ لَكُمْ كُلُّ شَيْءٍ إِلَّا النِّسَاءَ

"When one of you threw the pebbles and shaved his hair, everything including perfume becomes lawful for him except women (i.e. consummation)."

Thus, according to Shaykh Al-Islām Ibn Taimyyah (رَحِمَهُ ٱللَّهُ)[101] and some other scholars and probably an opinion of Imam Ahmad too, "The marriage contract is allowed to be concluded after the first removal of *Ihram*." However, the well-known opinion in Imam Ahmad's school of Fiqh is that making a marriage contract after the first removal is as prohibited as before it. In the case when the contract has not been concluded yet, the Mufti should say it is not allowed to conclude it. However, the other opinion should be followed if the contract has already been concluded. It is difficult to renew the contract, especially after the possibility of pregnancy.

For example, a person performed Hajj, threw the pebbles, made Tawāf (circumambulation) and observed Sai', but he did not shave. And then he concluded the contract before shaving and making expiation (to compensate for missing the shaving). What can we say?

We say: This is lawful. But if he said, "I want to conclude the marriage contract," we should tell him to wait until he finishes the second removal of *Ihram*.

2. **One is not allowed to do anything hindering his worship or make it unlawful**, how? The *Muhrim* is not

[101] Ibn Taimyyah (رَحِمَهُ ٱللَّهُ) said, "It is agreed upon in the Imam Ahmad's school of Fiqh that if the *Muhrim* threw the pebbles, slaughtered, shaved or cut his hair, he is allowed to wear his clothes, use perfumes and fishing, concluding marriage contract." Sharh Al-Omda (3/535).

allowed to make consummation or conclude the marriage contract.

3. **The *Muhrim* is not allowed to propose or arrange proposals** as the Prophet (صَلَّى ٱللَّهُ عَلَيْهِ وَسَلَّمَ) said,

لَا يَـخْطَبُ، وَلَا يُـخْطَبُ

"Nor should he make the proposal of marriage," Ibn Hibban added, **"Nor arrange a marriage for others."**

4. **This *Ḥadīth* indicates the prohibition of what may lead to committing sins**, as he (صَلَّى ٱللَّهُ عَلَيْهِ وَسَلَّمَ) said,

لَا يَـخْطَبُ

"Nor arrange a marriage for others."

According to the literal meaning of the *Ḥadīth*, it is not allowed to propose directly or indirectly. One may argue that the complete proposal is the direct one, so the indirect proposal is allowed. For example, when a *Muhrim* encountered a man and said to him, "Your daughter is a treasure," or "I want your daughter." This is an indirect proposal. Preferably, he should not propose directly or indirectly.

Concerning the *Ḥadīth* of Ibn 'Abbās (رَضِيَ ٱللَّهُ عَنْهُ), **"The Prophet** (صَلَّى ٱللَّهُ عَلَيْهِ وَسَلَّمَ) **married Maimuna** (رَضِيَ ٱللَّهُ عَنْهَا) **while he was in the**

state of *lhram*." Maimuna Bint Al-Harith (رَضِيَ ٱللَّهُ عَنْهَا), the aunt of Abdullah Ibn 'Abbās (رَضِيَ ٱللَّهُ عَنْهُ),

وَهُوَ مُـحْرِمٌ

"While he was in the state of *lhram*," referring to the performance of *Umrah*. **"Married"** indicates that the Prophet (صَلَّى ٱللَّهُ عَلَيْهِ وَسَلَّمَ) married her while he was performing Umrah. And Muslim related on the authority of Maimuna (رَضِيَ ٱللَّهُ عَنْهَا), that the Prophet (صَلَّى ٱللَّهُ عَلَيْهِ وَسَلَّمَ) married her while he was not in the state of *Ihram*. There is another *Ḥadīth* narrated by Abu Rāfi' (رَضِيَ ٱللَّهُ عَنْهُ) that the Prophet (صَلَّى ٱللَّهُ عَلَيْهِ وَسَلَّمَ) married Maimuna (رَضِيَ ٱللَّهُ عَنْهَا) while he was not in the state of *Ihram* where he said,

وَكُنْتُ الرَّسُولَ بَيْنَهُمَا

"**I was the intercessor between them**."

Thus, Ibn 'Abbās' *Ḥadīth* is contradicted with *Aḥadīth* of Maimuna and Abu Rāfi' (رَضِيَ ٱللَّهُ عَنْهُمْ). Scholars hold different opinions about whose statement takes precedence. Some scholars preferred *Ḥadīth* of Ibn 'Abbās (رَضِيَ ٱللَّهُ عَنْهُ) due to the chain of narration, as it is agreed upon by Bukhari and Muslim and because Maimuna (رَضِيَ ٱللَّهُ عَنْهَا) is his aunt and he knows her state best.

Others preferred *Hadīth* of Maimuna (رَضِيَ ٱللَّهُ عَنْهَا) as:

1. She is the subject matter of the story.

2. It is supported by the *Ḥadīth* of Abu Rāfi' (رَضِيَ ٱللَّهُ عَنْهُ) who was the intercessor between them.

3. It coincides with what the Prophet (صَلَّى ٱللَّهُ عَلَيْهِ وَسَلَّمَ) said,

لَا يَنْكِحُ الْمُحْرِمُ

"A Muhrim should neither marry himself."

Fundamentally speaking, if the Prophet's actions are not held as exclusive to him (صَلَّى ٱللَّهُ عَلَيْهِ وَسَلَّمَ), then the Prophet (صَلَّى ٱللَّهُ عَلَيْهِ وَسَلَّمَ) did not marry in the state of *Ihram*. Based on this opinion, what is legislated upon the Ummah is legislated upon him as well. Whereas, what is exclusive to him cannot be extended to include the Ummah unless there is a proof saying so.

The second opinion is the right one and that is that the Prophet (صَلَّى ٱللَّهُ عَلَيْهِ وَسَلَّمَ) married her while he was not in the state of *Ihram*.

One may argue, "What about the *Hadīth* of Ibn 'Abbās (رَضِيَ ٱللَّهُ عَنْهُ)?"

The answer: Ibn 'Abbās (رَضِيَ ٱللَّهُ عَنْهُ) did not know about her marriage except after the Prophet (صَلَّى ٱللَّهُ عَلَيْهِ وَسَلَّمَ) made *Ihram*. He thought that he (صَلَّى ٱللَّهُ عَلَيْهِ وَسَلَّمَ) married her in the state of *Ihram* and narrated what he knew. Thus, the right opinion is that he (صَلَّى ٱللَّهُ عَلَيْهِ وَسَلَّمَ) married her while he was not in the state of *Ihram*. Considering this ruling leads to the conclusion that the Prophet's (صَلَّى ٱللَّهُ عَلَيْهِ وَسَلَّمَ) marriage in this case is not exclusive to him. However, those who preferred the *Ḥadīth* of Ibn 'Abbās (رَضِيَ ٱللَّهُ عَنْهُ) believed that this is exclusive to the Prophet

(صَلَّى ٱللَّهُ عَلَيْهِ وَسَلَّمَ) as many issues concerning the affair of marriage were made exclusive to the Prophet (صَلَّى ٱللَّهُ عَلَيْهِ وَسَلَّمَ).

NIKĀH CONDITIONS

996- Uqbah bin Amir Al-Juhani (رَضِيَ ٱللَّهُ عَنْهُ) narrated that the Messenger of Allāh (صَلَّى ٱللَّهُ عَلَيْهِ وَسَلَّمَ) said,

إِنَّ أَحَقَّ الشُّرُوطِ أَنْ يُوَفَّى بِهِ، مَا اسْتَحْلَلْتُمْ بِهِ الْفُرُوجَ.

"Indeed, the conditions most deserving to be fulfilled are those that make the private parts lawful."[102] Related by Bukhari and Muslim.

Explanation

What is the meaning of **"That make the private parts lawful?"** The wife and her family hinged making the private parts lawful on the compliance with whatever condition involved in the contract. Thus, he said,

مَا اسْتَحْلَلْتُمْ بِهِ الْفُرُوجَ

"That make the private parts lawful." Otherwise, the private parts are considered lawful after concluding the marriage contract, but the conditions in the contract are an integral part of it.

[102] Related by Bukhari (5151), Muslim (1418), Tuhfat Al-Ashraf (9953).

The word "**condition**" applies to two categories. They are the conditions of validity and the conditions of obligation. The general conditions of a contract are called "validity conditions." The special conditions of a contract are called "irrevocability conditions." Scholars differentiate between the conditions of marriage and those included in a marriage contract similar to how they differentiate between the general conditions of business transactions and the those in the contract of the business transactions.

The condition of a contract is that upon which the validity of the contract is based. The contract will be unlawful if this condition is not fulfilled. Knowing about the product and its price is an essential condition in a business transaction, for example. Also, the existence of a guardian in marriage is a condition that makes the contract valid. As for the issue of obligation, it is dependent upon the conditions laid down in the contract itself. The contract will be lawful even if the conditions are not fulfilled.

There is another difference. The conditions of the validity of a contract are set by the Sharia Law and no one can renounce them, bu conditions in the contract are set by the contractors and either one of the contracting parties has the option to revoke it.

إِنَّ أَحَقَّ الشُّرُوطِ أَنْ يُوَفَّى بِهِ

"Indeed, the conditions most deserving to be fulfilled."

Does the Prophet (صَلَّى ٱللَّهُ عَلَيْهِ وَسَلَّمَ) mean the conditions of the contract or the condition 'in' the contract? He (صَلَّى ٱللَّهُ عَلَيْهِ وَسَلَّمَ) referred to the second. In case anyone stipulated some conditions, these conditions will be an integral part of the contract and of this verse,

﴿ يَٰٓأَيُّهَا ٱلَّذِينَ ءَامَنُوٓاْ أَوۡفُواْ بِٱلۡعُقُودِۚ ﴾

"O' you who believe! Fulfill (your) obligations." [*Sūrah al-Mā'idah* 5:1]

It means fulfilling its essential and integral terms. One is obligated to fulfill the conditions in a business transaction. Is he similarly obligated to fulfill the conditions in the marriage contract? Yes, it is even more important, because the Prophet (صَلَّى ٱللَّهُ عَلَيْهِ وَسَلَّمَ) said,

إِنَّ أَحَقَّ الشُّرُوطِ

"**Indeed the conditions most deserving**."

They are the most deserving conditions because conditions in a marriage make private parts lawful. Whereas, the conditions in a business transaction make a commodity lawful. Making private parts lawful is more dangerous than business deals. So, the conditions in marriage are most deserving to be fulfilled.

الْفُرُوجَ

"**Private parts**" refers to the those of women, which Allāh makes lawful.

As for the conditions in marriage which are mentioned in the *Ḥadīth*. They are divided into three categories:

1. A condition that the contract depends on;
2. A condition for the sake of the two parties that does not violate the contract;
3. And a condition that violates the contract.

First: A condition which is an integral part of the contract. It is whether either stipulated or not, such as providing the wife's expenses. If the wife stipulated that the husband must provide her expenses, this is just a confirmation. If the wife stipulated that the husband allots certain nights to spend with her like his other wife, this is also just a confirmation. If the husband stipulated that that the wife must obey him in obligatory matters, this is just a confirmation.

Second: A condition which violates the contract. It is considered a prohibited condition. For example, the husband stipulated that the wife must allow him to have intercourse with her during her menses. This condition is unlawful and must not be fulfilled. Similarly, when the wife stipulates that the husband should allot more nights for her than his other wife, this is also unlawful condition. Conditions are lawful except the ones which are against Sharia Law. For example, it is allowed to stipulate a particular dowry (i.e. one thousand dirham) and the husband stipulates that the dowry will not be more than one thousand dirhams. Also, it is allowed to stipulate that she wants to stay in her country or her house.

Moreover, it is allowed to stipulate that a maid servant should wait on her. Allotting nights for women is allowed except what is prohibited by evidence. According to the right opinion, it is allowed if the husband stipulated not to allot nights for her and to make consummation whenever he wants. Furthermore, the husband is not allowed to allot nights for a wife if she waives her right. For example, Sauda Bint Zama' (رَضِيَٱللَّهُعَنْهَا) waived her right for Ai'shah (رَضِيَٱللَّهُعَنْهَا).[103]

The wife is allowed to stipulate that the husband accompanies her in Hajj. The wife is not allowed to stipulate that she will not breastfeed the baby. However, it is said to be allowed unless the baby is in dire need of it. In short, this is fundamentally lawful except what is prohibited by evidence.

To conclude, there are three categories. First, for what is considered an integral part of the contract, stipulating it in the contract is only a confirmation. Second, what is considered unlawful must not be fulfilled. Third, when neither of the earlier conditions is met, then in this it is originally allowed except what is prohibited by evidence.

If the wife stipulated that she has the choice to dissolve the marriage if not suitable with her? Shaykh Al-Islām Ibn Taimyyah (رَحِمَهُٱللَّهُ)[104] said this is a lawful condition, particularly if she said, "If it is not suitable to stay with your family, I have the choice to annul marriage or stay in another house," as staying with the family is often not suitable. So, this is a lawful condition and in accordance with the contract. But

---

[103] This will be addressed later.

[104] Al-Fatawa (32/149).

if the wife stipulated that she wants to finish her studies, this condition shall be limited. One can say that she will be enabled to study for four years only in case the period of study is three years. This is because some women do not care about studying and passing exams. Anyway, this shall be limited so that the husband's right would be kept.

The Benefits of the Ḥadīth:

1. **It is allowed to stipulate conditions in contracts** as the Prophet (صَلَّى ٱللَّهُ عَلَيْهِ وَسَلَّمَ) allowed them unrestrictedly. But this shall be limited on the basis of what is related by Bukhari and Muslim on the authority of A'ishah (رَضِيَ ٱللَّهُ عَنْهَا) that the Prophet (صَلَّى ٱللَّهُ عَلَيْهِ وَسَلَّمَ) said,

   كُلُّ شَرْطٍ لَيْسَ فِي كِتَابِ اللهِ فَهُوَ بَاطِلٌ، وَإِنْ كَانَ مِئَةَ شَرْطٍ

   "Every condition that is not in the Book of Allāh (سُبْحَانَهُ وَتَعَالَىٰ) is invalid, even if there are one hundred conditions."

   Also, the Prophet (صَلَّى ٱللَّهُ عَلَيْهِ وَسَلَّمَ) said,

   الْمُسْلِمُونَ عَلَى شُرُوطِهِمْ، إِلَّا شَرْطًا أَحَلَّ حَرَامًا أَوْ حَرَّمَ حَلَالًا

   "And the Muslims will be held to their conditions, except the conditions that make the lawful unlawful or the unlawful lawful."

2. **Islāmic Sharīʿah is so flexible** that it has not narrowed the window of stipulating conditions (in the marriage contract) because the Muslim may need to incorporate conditions in order to be committed to them.

3. **Conditions in marriage are lawful and fulfilling** them should be one's priority.

4. **Refuting the opinion of those who make marriage conditions so limited** that no condition is to be lawful except what is fundamental for the contract. If we were to follow this opinion, this *Ḥadīth* would consequently be useless. Fundamental conditions of the contract are, nevertheless, needless of stipulating them or otherwise.

5. **What is hinged on a condition cannot be effective without fulfilling that condition.** The Prophet (صَلَّى ٱللَّٰهُ عَلَيْهِ وَسَلَّمَ) said,

مَا اسْتَحْلَلْتُمْ بِهِ الْفُرُوجَ

"That make the private parts lawful."

The marriage contract is therefore ineligible to move forward unless that condition is fulfilled.

6. **It is noteworthy to indicate what Allāh said,**

﴿ يَٰٓأَيُّهَا ٱلَّذِينَ ءَامَنُوٓاْ أَوۡفُواْ بِٱلۡعُقُودِ ﴾

"O' you who believe! fulfill (your) obligations." [*Sūrah al-Mā'idah* 5:1]

Includes compliance with the fundamental and integral conditions of the contract. Fulfilling the integral condition is therefore a must. To conclude, when Allāh (سُبْحَانَهُۥ وَتَعَالَىٰ) said,

"**Fulfill (your) obligations**," this includes compliance with the fundmental as well as the integral conditions of contracts. This sheds light on what people do nowadays. They cheat in contracts which are concluded between them and between their countries. They think that the conditions in these contracts are not included in this verse,

"Fulfill (your) obligations."

This is a misconception because the contract includes the contract as an entity and the conditions therein.

7. Private parts are normally prohibited as the Prophet (صَلَّى ٱللَّهُ عَلَيْهِ وَسَلَّمَ) said,

مَا اسْتَحْلَلْتُمْ بِهِ الْفُرُوجَ

"**That make the private parts lawful**."

Thus, in case anybody's sister (by reason of breastfeeding) is confused with another woman, he is not allowed to marry any of them. Concerning the breastfeeding, sometimes one is uncertain if the elder or the younger girl was breastfed by his mother, so he must avoid marrying the two girls until lawfulness is proven because private parts are normally unlawful. The Prophet (صَلَّى ٱللَّٰهُ عَلَيْهِ وَسَلَّمَ) said,

مَا اسْتَحْلَلْتُمْ بِهِ الْفُرُوجَ

"That make the private parts lawful."

THE RULING OF NIKAH AL-MUT'AH (TEMPORARY MARRIAGE)

997- Narrated Salama Ibn Al-Akwa' (رَضِيَ ٱللَّهُ عَنْهُ),

رَخَّصَ رَسُولُ اللهِ (صَلَّى اللهُ عَلَيْهِ وَسَلَّمَ) عَامَ أَوْطَاسٍ فِي الْمُتْعَةِ ثَلَاثَةَ أَيَّامٍ، ثُمَّ نَهَى عَنْهَا.

"Allāh's Messenger (صَلَّى ٱللَّهُ عَلَيْهِ وَسَلَّمَ) gave sanction for contracting temporary marriage for three nights in the year of Autas, but then forbade it."[105] Related by Muslim.

Explanation

Autas, the conquest of *Makkah* and the conquest of *At-Ta'if* took place in the same year, but the conquest of Makkah took place in Ramaḍān. Whereas, the conquest of Autas happened in Dhul-Qa'dah. It is sometimes called the year of the conquest of Makkah or Autas. So, this *Ḥadīth* does not

[105] Related by Muslim (1405).

contradict the authentic *Ḥadīth* where he (ﷺ) prohibited it during the conquest of Makkah in the same year.

This statement,

رَخَّصَ رَسُولُ اللهِ (صَلَّى اللهُ عَلَيْهِ وَسَلَّمَ) عَامَ أَوْطَاسٍ فِي الْمُتْعَةِ ثَلَاثَةَ أَيَّامٍ.

> **"Allāh's Messenger (ﷺ) gave sanction for contracting temporary marriage for three nights in the year of Autas,"**

Indicates that *Mut'ah* marriage was prohibited at first because permission is given for (what was) unlawful only. The *Mut'ah* marriage was prohibited at first and then made permissible for only three days, but later returned to being forbidden. So, it was forbidden twice and then became allowed and finally forbidden. Like (the sanctity of) *Makkah,* many scholars[106] said it is forbidden, but a concession was made for the Messenger of Allāh (ﷺ) for an hour of the day and then became forbidden.

Scholars have different opinions about the *Mut'ah* marriage. Was it prohibited once or twice? Some scholars said, "It was prohibited once," while others said, "Twice;" citing this *Hadīth,*

---

[106] Mughni Al-Muhtag (3/142), Al-Bahr Ar-Ra'q (3/116).

رَخَّصَ رَسُولُ اللهِ (صَلَّى اللهُ عَلَيْهِ وَسَلَّمَ) عَامَ أَوْطَاسٍ فِي الْمُتْعَةِ ثَلَاثَةَ أَيَّامٍ، ثُمَّ نَهَى عَنْهَا.

"That Allāh's Messenger (ﷺ) gave sanction for contracting temporary marriage for three nights in the year of Autas and then forbade it."

ḤADĪTH 998

998- Narrated `Ali (رَضِيَ اللَّهُ عَنْهُ),

نَهَى رَسُولُ اللهِ (صَلَّى اللهُ عَلَيْهِ وَسَلَّمَ) عَنِ الْمُتْعَةِ عَامَ خَيْبَـرَ

"Allāh's Messenger (صَلَّى اللَّهُ عَلَيْهِ وَسَلَّمَ) prohibited *Mut'ah* marriage in the year of the *Khaibar* battle."[107] Related by Bukhari and Muslim.

Explanation

The Battle of Khaibar took place in the sixth year before the *Autas* Battle, which took place in the Eighth Hijri year. So, according to many scholars, it was prohibited during *Khaibar* battle and then made lawful in *Autas* battle for three days and eventually made unlawful. However, some scholars said, "It was forbidden only once during the conquest of Makkah." *Hadīth* of 'Ali (رَضِيَ اللَّهُ عَنْهُ):

نَهَى عَنِ الْمُتْعَةِ عَامَ خَيْبَـرَ

[107] Related by Bukhari (5115), Muslim (1407), Tuhfat Al-Ashraf (10263).

"Allāh's Messenger (ﷺ) prohibited *Mut'ah* marriage in the year of the *Khaibar* battle."

There is another narration,

نَهَى عَنِ الْمُتْعَةِ عَامَ خَيْبَـرَ، وَعَنْ لُـحُومِ الْـحمر الْأَهْلِيَّةِ.

"Allāh's Messenger (ﷺ) prohibited *Mut'ah* marriage and the eating of donkey's meat in the year of the *Khaibar* battle." Related by Bukhari and Muslim.

So, eating donkey's meat was made forbidden in the year of the *Khaibar* battle, but according to Ibn Al-Qayim (رَحِمَهُ ٱللَّهُ) in *"Zad el-Ma'ad,"* some narrators thought that the *Mut'ah* marriage was coupled with the prohibition of eating the donkey's meat.

What is *Mut'ah* marriage? It means a marriage for a limited period of time. For example, someone says, "May I marry your daughter for a month?" A man went to a country where he wanted to marry, but for a certain time, so he asked the woman's guardian to marry for a month, upon which the guardian agreed.

We say this is a *Mut'ah* marriage. Why is it called *Mut'ah* marriage? Because it targets satisfying sexual desires only, not having a wife to find repose with, to have children with and so that he could have a life partner. He solely wants to gratify his desire like an animal. And when the decided time comes, the marriage is annulled. In the event, the man said he wants to keep the wife, this will be rejected. The husband has no choice and no waiting period. All that is left to do is waiting to make sure of whether there are children from that man or not.

The marriage contract of this kind involves no dowry, no division of stay and no limited number of wives.

In addition, if one has a financial and physical capacity to give this kind of marriage, then marrying lots of women is not a problem. In reality, it is not a valid marriage and no rulings are to be based on it. Even the children cannot be attributed to the man except with a condition, otherwise they are adulterine (children born to an adulterous relationship).

At first, *Mut'ah* marriage was forbidden on the basis that if the Islamic Sharia did not prohibit any of the rulings of the pre-Islāmic period, these rulings would remain unchangeable. And it is agreed upon that the Prophet (صَلَّى ٱللَّهُ عَلَيْهِ وَسَلَّمَ) forbade it in the conquest of Makkah. Was it lawful before and then made forbidden in *Khaibar* and then made lawful in the conquest of Makkah and then made forbidden? This is the question. Anyway, according to *Ḥadīth* of Sabra Ibn Ma'bad Al-Juhani (رَضِيَ ٱللَّهُ عَنْهُ), *Mut'ah* is prohibited until the Day of Judgment. The Prophet (صَلَّى ٱللَّهُ عَلَيْهِ وَسَلَّمَ) said, in Fath Makkah,

إِنِّي كُنْتُ أَذِنْتُ لَكُمْ فِي الِاسْتِمْتَاعِ مِنَ النِّسَاءِ، وَإِنَّ اللهَ قَدْ حَرَّمَ ذَلِكَ إِلَى يَوْمِ الْقِيَامَةِ.

> **"So he who has any (woman with this type of marriage contract) he should let her off and do not take back anything he has given to them (as dowry)." And then**

he (صَلَّى ٱللَّهُ عَلَيْهِ وَسَلَّمَ) said, "But Allāh has forbidden it (now) until the Day of Resurrection."

In Sahih Muslim, it is prohibited till the Day of Resurrection. But scholars have different opinions about this subject. Ibn 'Abbās (رَضِيَ ٱللَّهُ عَنْهُ) believed that *Mut'ah* marriage is lawful, but 'Ali Ibn Abu Tālib (رَضِيَ ٱللَّهُ عَنْهُ) held a discussion with him in which he said to him at the end of it,

إِنَّكَ امْرَؤٌ تَائِهٌ

"You are at a loss."[108]

He told him that the Prophet (صَلَّى ٱللَّهُ عَلَيْهِ وَسَلَّمَ) forbade it. Scholars differed over the question of whether Ibn 'Abbās (رَضِيَ ٱللَّهُ عَنْهُ) considered it boundlessly lawful or only when necessary? The most famous opinion is that he made it allowed when necessary.

For instance, it applies when a man goes to a country and he is in a dire need of marriage out of fear of adultery. Then, when people misused this fatwa, he changed his opinion. And later, the Shiite scholars considered it lawful. It is astonishing that they regard 'Ali Ibn Abi Tālib (رَضِيَ ٱللَّهُ عَنْهُ) their Imam and consider that he is infallible while they do not follow his opinion in this respect. 'Ali Ibn Abi Tālib (رَضِيَ ٱللَّهُ عَنْهُ) so strongly condemned this matter that he calls his cousin, Ibn 'Abbās (رَضِيَ ٱللَّهُ عَنْهُ), "lost". They also do not follow 'Ali Ibn Abi Tālib (رَضِيَ ٱللَّهُ عَنْهُ) regarding wiping over boots. They believe that it is not allowed to wipe over boots though Ibn Abi Tālib

108 Related by Muslim (1407).

(رَضِيَٱللَّهُعَنْهُ) is the one who narrated the exact period of time allowed for wiping over boots.

The Sunni scholars believe that *Mut'ah* is unlawful. In addition, the recent Shiite scholars denounced *Mut'ah* marriage, considering it a crime against women in which women are but a prey for vicious animals. If a man had intercourse with a woman in such a way, will anyone desire to marry her? No, women will be undesirable, children will be lost and people will be like beasts. Thus, they maintained it to be forbidden.

Anyway, the most famous Imams hold it as forbidden. Even Ibn 'Abbās (رَضِيَٱللَّهُعَنْهُ) believed it is allowed only when necessary in case a problem would arise. Otherwise, it is forbidden like any permissible act.

One may argue, "What is the reason for prohibition of this kind of marriage?"

First: Allāh made marriage an affection between the spouses, Allāh (سُبْحَانَهُۥوَتَعَالَىٰ) said,

﴿ وَمِنْ ءَايَـٰتِهِۦٓ أَنْ خَلَقَ لَكُم مِّنْ أَنفُسِكُمْ أَزْوَٰجًا لِّتَسْكُنُوٓا۟ إِلَيْهَا وَجَعَلَ بَيْنَكُم مَّوَدَّةً وَرَحْمَةً ﴾

"And among His signs is that He created for you wives from among yourselves, that you may find repose in them and He has put between you affection and mercy." [*Sūrah ar-Rūm* 30:21]

This is one of the ultimate purposes of marriage, which is obviously missed in *Mut'ah* marriage. The man feels that he only wants to satisfy his desire and the woman feels she is borrowed for such purposes. There is no repose, no affection and no mercy found. In addition, the one who is involved in such marriage cannot be satisfied with this woman, so he searches for another one and so on. He may have intercourse with ten women before sunset.

Question:[109] "Is having the intention of temporary marriage *(Mut'ah)* similar to conditioning it? For example, a man was in a foreign country where he wanted to marry a woman, but with the intention of marrying for a limited period."

The answer: Scholars have two different opinions[110] about this matter. According to the school of Ahmad, this is unlawful. They said there is evidence backed with an analogical proof as well. Concerning the evidence, they said,

إِنَّ النَّبِـيَّ (صَلَّى اللهُ عَلَيْهِ وَسَلَّمَ) قَالَ: إِنَّمَا الْأَعْمَالُ بِالنِّيَّاتِ.

"The Prophet (ﷺ) said, 'Actions are dependent on their intentions.'"

So, this person has the intention of a temporary marriage. Concerning the analogical proof, they said, "If anybody has the intention of marrying a woman to make her lawful for her husband who divorced her three times, the marriage will be

---

[109] This question was posed to Sheikh Ibn Othaimeen (رَحِمَهُ ٱللَّهُ) who spoke elaborately about it due to its importance. He will go back to the reasons of forbidding Mut'ah in the following page.

[110] Al-Fatawa (32/148).

illegal, exactly as if this condition was stipulated in the contract." They reasoned, "If the above kind of marriage is made just by the intention, without conditioning it in the contract, so is *Mut'ah* marriage.

Those who said that *Mut'ah* marriage is allowed, they clarified the difference. When the period of the *Mut'ah* marriage is finished, marriage will be annulled on the basis of the condition that is stipulated by the husband and the wife. However, the intention does not annul the marriage because his intention may change, and he may have the desire to keep her as a wife. But I believe this is unlawful, even if it is said to not be like *Mut'ah,* because he is cheating the wife and her family. If the wife knows that this man wants only to satisfy his sexual desire and then divorce her, she and her family will not accept, particularly because she will be undesirable after losing her virginity and becoming a divorced woman.

In addition, they believe in some non-Muslim countries that the divorced woman can never marry, which may make this woman vulnerable to adultery. So, I believe it is unlawful not only because of the intention but because of deception. If a person wants to marry your daughter or sister with such an intention, doesn't he deceive her? Undoubtedly, yes. If you know that this is his intention, you will not marry your daughter to him. So, deal with it as if this is your own business.

One may argue, "Had Mut'ah marriage been allowed, it would have been for the sake of strangers and would protect them from adultery?

The answer: This is very easy to rebut. The Prophet (ﷺ) clarified the cure that prevents from adultery,

يَا مَعْشَرَ الشَّبَابِ! مَنِ اسْتَطَاعَ مِنْكُمُ الْبَاءَةَ فَلْيَتَزَوَّجْ، فَإِنَّهُ أَغَضُّ لِلْبَصَرِ وَأَحْصَنُ لِلْفَرْجِ، وَمَنْ لَمْ يَسْتَطِعْ فَعَلَيْهِ بِالصِّيَامِ.

"O' young men! Those among you who can afford to marry a wife should marry for it restrains eyes (from casting evil glances) and preserves one from immorality; but he who cannot afford it should observe fast for it is a means of controlling the sexual desire."

If anyone can conclude a lawful marriage, he shall marry with no intention to divorce. If one cannot, one should fast instead. This is what the Prophet (ﷺ) clarified.

And it is not allowed to commit illegal acts to satisfy sexual desire. The Prophet (ﷺ) provided the solution. And as for deception and committing sins, this is not allowed.

Now, we go back to the reasons for forbidding the *Mut'ah* marriage. It is against the purpose of marriage, which aims at affection, establishing family, having children. The *Mut'ah* marriage is not as such. Why? Because the husband will divorce sooner or later and this strains the relations between the two spouses.

Second: In this case, the husband will earnestly try to stop the woman from having children because they will break up sooner or later.

Third: This is harmful for women as the man would, therefore, be able to marry an unlimited number of women. One may marry more than ten women in just one night. Thus three hundred women may lose their virginity in one month. In addition, if the ones who marry in such way are tens of people, many more women will lose their virginity. Then no one will marry a woman as such, but one who is unable to marry a virgin.

It is also degrading for women, because the husband in this case will be like the just like an animal, desiring nothing but sexual gratification.

Fourth: All the rulings that normally result from marriage such as inheritance, dowry and having children are absent in *Mut'ah* marriage. It is only gratification of sexual desire. Thus, Allāh (سُبْحَانَهُۥوَتَعَالَىٰ) has forbidden *Mut'ah* marriage. According to the *Ḥadīth* of Sabra (رَضِيَٱللَّهُعَنْهُمْ), the Prophet (صَلَّىٱللَّهُعَلَيْهِوَسَلَّمَ) has forbidden it till the Day of Resurrection. Consequently it will never be abrogated, as the Prophet (صَلَّىٱللَّهُعَلَيْهِوَسَلَّمَ) said,

حَرَّمَهَا إِلَى يَوْمِ الْقِيَامَةِ.

"till the Day of Resurrection."

And if we were to say that abrogation is allowed in this case, it would necessarily imply that the saying of the Prophet (صَلَّىٱللَّهُعَلَيْهِوَسَلَّمَ) may be false, which is impossible.

ḤADĪTH 999

999- It was narrated from 'Abdullāh and Al-Hasan, the sons of Muhammad bin 'Ali, from their father, from 'Ali bin Abi Tālib (رَضِيَٱللَّهُعَنْهُمْ),

أَنَّ رَسُولَ اللهِ (صَلَّى اللهُ عَلَيْهِ وَسَلَّمَ) نَهَى عَنْ مُتْعَةِ النِّسَاءِ، وَعَنْ أَكْلِ لُحُومِ الْحُمْرِ الأَهْلِيَّةِ يَوْمَ خَيْبَرَ.

"That the Messenger of Allāh (صَلَّىٱللَّهُعَلَيْهِوَسَلَّمَ) on the Day of *Khaibar* forbade temporary marriage to women (*Mut'ah*), and (he also forbade) the meat of tame donkeys."[111] Related by the seven Imams except Abu Dawud.

Explanation

The author mentioned this narration to separate between the prohibition of the *Mut'ah* marriage and eating the meat of tame donkeys. He (صَلَّىٱللَّهُعَلَيْهِوَسَلَّمَ),

---

111 Related by Bukhari (4216), Muslim (1407), At-Tirmidhi (1121), An-Nassai (6/126), Ibn Majah (1961), Ahmad (1/142), Tuhfat Al-Ashraf (10263).

نَهَى عَنْ مُتْعَةِ النِّسَاءِ، وَعَنْ أَكْلِ لُحُومِ الْحُمُرِ الْأَهْلِيَّةِ

> **"Forbade temporary marriage to women," and then, "the meat of tame donkeys."**

He (صَلَّى ٱللَّهُ عَلَيْهِ وَسَلَّمَ) "**forbade temporary marriage to women**" to differentiate between *Tamattu'*(literally: enjoyment) in Hajj and the *Mut'ah* marriage. *Tamattu'* in Hajj is not forbidden. Rather, it is either obligatory or desirable. It is to perform Umrah in one of the months of Hajj and then remove the *Ihram* (after finishing the rituals of Umrah) and then perform Hajj at the same year. So, Umrah will be separated from Hajj and the one who performed Umrah is allowed to do what he wants,

> **"And whosoever performs the Umrah in the month of Hajj"** [*Sūrah al-Baqarah* 2:196]

What does the perfomer of this type of Hajj enjoy? The enjoyment is with observing what Allāh made lawful. If you go to Makkah in the months of Hajj and passed by the *Miqāt* (appointed place for wearing the *Ihram* cloth) while you want to perform Hajj, you would have to make *Ihram* from the *Miqāt* and stay wearing *Ihram* until the Day of Eid.

So, you are not allowed to enjoy women, perfume or anything forbidden on the basis of *Ihram*. If you have the intention of Umrah from the Miqāt and go to Makkah, make Tawāf, Sai' and hair cutting, then you remove the *Ihram* and enjoy the preforbidden acts, until when? Until Hajj. If you arrive in Dhul Qa'dah, you make *Tamattu'* until the Eighth of Dhul Hijjah. This *Tamattu'* is desirable and obligatory. According to Sheikh Al-Islam Ibn Taymyyah (رَحِمَهُ ٱللَّهُ), the

Companions (رَضِيَ ٱللَّهُ عَنْهُمْ) were obliged to perform this *Mut'ah,* but it is desirable for the Muslims. It is related by Muslim that Abu Zar (رَضِيَ ٱللَّهُ عَنْهُ) said about *Mut'ah,*

"We are obligated to perform *Mut'ah* in Hajj."

Concerning the other Muslims, Suraqa Ibn Malik (رَضِيَ ٱللَّهُ عَنْهُ) asked the Prophet (صَلَّى ٱللَّهُ عَلَيْهِ وَسَلَّمَ),

أَلِعَامِنَا هَذَا، أَمْ لِأَبَدٍ؟

"Is this Tamattu' for this year only or forever?'

He (صَلَّى ٱللَّهُ عَلَيْهِ وَسَلَّمَ) said,

بَلْ لِأَبَدِ الأَبَدِ

"**No, it is forever and ever.**" It is desirable. The Companions (رَضِيَ ٱللَّهُ عَنْهُمْ) were obliged to make Tamattu' because they are directly addressed. If they obeyed, this would annul this act. The opinion of Sheikh Al-Islam (Ibn Taymiyyah (رَحِمَهُ ٱللَّهُ)) is better than that of Ibn Al-Qayyim (رَحِمَهُ ٱللَّهُ) who believed that it is obligatory to make Tamattu' or annulling Hajj when performing Umrah. We can say that it is Wājib for the Companions (رَضِيَ ٱللَّهُ عَنْهُمْ), but Sunnah for the other Muslims.

So, he (صَلَّى ٱللَّهُ عَلَيْهِ وَسَلَّمَ) said, "**Temporary marriage to women.**" What is meant by the temporary marriage to women? It is to marry a woman for a limited period of time. The Prophet (صَلَّى ٱللَّهُ عَلَيْهِ وَسَلَّمَ) forbade it and eating the meat of tame donkeys on the day of Khaibar.

وَعَنْ أَكْلِ الْـحُمْرِ الأَهْلِيَّةِ

"**Tame donkeys,**" He (صَلَّىٱللَّهُعَلَيْهِوَسَلَّمَ) said tame to differentiate between it and the wild donkeys which can be hunted. As-Saab Ibn Jathama (رَضِيَٱللَّهُعَنْهُ), who was so generous and ran faster than the zebra, when presented the meat of a zebra the Prophet (صَلَّىٱللَّهُعَلَيْهِوَسَلَّمَ) while he was in the area known as al-Abwā' or Waddan. The Prophet (صَلَّىٱللَّهُعَلَيْهِوَسَلَّمَ) very politely declined it, and said to him,

إِنَّا لَمْ نَرُدَّهُ إِلَّا أَنَّا حُرُمٌ

> **"We declined your present only because we are in the state of *Ihram*."**

Anyway, the wild donkeys are halal, but the tame donkeys are unlawful. However, it is said that on the day of Khaibar, it was considered Halal so that it could be slaughtered and eaten. Allāh is Glorified! Before making it unlawful, it was edible. Then, after making it unlawful, it is considered impure. Who can only rule? Allāh. After Allāh (عَزَّوَجَلَّ) makes it unlawful, He put impurities in it, though it was edible like cows at first. Thus, the Prophet (صَلَّىٱللَّهُعَلَيْهِوَسَلَّمَ) ordered Abu Talha (رَضِيَٱللَّهُعَنْهُ) on the day of Khaibar to say, "Allāh and His Messenger (صَلَّىٱللَّهُعَلَيْهِوَسَلَّمَ) forbade the meat of tame donkeys as it is filthy.

Benefits from the Ḥadīth:

1. **<u>In this *Ḥadīth, Mut'ah* marriage is prohibited</u>**. If the contract is concluded, is it lawful or not? It is unlawful based on the ruling that every forbidden act is itself unlawful, even if it is already done. If a person wants to perform prayers with submissiveness for no reason at the forbidden times, his prayers will be unlawful.

   If a person has concluded a *Mut'ah* marriage, this marriage would be unlawful. If a person sold a commodity after the second call of Jumu'ah, it would be unlawful and the commodity is still owned by the seller and the price is still owned by the buyer.

   One may ask, "What is the reason behind that? Why don't you say, 'If he committed the unlawful act, he would be sinful whereas the contract is still lawful?'"

   <u>The answer:</u> Making the contract lawful is against Allāh's Will and His Messenger's (صَلَّى ٱللَّٰهُ عَلَيْهِ وَسَلَّمَ), because making it lawful after the Sharia judged it to be unlawful would give it standing which is is the complete opposite of the intent of the Sharia. For example, if a person sold a house after the second call of Jumu'ah prayers, the sale would be unlawful and the contract is invalid. If we said that the sale is unlawful and the two parties committed sin but the contract is effective, this will be against the Sharia. Sharia makes it forbidden in order to avoid concluding contract and the property being handed to the buyer and the price being handed to the seller. Thus, the rule indicates that all what is fundamentally forbidden such as worship or transaction will be considered unlawful if it is committed.

2. The meat of tame donkeys is prohibited despite being young and fleshy. However, it is allowed to eat them when necessary as Allāh (سُبْحَانَهُ وَتَعَالَىٰ) said,

﴿ حُرِّمَتْ عَلَيْكُمُ ٱلْمَيْتَةُ وَٱلدَّمُ وَلَحْمُ ٱلْخِنزِيرِ وَمَآ أُهِلَّ لِغَيْرِ ٱللَّهِ بِهِۦ وَٱلْمُنْخَنِقَةُ وَٱلْمَوْقُوذَةُ وَٱلْمُتَرَدِّيَةُ وَٱلنَّطِيحَةُ وَمَآ أَكَلَ ٱلسَّبُعُ إِلَّا مَا ذَكَّيْتُمْ وَمَا ذُبِحَ عَلَى ٱلنُّصُبِ وَأَن تَسْتَقْسِمُوا۟ بِٱلْأَزْلَٰمِ ۚ ذَٰلِكُمْ فِسْقٌ ۗ ٱلْيَوْمَ يَئِسَ ٱلَّذِينَ كَفَرُوا۟ مِن دِينِكُمْ فَلَا تَخْشَوْهُمْ وَٱخْشَوْنِ ۚ ٱلْيَوْمَ أَكْمَلْتُ لَكُمْ دِينَكُمْ وَأَتْمَمْتُ عَلَيْكُمْ نِعْمَتِى وَرَضِيتُ لَكُمُ ٱلْإِسْلَٰمَ دِينًا ۚ فَمَنِ ٱضْطُرَّ فِى مَخْمَصَةٍ غَيْرَ مُتَجَانِفٍ لِّإِثْمٍ ۙ فَإِنَّ ٱللَّهَ غَفُورٌ رَّحِيمٌ ۝٣ ﴾

"Forbidden to you (for food) are: Al-Maitah (the dead animals - cattle - beast not slaughtered), blood, the flesh of the swine, and that on which Allāh's Name has not been mentioned while slaughtering, (that which has been slaughtered as a sacrifice for others than Allāh, or has been slaughtered for idols) and that which has been

> **killed by strangling, or by a violent blow, or by a headlong fall, or by the goring of horns, and that which has been (partly) eaten by a wild animal, unless you are able to slaughter it (before its death), and that which is sacrificed (slaughtered) on An-Nusub (stone-altars). (Forbidden) also is to use arrows seeking luck or decision; (all) that is Fisqun (disobedience of Allāh and sin). This Day, those who disbelieved have given up all hope of your religion; so fear them not but fear Me. This day, I have perfected your religion for you, completed My Favor upon you, and have chosen for you Islam as your religion. But as for him who is forced by severe hunger, with no inclination to sin (such can eat these above-mentioned meats), then surely, Allāh is Oft-Forgiving, Most Merciful.**" [*Sūrah al-Mā'idah* 5:3]

If it is allowed when necessary to eat the flesh of swine, which is filthier than tame donkeys, so donkeys are allowed when necessary. We said, swine is filthier than the tame donkey because swine has always been unlawful, but the tame donkey was lawful at the past.

ḤADĪTH 1000

1000- Rabi' ibn Sabra reported on the authority of his father (رَضِيَ اللَّهُ عَنْهُمْ) that while he was with Allāh's Messenger (صَلَّى اللَّهُ عَلَيْهِ وَسَلَّمَ), he (صَلَّى اللَّهُ عَلَيْهِ وَسَلَّمَ) said,

إِنِّي كُنْتُ أَذِنْتُ لَكُمْ فِي الِاسْتِمْتَاعِ مِنَ النِّسَاءِ، وَإِنَّ اللهَ قَدْ حَرَّمَ ذَلِكَ إِلَى يَوْمِ الْقِيَامَةِ، فَمَنْ كَانَ عِنْدَهُ مِنْهُنَّ شَيْءٌ فَلْيُخَلِّ سَبِيلَهَا، وَلَا تَأْخُذُوا مِمَّا آتَيْتُمُوهُنَّ شَيْئًا.

"O' people, I had permitted you to contract temporary marriage with women, but Allāh has forbidden it (now) until the Day of Resurrection. So, he who has any (woman with this type of marriage contract), he should let her off and do not take back anything you have given to them (as dowry)."[112] Related by Muslim, Abu Dawud, An-Nassai, Ibn Majah, Ahmad and Ibn Hibban.

Explanation

---

[112] Related by Muslim (1406), Abu Dawud (2072), An-Nassai (6/126), Ibn Majah (1962), Ahmad (3/405), Ibn Hibban (4147).

إِنِّي كُنْتُ أَذِنْتُ

"I had permitted." Meaning gave permission. This does not indicate that it was previously prohibited. Permission can be given orally, as it was here and by acknowledgement. In this *Ḥadīth,* prohibition is attributed to having been made by Allāh to render it more impactful and acceptable, even if what is ruled by the Prophet (صَلَّى ٱللَّهُ عَلَيْهِ وَسَلَّمَ) is the same as was ruled by Allāh (عَزَّوَجَلَّ). However, in this case, it is most impactful because the ruling is the right of Allah while the Prophet reports it.

يَوْمِ الْقِيَامَةِ

"The Day of Resurrection," it is called as such because it is the Day when mankind will stand before the Lord of all that exists and the witnesses will stand forth,

﴿ إِنَّا لَنَنصُرُ رُسُلَنَا وَٱلَّذِينَ ءَامَنُوا۟ فِى ٱلْحَيَوٰةِ ٱلدُّنْيَا وَيَوْمَ يَقُومُ ٱلْأَشْهَٰدُ ﴿٥١﴾ ﴾

> **"Verily, We will indeed make victorious Our Messengers and those who believe (in the Oneness of Allāh - Islamic Monotheism) in this world's life and on the Day when the witnesses will stand forth, (i.e. Day of Resurrection)."** [*Sūrah Ghafir* 40:51]

And the balances of justice will be set up,

﴿ وَنَضَعُ ٱلْمَوَٰزِينَ ٱلْقِسْطَ لِيَوْمِ ٱلْقِيَـٰمَةِ ﴾

"And We shall set up balances of justice on the Day of Resurrection." [*Sūrah* al-'Anbiyā' 21:47]

فَلْيُخَلِّ سَبِيلَهَا

"**He should let her off.**" The Prophet (ﷺ) forbade even continuing this marriage. However, the scholars maintained that continuity (of marriage, in this case) is more appropriate than to start another marriage. Yet, in this *Ḥadīth*, continuity of marriage was given secondary importance after starting another marriage.

فَمَنْ كَانَ عِنْدَهُ مِنْهُنَّ شَيْءٌ

"**So, he who has any (woman with this type of marriage contract).**" Meaning whoever concluded a *Mut'ah* marriage contract, they should let their respective wives off. The Prophet (ﷺ) did not say, "He should divorce." Rather, he said, "**Let her off**."

لَا تَأْخُذُوا مِمَّا آتَيْتُمُوهُنَّ شَيْئًا

"And do not take back anything you have given to them (as dowry)."

Allāh forbade to take back anything given to them (as dowry) because they deserved the dowry to make sexual intercourse lawful with them, which is indicated in the previous *Ḥadīth*.

<u>**The Benefits of the Ḥadīth**</u>:

1. <u>**The lawfulness of Mut'ah is abolished by the commandment of Allāh**</u>, Because He made it unlawful.

2. <u>**As He has forbidden it without any chance of making it lawful again**</u>. According to this *Ḥadīth,*

إِلَى يَوْمِ الْقِيَامَةِ

"**Until the Day of Resurrection**."

3. Whoever concluded unlawful contract must let it off as the Prophet (ﷺ) said,

فَمَنْ كَانَ عِنْدَهُ مِنْهُنَّ شَيْءٌ فَلْيُخَلِّ سَبِيلَهَا

"**So, he who has any (woman with this type of marriage contract), he should let her off**."

Thus, if two men made an unlawful deal because of the absence of a condition or the existence of a prohibitive, this deal must be annulled and abandoned. We can say that it is necessary to abandon it, but we shall not say annulment. Why? Because annulment indicates its lawfulness.

THE RULING OF NIKAH *AT-TAHLIL* MARRIAGE

1001- It was narrated that Ibn Masūd (رَضِيَٱللَّهُعَنْهُ) said,

لَعَنَ رَسُولُ اللهِ (صَلَّى اللهُ عَلَيْهِ وَسَلَّمَ) الْمُحَلِّلَ، وَالْمُحَلَّلَ لَهُ

"The Messenger of Allāh (صَلَّىٱللَّهُعَلَيْهِوَسَلَّمَ) cursed the one who marries a divorced woman with the intention of making her lawful for her former husband (Al-Muhallil) and upon the one for whom she is made lawful (Al-Muhallal Lahu)."[113] Related by Ahmad, An-Nassa'i and At-Tirmidhi who graded it as Sahih.

1002- There is another narration by 'Ali (رَضِيَٱللَّهُعَنْهُ) related by the four Imams except An-Nasā'ī.[114]

---

[113] Al-Musnad (1/450), An-Nassai filKobra (5536), At-Tirmidhi (1120), said in Drayah (2/73): its narrators are trustworthy, Sheikh Taqi Eldein said, it is on the condition of Bukhari, authenticated by Ibn Al-Qattan as in At-Talkhis (3/170).

[114] Related by Abu Dawud (2076), At-Tirmidhi (1119) who graded it as weak, Ibn Majah (1935), the hadith is weakened by Al-Harith, see Nasb Ar-Raya (3/239).

Explanation

One must know who al-Muhallil is. Al-Muhallil is he who marries a woman who has been divorced irrevocably to make it lawful for her former husband to marry her. So, the woman cannot be lawful for him again except after she marries someone else. Allāh (سُبْحَانَهُ وَتَعَالَىٰ) said:

﴿ ٱلطَّلَٰقُ مَرَّتَانِۖ فَإِمْسَاكُۢ بِمَعْرُوفٍ أَوْ تَسْرِيحُۢ بِإِحْسَٰنٍۗ وَلَا يَحِلُّ لَكُمْ أَن تَأْخُذُوا۟ مِمَّآ ءَاتَيْتُمُوهُنَّ شَيْـًٔا إِلَّآ أَن يَخَافَآ أَلَّا يُقِيمَا حُدُودَ ٱللَّهِۖ فَإِنْ خِفْتُمْ أَلَّا يُقِيمَا حُدُودَ ٱللَّهِ فَلَا جُنَاحَ عَلَيْهِمَا فِيمَا ٱفْتَدَتْ بِهِۦۗ تِلْكَ حُدُودُ ٱللَّهِ فَلَا تَعْتَدُوهَاۚ وَمَن يَتَعَدَّ حُدُودَ ٱللَّهِ فَأُو۟لَٰٓئِكَ هُمُ ٱلظَّٰلِمُونَ ﴿٢٢٩﴾ فَإِن طَلَّقَهَا فَلَا تَحِلُّ لَهُۥ مِنۢ بَعْدُ حَتَّىٰ تَنكِحَ زَوْجًا غَيْرَهُۥۗ ﴾

"The divorce is twice, after that, either you retain her on reasonable terms or release her with kindness. And it is not lawful for you (men) to take back (from your wives) and of your Mahr (bridal-money given by the husband to his wife at the time of marriage) which you have given them, except when both parties fear that they would be unable to keep the limits ordained by Allāh (e.g. to deal with each other on a fair basis). Then if you fear that they would not be able to keep the limits ordained by Allāh, then there is no sin on either of them if she gives back (the Mahr or part of it) for her Al-Khul' (divorce). These are the limits ordained by

> **Allāh, so do not transgress them. And whoever transgresses the limits ordained by Allāh, then such are the wrong-doers). And if he has divorced her (the third time), then she is not lawful unto him thereafter until she has married another husband."** [*Sūrah al-Baqarah* 2:229-230]

This is the third time. There are previous two times.

"**Then she is not lawful to him.**" Meaning to the divorced husband. "**Thereafter.**Meaning after this divorce.

"**Until she has married another husband.**" The word "marriage" refers to the contract whenever mentioned in the Qur'ān.

﴿ وَلَا تَنكِحُوا۟ مَا نَكَحَ ءَابَآؤُكُم مِّنَ ٱلنِّسَآءِ ﴾

> **"And marry not women whom your fathers married."** [*Sūrah an-Nisā'* 4:22]

However, in this verse, it refers to the consummation of marriage as Allāh (سُبْحَانَهُ وَتَعَالَىٰ) said,

﴿ وَلَا تَنكِحُوا۟ مَا نَكَحَ ءَابَآؤُكُم مِّنَ ٱلنِّسَآءِ ﴾

> **"And marry not women whom your fathers married."**

He attributed marriage to men who cannot marry without a contract. Whenever the Qur'ān mentions marriage after the wife, it indicates consummation, otherwise it would have been, "until she has married another (man)."

So, marriage here indicates consummation as in the *Ḥadīth* mentioned in the footnotes that is of Rifa'ah Al-Qurazi (رَضِيَ ٱللَّهُ عَنْهُ)[115], where the wife of Rifa'ah said,

فَطَلَّقَنِي فَبَتَّ طَلَاقِي

"Divorced me and made it irrevocable."

Thus, if anyone divorced a woman three times, she would be unlawful to him until she marries another man. This man divorced his wife three times and his friend married her on the condition of making her lawful to her previous husband. So, he consummated the marriage and then divorced her. We say this Muhallil is cursed, and he does not deserve Mercy of Allāh.

Who is the Muhallil? How is the former husband cursed? He is cursed because he accepted this while he knew about it. However, if he did not know, then he would not be cursed. Certainly, he knew and may have told a friend of his, 'I divorced my wife the final divorce. May you marry her to make her lawful to me."

So, his friend married her and had consummation with her to make her lawful for her previous husband. We say: the latter is Muhallal and the former is Muhallil. Both of them are cursed by the Prophet (صَلَّى ٱللَّهُ عَلَيْهِ وَسَلَّمَ). Now, is she lawful to the former husband or not? No, she is unlawful to the former husband who is additionally cursed.

---

115 Related by Bukhari (2639), Muslim (1433) on the authority of 'Aishah (رَضِيَ ٱللَّهُ عَنْهَا), Tuhfat Al-Ashraf (16436).

لَعَنَ رَسُولُ اللهِ (صَلَّى اللهُ عَلَيْهِ وَسَلَّمَ) الْمُحَلِّلَ

"**The Messenger of Allāh** (ﷺ) **cursed the Muhallil.**" He indicates that he is damned. He is invocating against him. It may be a statement too because the Prophet (ﷺ) receives the Revelation from Allāh, which probably makes it a statement, not an invocation. If the sentence reads, "May Allāh curse something," then this is an invocation, unless it is attached to a legal ruling indicating an invocation such as "May Allāh curse anyone who curses his parents." This is a statement. And if the Prophet (ﷺ) did this, it might be an invocation or a statement. In short, whether it is an invocation or a statement, it indicates that this doer deserves to be cursed because the Prophet (ﷺ) cannot invocate against anyone unless he deserves it.

The Muhallil is the one who marries a woman after being divorced three times in order to make her lawful for her former husband.

There are two conditions to make it lawful:

First: The lawfulness of the marriage, in the sense that they are married out of mutual desire, neither Tahlil marriage nor *Mut'ah* marriage. If the marriage is proved to be unlawful, she will not be lawful to her former husband. For example, a man married a woman after being divorced by her former husband three times and then it is discovered that she is his sister by suckling. What is the ruling of this marriage? It is unlawful. Would she still be lawful to her former husband in this situation? No, because the marriage is unlawful. If he married her with no guardian, she would be also unlawful to her former husband because the marriage is unlawful.

Second: To consummate marriage, as will be mentioned in the coming *Ḥadīth* of ʻAishah (رَضِيَ ٱللَّهُ عَنْهَا). And Allāh (سُبْحَانَهُ وَتَعَالَىٰ) said,

﴿ فَإِن طَلَّقَهَا فَلَا تَحِلُّ لَهُۥ مِنۢ بَعْدُ حَتَّىٰ تَنكِحَ زَوْجًا غَيْرَهُۥ ﴾

"And if he has divorced her (the third time), then she is not lawful to him, thereafter, until she has married another husband." [*Sūrah al-Baqarah* 2:230]

The evidence lies in the statement,

﴿ حَتَّىٰ تَنكِحَ زَوْجًا غَيْرَهُۥ ﴾

"Until she has married another husband."

Marriage here indicates consummation, not the marriage contract because "**another husband**" indicates that the marriage must be before consummation. So, marriage here must be interpreted as consummation.

Important notes:

If the woman returned to the former husband after a lawful marriage, does he have the right to divorce her three times or one time? Scholars said, "He has the right to divorce three times." The former husband was entitled to divorce three times and the previous divorces do not count. The former husband has the right to reunite if he divorced her after remarriage.

If he divorced for the second time, he is entitled to reunite. However, if he divorced for the third time, he is not entitled to reunite. Thus, she can be reunited with the former husband on the basis of three divorces as if he just married her at the present time because the latter husband's marriage abolished the former divorce.

If the woman is divorced two times and then married another husband who consummated the marriage and then divorced her and then she reunited with the former husband, is she reunited on the basis of three divorces or the remaining divorce? There are different opinions. Some scholars[116] believed that the latter marriage abolished the previous divorces. So, she can be reunited with the former husband on the basis of three divorces. Other scholars believed that this marriage does not abolish the previous divorces. So, she can be reunited with the former husband on the basis of the remaining divorces.

So, if she is reunited with the former husband who divorced her one time, she is not lawful to him because this divorce is based on the previous ones. Thus, if she is divorced three times, then married another one, then reunited with the former one, she might be divorced three times. If she is divorced less than three times and then married, then reunited with the former one, she will be reunited on the basis

116 Al-Umm by Ash-Shafie (7/162), Moghni Al-Mohtaj by Ash-Shirbini (3/293).

of the remaining divorce, this is according to Imam Ahmad (رَحِمَهُ ٱللَّهُ), which is the correct opinion.

One may argue, "How can the latter marriage abolish the three divorces and not the one with two divorces?

The Answer: Because marriage of the latter husband affects only in case of the three divorces. It makes the wife lawful. But the marriage of the latter husband after two divorces or one divorce has no effect because it is not of use for the former husband. Allāh (سُبْحَانَهُ وَتَعَالَىٰ) said,

﴿ ٱلطَّلَٰقُ مَرَّتَانِۖ فَإِمۡسَاكُۢ بِمَعۡرُوفٍ أَوۡ تَسۡرِيحُۢ بِإِحۡسَٰنٖ ﴾

"The divorce is twice, after that, either you retain her on reasonable terms."

And then said,

﴿ فَإِن طَلَّقَهَا فَلَا تَحِلُّ لَهُۥ مِنۢ بَعۡدُ حَتَّىٰ تَنكِحَ زَوۡجًا غَيۡرَهُۥۗ ﴾

"And if he has divorced her (the third time), then she is not lawful to him thereafter until she has married another husband." [*Sūrah al-Baqarah* 2:230]

The opinion of Ahmad's school is right.

MARRIAGE OF THE ADULTERER AND ADULTERESS

1003- Narrated Abu Hurairah (رَضِيَٱللَّهُعَنْهُ), "The Prophet (صَلَّىٱللَّهُعَلَيْهِوَسَلَّمَ) said,

لَا يَنْكِحُ الزَّانِي الْمَجْلُودُ إِلَّا مِثْلَهُ

'The adulterer who has been flogged shall not marry save one like him.'"[117] Related by Ahmad, Abu Dawud, its narrators are trustworthy.

Explanation

لَا يَنْكِحُ

"**Shall not marry.**" The interpreters of the Qur'ān differed over the meaning of this *Ḥadīth* and this gracious verse,

[117] Related by Ahmad (2/324), Abu Dawud (2053), Ibn Ady fi Al-Kamel (2/409) Habib Abu Mohamed and said, his narrations are authentic, and also authenticated by Al-Hakim (2/180), (3/211).

﴿ ٱلزَّانِى لَا يَنكِحُ إِلَّا زَانِيَةً أَوْ مُشْرِكَةً ﴾

"The adulterer-fornicator marries not but an adulteress-fornicatress or a polytheist." [*Sūrah an-Nūr* 24:3]

What is meant by "**Shall not marry**"? It is said to be the consummation. So, it indicates that the adulterer-fornicator is not to marry anyone but an adulteresss-fornicatress. Thus, marriage here refers to consummation which is considered adultery in such cases. But this opinion is extremely weak because the lawful marriage upon which great rules are based such as lawfulness and unlawfulness, expenses, and inheritance cannot be identitfed with adultry. The same judgment holds if it were to refer to intercourse when attributed to the wife.

We cannot say, "A man had sexual intercourse with another woman for a year." This is weak opinion and irrationale, as how would it mean to say an adulterer would not have committed adultery except with an adulteress?! If he means a woman practices adultery, this is untrue because the adulterer may have committed adultery with a virgin and a chaste woman. But if it means a woman known to be practicing adultery, which would mean the adulterer would not have committed adultery but with an adulteress; is this meaningful? This is like, "The land is under us. The sky is over us." Or, "The bread eater is the bread eater." This is meaningless. Therefore, the right opinion is that *Ḥadīth* and verse,

﴿ ٱلزَّانِى لَا يَنكِحُ إِلَّا زَانِيَةً أَوْ مُشْرِكَةً ﴾

"The adulterer-fornicator marries not but an adulteress-fornicatress or a polytheist." [*Sūrah an-Nūr* 24:3]

"**Marries not.**" Meaning does not marry, but an adulteress or a disbeliever. Why? We say, "The adulterer shall not marry but an adulteress if marrying the adulterer to a chaste woman is unlawful (haram). If the woman is married by an adulterer, though she knew it is unlawful as Allāh said,

﴿ وَحُرِّمَ ذَٰلِكَ ﴾

"Such a thing is forbidden to the believers (of Islamic Monotheism)." [*Sūrah an-Nūr* 24:3]

If she rejected the ruling of unlawfulness and said it is not Haram, she would be a polytheist because she believed that this man had sexual intercourse by a lawful contract. She was not convinced by the ruling of unlawfulness. And whoever is not convinced by the rulings of Allāh is considered a polytheist. And if she approved of the marriage and believed it to be unlawful, yet she acted heedlessly and she consummated an unlawful marriage with an unlawful contract, then she is an adulteress.

This meaning is very clear. We say that if an adulterer married a chaste woman who believes in the unlawfulness of this marriage, she would be an adulteress because she believes it is unlawful. The other situation would be if she rejected

Allāh's rulings, which would make her a polytheist. She made herself an associate with Allāh regarding legislation and lawmaking. This is the opinion of Ibn Al-Qayyim[118] (رَحِمَهُ ٱللَّهُ) which, I think, Ibn Taimyyah (رَحِمَهُ ٱللَّهُ) previously advocated. This is a clear opinion.

As for the ruling of the issue under discussion, the Prophet (صَلَّى ٱللَّهُ عَلَيْهِ وَسَلَّمَ) said:

لَا يَنْكِحُ الزَّانِي الْمَجْلُودُ إِلَّا مِثْلَهُ

> **"The adulterer who has been flogged shall not marry except one like him."**

The one who is flogged because of adultery. He (صَلَّى ٱللَّهُ عَلَيْهِ وَسَلَّمَ) said, "**Who has been flogged,**" to ascertain that he is flogged because of adultery. He "**Shall not marry except one like him,**" indicates that an adulteress who knew the unlawfulness of adultery, but she committed unlawful act which made her an adulteress. Therefore, this *Ḥadīth* indicates that it is not allowed to marry the adulterer until he repents. If one committed this unlawful act after marriage, would his marriage be terminated? No. Why? Because continuity of marriage in this situation would be better than terminating it to start another one.

---

118 E'lam Al-Moaqieen (4/343) and said, the Prophet صلى الله عليه وسلم said that the flogged adulterous shall not marry but one like him, Imam Ahmad رحمه الله had the same opinion which is one of the best opinions of his Madhab.

Therefore, we say the adulterer shall not be married until he repents. If one committed adultery after marriage, the marriage should not be terminated:

﴿ وَٱلزَّانِيَةُ لَا يَنكِحُهَآ إِلَّا زَانٍ أَوْ مُشْرِكٌۚ ﴾

> **"And the adulteress-fornicatress none marries her except an adulterer-fornicator or a polytheist."** [*Sūrah an-Nūr* 24:3]

In this verse, "**Except an adulterer-fornicator or a polytheist,**" and "**but an adulteress-fornicatress or a polytheist.**" This man who marries her is either satisfied with the ruling of Allāh and believes that he commits a sinful act, so he is considered adulterer; or he does not accept the ruling of Allāh and believes that it is harmless to marry an adulteress, so he is a polytheist. In the case where he married an adulteress before forgiveness, the marriage would be unlawful. They should be separated because if she repented, she would be no longer an adulteress. She would be chaste. So, how can we know that she repented? Some scholars said, "Thee sign of her repentance is that, if she is seduced, she will refuse. If a man seduced her, she would refuse." However, this is very weak opinion. Not being seduced is not an indication of her repentance. If the one who seduced her is known to be chaste and pious, she will refuse even though she desires. And if he is known to be an adulterer, he will commit a sinful act which is adultery. Thus, this is a wrong way to know if she repents or not.

How can we be sure about her repentance? We know of her repentance by the women who are closer to her. Also, if she asked the scholars about that; to say that she committed a sinful act and said that she repents, does Allāh accept her repentance? These are signs of repentance.

لَا يَنْكِحُ الزَّانِي الْمَجْلُولُ إِلَّا مِثْلَهُ

"The adulterer who has been flogged shall not marry save the one like him."

Can this *Ḥadīth* be generalized? And can one consider man and woman included? Yes. Therefore, this *Ḥadīth* will be in accordance with this detailed verse,

﴿ ٱلزَّانِى لَا يَنكِحُ إِلَّا زَانِيَةً أَوْ مُشْرِكَةً وَٱلزَّانِيَةُ لَا يَنكِحُهَآ إِلَّا زَانٍ أَوْ مُشْرِكٌ ۚ وَحُرِّمَ ذَٰلِكَ عَلَى ٱلْمُؤْمِنِينَ ۝٣ ﴾

"The **adulterer-fornicator marries not but an adulteress-fornicatress or a polytheist, and the adulteress- fornicatress none marries her except an adulterer-fornicator or a Mushrik [and that means that the man who agrees to marry (have a sexual relation with) a Mushrikah (female polytheist, pagan, or idolatress) or a prostitute, then surely he is either an adulterer-fornicator, or a Mushrik (polytheist, pagan, or idolatress). And the woman who agrees to marry (have a sexual relation with) a Mushrik (polytheist, pagan, or idolatress) or an adulterer-fornicator, then she is either a prostitute or a Mushrikah (female polytheist, pagan, or idolatress)]. Such a thing is**

forbidden to the believers (of Islamic Monotheism).” [*Sūrah an-Nūr* 24:3]

Ironically, most scholars believe that it is lawful if a chaste married an adulterer and vice versa. This is astonishing because Allāh (سُبْحَانَهُ وَتَعَالَىٰ) said,

﴿ وَحُرِّمَ ذَٰلِكَ عَلَى ٱلْمُؤْمِنِينَ ۝٣ ﴾

“Such a thing is forbidden to the believers (of Islamic Monotheism).” [*Sūrah an-Nūr* 24:3]

This is clear forbiddance. But they believed this verse means, **“The adulterer-fornicator marries not,”** has sexual intercourse with none “**but an adulteress-fornicatress.**” We say, “This is weak opinion.” Thus, if one is accused of being an adulterer, do we accept his proposal? No, because his religion and his morals are not accepted. Some sins have a bad effect on religion and the morals and some destroy religion only. Adultery destroys religion and the morals. We seek refuge from Allāh. Thus, adultery is an example of disintegration and bad manners.

Some benefits can be taken form this *Hadīth*:

1. It is not allowed to marry off an adulterer to a chaste woman except with repentance. It is allowed, however, to marry him if he repents. What is the evidence? It is because he is no longer an adulterer if he repented.

2. **Islamic Sharia protects good morals**. The adulterer does not care if his wife committed adultery as he committed adultery with another woman. The sinner does not blame the other sinners.

3. **It is desirable or rather obligatory to prevent the adulterer from marriage,[119] even if he performs other righteous good deeds**. He may perform prayer, give charity, perform fasting, Hajj and Umrah, but he commits adultery. Is this one allowed to be married on the basis that he is religious and may repent? No. It is not allowed. But if he does not perform prayer, this is more dangerous. Some people say, "We can let him marry so that he may be guided." Then, when they marry him to a pious girl, he will make her life full of sorrow. We say, "May Allāh guide him, but he may lead her astray. Thus, we shall give this advice if we are consulted in these matters,

﴿ ۞ يَٰٓأَيُّهَا ٱلَّذِينَ ءَامَنُوا۟ كُونُوا۟ قَوَّٰمِينَ بِٱلْقِسْطِ شُهَدَآءَ لِلَّهِ وَلَوْ عَلَىٰٓ أَنفُسِكُمْ أَوِ ٱلْوَٰلِدَيْنِ وَٱلْأَقْرَبِينَ ﴾

---

119 Sheikh was asked if anyone is known for homosexuality like the adulterer? He said this is more dangerous and must be stopped because Lūt (عَلَيْهِ ٱلصَّلَاةُ وَٱلسَّلَامُ) said to his people, "Go you in unto the males of the Alamin (mankind)." [*Sūrah Ash-Shu'arā'* 26:165]. This is considered disintegration.

> **"O' you who believe! Stand out firmly for justice, as witnesses to Allāh, even though it be against yourselves, or your parents, or your kin**." [*Sūrah an-Nisā'* 4:135]

ḤADĪTH 1004

1004- 'Aishah (رَضِيَ اللَّهُ عَنْهَا) reported,

طَلَّقَ رَجُلٌ اِمْرَأَتَهُ ثَلَاثًا، فَتَزَوَّجَهَا رَجُلٌ، ثُمَّ طَلَّقَهَا قَبْلَ أَنْ يَدْخُلَ بِهَا، فَأَرَادَ زَوْجُهَا أَنْ يَتَزَوَّجُهَا، فَسُئِلَ رَسُولُ اللهِ (صَلَّى اللهُ عَلَيْهِ وَسَلَّمَ) عَنْ ذَلِكَ؛ فَقَالَ: لَا، حَتَّى يَذُوقَ الْآخَرُ مِنْ عُسَيْلَتِهَا مَا ذَاقَ الْأَوَّلُ.

"A person divorced his wife by three pronouncements. Then another person married her and he also divorced her without having consummation. Then her first husband intended to remarry her. It was about such a case that Allāh's Messenger (صَلَّى اللَّهُ عَلَيْهِ وَسَلَّمَ) was asked. Whereupon he (صَلَّى اللَّهُ عَلَيْهِ وَسَلَّمَ) said, 'No, until the second one has tasted her sweetness as the first one had tasted."[120] Related by Bukhari and Muslim, but this wording is related by Muslim.

Explantion

طَلَّقَ رَجُلٌ اِمْرَأَتَهُ ثَلَاثًا

"A person divorced his wife by three pronouncements." He (صَلَّى اللَّهُ عَلَيْهِ وَسَلَّمَ) meant three consecutive divorces in one utterance because this was considered one divorce in the era of the

[120] Related by Bukhari (5261), Muslim (1433), Tuhfat Al-Ashraf (17536).

Prophet (صَلَّى ٱللَّهُ عَلَيْهِ وَسَلَّمَ). Wherever you come across "A person divorced his wife by three pronouncements," this indicates one divorce after another. So, there are many narrations like (divorced her three divorces).

It was mentioned earlier that the latter husband must consummate the marriage. So, if he made the contract, but without consummation, then divorced her, she will not be lawful to the former husband.

مِنْ عُسَيْلَتِهَا

"**Has tasted her sweetness.**" Does sweetness indicate ejaculation or just having sexual intercourse? The right opinion indicates it is just sexual intercourse. So, she is lawful to the former husband despite the absence of ejaculation because sexual intercourse itself is enough as the Prophet (صَلَّى ٱللَّهُ عَلَيْهِ وَسَلَّمَ) said, "**Sweetness.**" Although, ejaculation is more assuring.

Therefore, we can say she is not lawful to the former husband until the latter husband consummates the marriage. However, if he divorced her without having sexual intercourse, despite having privacy, kissing or hugging, she would not be lawful to the former husband without the consummation.

Another point: Whose intention is to be taken into account: the wife's, the husband's or the guardian's? Jurists (رَحِمَهُمُ ٱللَّهُ) said, "Whoever has no right to breakup, his intention has no effect."[121] So, the husband's intention shall be regarded because he is the one who is entitled to divorce, the wife's intention has no effect. In the case where the wife said, "I want to be divorced," and the husband answered, "No," his intention is effective. Some scholars said, "Both the wife's and husband's intentions are to be considered." However, it is clear that the husband's intention is effective and the marriage tie is in the husband's hands, but the wife's intention is regarded because she may try to break up by anyway. She can annoy him. If he said to her, "Make me a cup of tea," she may make something else or she may say, "I will not make anything."

When they are in bed, she may make troubles in order to make him divorce her. Some women challenge their husband. She may tell him, "Are you a man?" When he says, "Yes," then she may add, "If you are a man, divorce me." So, he may nervously divorce her. Also, the man may be indebted or needy, in which case she may offer her money in exchange for a divorce.

Anyway, this opinion is strong if we know the bad intention of the wife who caused troubles to be divorced in order to reunite with the former husband. So, we shall prevent her from marrying him because she prohibitively tried to reunite with the former husband. She is not allowed to disobey her husband or violate his rights.

Now she may be sorry for losing the latter husband. What if the judge wisely said to her, "It is obvious that you desire to reunite with the former husband and you seek a middleman,

---

[121] Al-Forou' (5/164), Al-Mobdi' (7/86), Al-Insaf by Al-Mardawi (8/162).

so you are not lawful to reunite with the former husband?" I think that she will be sorry for the latter one and try to reunite with him, at which time he would express how late her decision is. Then she will be left hanging.

Anyway, the husband's intention is fundamentally considered and the fact that it is based on the husband's intention is strong opinion. We said, at the time of the Prophet (صَلَّى ٱللَّهُ عَلَيْهِ وَسَلَّمَ), Abu Bakr (رَضِيَ ٱللَّهُ عَنْهُ) and the first two years of Umar's reign (رَضِيَ ٱللَّهُ عَنْهُ), that three divorces in one utterance was regarded as one divorce. But later in Umar's reign, he (رَضِيَ ٱللَّهُ عَنْهُ) said,

> **"Verily the people have begun to hasten[122] in the matter in which they are required to observe respite. So if we had imposed this upon them, and he imposed it upon them."**

What is the meaning of, "**They are required to observe respite**"? There is no problem if they divorce one time. If you divorced one time, must you reunite with your wife? No, but because of the ignorance some people, they say, ***"I can divorce her three times in order not to reunite."***

We say that if you divorced one time, you are not obliged to reunite with her. You can let her off until her prescribed period is finished and then you can reunite with her as Umar (رَضِيَ ٱللَّهُ عَنْهُ) said, "**If we had imposed this upon them.**" And he (رَضِيَ ٱللَّهُ عَنْهُ) imposed it upon them. This is an authentic narration that is related by Muslim.

---

[122] Meaning "They are at a loss."

Some scholars said, "Because the scholars believed in this point of view, it became the consensus." Some scholars said, "Divocring three times in one setting makes the woman irrevocably divorced." Other scholars maintained that the consensus is in the opposite direction on the basis of *Ḥadīth* of ibn 'Abbās (رَضِيَ ٱللَّهُ عَنْهُ) which is related by Muslim, Ibn 'Abbās (رَضِيَ ٱللَّهُ عَنْهُ) reported that the pronouncement of three divorces, during the lifetime of Allāh's Messenger (صَلَّى ٱللَّهُ عَلَيْهِ وَسَلَّمَ) and that of Abu Bakr (رَضِيَ ٱللَّهُ عَنْهُ) and the two years of the caliphate of Umar (رَضِيَ ٱللَّهُ عَنْهُ), was treated as one.

So, there are three lifetimes: the lifetime of Allāh's Messenger (صَلَّى ٱللَّهُ عَلَيْهِ وَسَلَّمَ) and that of Abū Bakr (رَضِيَ ٱللَّهُ عَنْهُ) and two years of the caliphate of Umar (رَضِيَ ٱللَّهُ عَنْهُ). They said, "If we narrated the consensus, on what basis would we base the consensus? It is on the basis that divorcing three times in one setting is treated as one. The preponderant opinion is that the pronouncement of divorce, whether three times or one time in one setting, is considered as one.

For instance, one may divorce his wife and then remarry. If he remarried, his wife will return to him. And then he divorced for the second time, he can still remarry. If he divorced for the third time or he said to his wife, You are divorced," and then she spends the prescribed period. Then he remarries and then divorces and then she spends the prescribed period. Then he remarries her and then divorces her, thus the third divorce is the irrevocable one. She (رَضِيَ ٱللَّهُ عَنْهَا) said, "A man divorced his wife thrice." The thrice divorces indicates the irrevocable one.

This *Ḥadīth* indicates that if the woman is divorced thrice, she will not be lawful to the former husband, except after lawful marriage to and consummation with the latter husband. It is important to be after the lawful marriage because the consummation with the latter husband is not allowed but after lawful marriage.

Thus, lawful marriage and consummation are necessary.

"Until the second one has tasted her sweetness."

"Sweetness" here indicates consummation. Some scholars said it indicates ejaculation and that if he consummated without ejaculation, she would not be lawful to the former husband. Consummation, regardless, is what is meant here, even in case of no ejaculation. And if he had sexual intercourse with her, she would be lawful to the former one, provided that the marriage is lawful.

However, if it is a Tahlil marriage, she will not be lawful, even if there was consummation because the Tahlil marriage is invalid and ineffective.

Benefits from the Ḥadīth:

1. Using the euphemism as she ('Aishah (رَضِيَ ٱللَّهُ عَنْهَا)) said, "Without having consummation," Allāh also said,

﴿ دَخَلْتُم بِهِنَّ ﴾

"To whom you have gone in." [*Sūrah an-Nisā'* 4:23]

2. If a woman married another husband and stayed a year[123] with him without consummation, and then he divorced her, she would not be lawful to the former husband as consummation with the second husband is a must.

3. If anyone committed an action against Sharia while he believed it to be lawful, this action is useless. When this woman was divorced, she thought she was lawful to the former husband but the Prophet (صَلَّىٰٱللَّهُعَلَيۡهِوَسَلَّمَ) said that she is unlawful without having consummation.

<u>The question of the honeymoon</u>: Can this *Ḥadīth* indicate the lawfulness of what is called a honeymoon?

<u>The answer:</u> No, because sweetness can be tasted in one night, the first night. So, this *Ḥadīth* is not an evidence of what is called a honeymoon. Furthermore, most people go abroad on such honeymoons where they spend a lot of money and they may commit sins. On the other hand, some people travel to Makkah or Madinah to perform Umrah and visit the Prophet's Masjid. Though this is not in accordance with Sharia, it is better.

---

[123] Shaykh said, "Even if his inability to have sexual intercourse with her is temporary, she is unlawful to the other husband. For example, if the woman is envied after being divorced by the former husband and the other cannot have sexual intercourse with her, either she stays like this or marries another man who is satisfied with this situation, according to what is said by the woman in *Ḥadīth* of Rifa'ah Al-Qurazi (رَضِيَٱللَّهُعَنۡهُ), "**And what he has is like the fringe of a garment**."